Praise for Dr. Chopra and *Uncon[...]*

"Brilliant, provocative, and poetic . . . Dr. Chopra's kindness and deep caring for people, and his desire for their liberation from suffering, shine through on every page."
—Jon Kabat-Zinn, Ph.D., Director, Stress Reduction and Relaxation Program, University of Massachusetts Medical Center, and author of *Full Catastrophe Living*

"Inspiring reading . . . Dr. Chopra presents a rare perspective—that of a scientist and a healer. Through beautifully told stories of his clinical experience, he demonstrates the possibilities of medicine with heart and spirit."
—Stephan Rechtschaffen, M.D., President, Omega Institute

And for His National Bestseller
Quantum Healing

"Dr. Chopra is a fine, evocative writer who maneuvers his way suavely through medicine, physics, and metaphysics. For anyone who has awaited a *Tao* of medicine, this book is a most welcome arrival."
—*The New England Journal of Medicine*

"Dazzling." —*The Washington Post*

"Brilliant and entertaining."
—*The London Daily Telegraph*

"A profound investigation of consciousness and health."
—*Yoga Journal*

"Drawing on both modern science and ancient wisdom, here is a model of health and illness that can stand the test of scientific scrutiny because of one simple fact: It works."
—Larry Dossey, M.D., author of *Space, Time & Medicine*

"A beautifully balanced web of dramatic examples and reasoned speculation."
—Craig A. Lambert, Ph.D., *Harvard Magazine*

"His case histories . . . take the old 'mind-body' controversy to new levels of complexity and fascination."
—*San Francisco Chronicle and Examiner*

"Illuminating and inspiring."
—*East West*

Other books by Deepak Chopra, M.D.

CREATING HEALTH
RETURN OF THE RISHI
QUANTUM HEALING
PERFECT HEALTH

Unconditional Life

~~~~~~

*Discovering the Power
to Fulfill Your Dreams*

Deepak Chopra, M.D.

BANTAM BOOKS
NEW YORK · TORONTO · LONDON · SYDNEY · AUCKLAND

UNCONDITIONAL LIFE
A Bantam Book

PUBLISHING HISTORY
Bantam hardcover edition published October 1991
Bantam trade paperback edition/October 1992

ISBN 0-553-37050-2

Published simultaneously in the United States and Canada

*Bantam Books are published by Bantam Books, a division of Bantam
Doubleday Dell Publishing Group, Inc. Its trademark, consisting of the
words "Bantam Books" and the portrayal of a rooster, is Registered in
U.S. Patent and Trademark Office and in other countries.
Marca Registrada. Bantam Books, 666 Fifth Avenue, New York,
New York 10103.*

PRINTED IN THE UNITED STATES OF AMERICA

BVG   0 9 8 7 6 5 4

Contents

꧁꧂

Unconditional
Life

Part One

~~~~~~~~~~~~~~~~~~~~

The Mystery of Personal Reality

1

⚬⚬⚬⚬⚬⚬⚬⚬⚬⚬⚬⚬

The Man Who Would Be Healed

"How much more of this do you think I can stand?" the patient demanded. He slumped in his chair, and his face darkened. "Six months ago all I could think about was staying alive. I listened to anyone who held out hope for a cure. They're all scared to come out and use the word 'cure,' of course, but I've been promised every kind of rose garden you can grow. It all sounds pretty funny now, doesn't it?"

"No," I said quietly, "I know how hard you have worked to get well." I put my hand on his shoulder, but the man stiffened and drew back. "Let's drop it," he muttered. "Only a fool would keep on like this."

"A condition like yours is going to have its ups and downs. That's only to be expected," I said gingerly, "but instead of being so disappointed about your white counts—"

"No," he interrupted bitterly, "no more white counts. I don't want that anymore."

"What do you want?" I asked.

"A way out."

"Meaning what?"

"Believe me, if I knew that—" There was a long, tense

silence. The man kept staring at the floor, his face set in a hard mask. We both waited to hear what I would say next.

My patient's name was Robert Amis. He was thirty-seven and had worked for a small computer firm on the outskirts of Boston. A year earlier his company had urged all employees to undergo a complete blood screening as part of a stepped-up emphasis on health. Robert complied without qualms. He was surprised when the test results came back showing a suspicious rise in his white blood cell count. Follow-up tests were run, and a few weeks later an oncologist somberly informed him that he had an incurable form of leukemia. Robert was deeply shaken. The average life expectancy for his particular disorder, called chronic myelocytic leukemia, or CML, was uncertain, but it could be as short as two to four years. With so little time left, he knew he had to act.

"The minute I left the doctor's office, it was as if a switch clicked," he told me at our first meeting. "I knew that my priorities had to change." He proposed to his live-in girlfriend and very quickly got married. Next he gave up his job in Boston and bought a condo in Miami. But the main thing that happened was that Robert threw himself with abandon into the project of curing himself. "I kept reading that there's an inner healer," he said, "and I was determined to find it."

He discovered no lack of channels for reaching his goal: self-hypnosis, visualization, psychotherapy, deep massage, and progressive relaxation were just the beginning. He started attending support group meetings with other leukemia patients and weekend seminars on self-healing, at which he heard inspiring stories from patients who had recovered from incurable illnesses. When I met him, he brandished the latest in a series of audiotapes he mailed out every month to update friends and family on developments in his life—meaning his disease, for that had become so nearly all-consuming that there was very little of Robert's life outside it.

After six months, when he was at the height of his new existence, Robert felt more emotionally secure than he ever had. He confidently went in for his next blood test, only to find that, far from coming under control, his white cell count had skyrocketed. His disorder seemed to be accelerating dangerously, and his oncologist took a stern tone, advising him either to start intensive chemotherapy or to take the more drastic step of having a bone marrow transplant. Neither course of action was likely to lead to a permanent cure, but conventional medicine had little else to offer.

Robert tried to remain resolute and refused both options. Soon afterward, however, he began to tailspin into a deep depression. He lost his appetite and found it increasingly difficult to sleep. By the time he was referred to me, he was bitter, lonely, and all but cut off from other people by his desperation.

He sat slumped in his chair in front of me, and I pondered what to tell him. Although everything he had pursued was "right"—his search for an inner healer, his attempt to break old, unfulfilling habits, his decision to avoid stressful situations—he had not really changed himself in any profound way.

"Let me make clear that what I want isn't for you to 'think' yourself into getting well," I said. "It's not a question of hoping hard enough that this disease will go away—every patient in your position desperately wants to get better. Why do some people have it happen?"

He shrugged his shoulders. "A stronger body, good genes, luck. Maybe God loves them more than other people."

"I'm not discounting any of these factors, and we can go into them one by one. But what I hear you asking for," I said, "is not just a cure but a reason why this has happened to you." Robert's expression remained frozen, but his eyes seemed to soften a little. I continued, "It would be easy for me to claim that your sickness is meaningless, that it is just the result of some random disruption in your body. That is more or less what medical training drums into us.

"It would also be easy to tell you exactly the opposite, that your disease has a simplistic emotional cause, that you don't love yourself enough or that some form of repressed psychic pain is making you sick. But that, too, is a half-truth. Both are prepackaged answers."

"What else is there?" he asked bitterly. In that question, which hung in the air between us with so much reproach and hopelessness, we both came to a turning point. He was at the limit of what he could ask for. I was at the limit of what medicine said I could offer. Yet it was absolutely clear, in human rather than medical terms, what was being demanded. The old questions—"What does life mean? Why can't I have what I want?"—had come back up to the surface of Robert's mind, triggered by the crisis of his disease.

A Cry for Meaning

Over the past ten or twenty years, medicine has had to open itself to issues that it never felt comfortable facing in the past. Patients want to know why they hurt, which is certainly not new, but as they aim the question, its deeper implications refuse to remain buried. They are not content just to be told why the stomach, the intestines, or the breast hurts. "Why do *I* hurt?" is their dilemma, and even after you salve the ulcer, unblock the intestine, or cut out the breast tumor, the patient returns with trouble in his eyes.

Pushed to the edge of my so-called expertise, I have thought about this hurt and tried to observe as closely as possible the people who are honest enough to confront me with it. I have made some surprising discoveries. There seems to be a hole in the middle of everyday life, as if a rock had been thrown through a plate-glass window. But instead of being a physical hole, one could call this a "meaning hole," an absence that cannot be defined except to say that it hurts. Even if they cannot analyze the effect that lack of meaning is having on their lives, people feel it, and as a result a sick sadness hangs over things, even the best things. How many people experience love, freedom, faith, or devotion as deeply as they really want to? How many cannot feel these things at all and are left with guilt and blame instead?

On the surface, all my patients are seeking help because they are ill, sometimes gravely ill. But what often shocks me is that many seem, in some barely concealed way, *relieved.* In the midst of all his struggle, Robert showed an undercurrent of this feeling. He hated his disease, but it had also opened up opportunities denied to him by ordinary life. "I didn't believe in God until I got this cancer," one woman in her sixties said, "but now He feels very close." I cannot judge her experience; certainly I am glad that she has found solace near the end of her life rather than being shattered by bitterness. But her words also seem to say, "My life didn't mean much until I was forced out of it."

One of the strangest phenomena of postmodern culture is this optimism over death: doctors and therapists are urging us to make death, not just a positive experience, but *the* positive experience of a lifetime. Sickness has always had an element of escapism in it. As children we were coddled by our mothers whenever we ran a fever, and seriously ill adults are still given "intensive care." But if a terminal illness is seen as escapism carried to its ultimate, one cannot help but ask, "Is this life so terrible that escape is its greatest reward?" A patient of mine with multiple metastatic colon cancer attended a seminar on "the will to live," which is said to help people recover from incurable illness. She opened her program book and was horrified to see that the main sponsors for the event were six funeral homes. No one else seemed to notice, or at least comment upon, this savage irony.

I do not want to parody this issue, having strong beliefs of my own that the fear of death is very crippling and needs to be overcome at the deepest level. But it is disturbing to think that our culture provides us with so little opportunity to confront the basic meaning of life that sickness and death have filled the void by becoming conversion experiences. Robert was desperate to have such an experience and furious that it was denied to him. Other patients of mine, however, have found their conversion and embraced it with disquieting results.

One of these patients was Barbara. The minute she walked into my office, it was hard not to be bewitched. Even though I knew she was consulting me about a serious illness, she looked radiant, with sparkling eyes and a perfect complexion. A native Californian, she had flown to the East Coast for our appointment, and when she saw me staring as we shook hands, she laughed and told me a story:

"I tried to fly to Boston to see you last week, but a family emergency made me miss my flight. I asked my doctor in San Diego to write a medical excuse so I could get a refund on my ticket. On the phone I simply told his secretary to ask for a note stating that I had the flu.

"When I got to the airport and handed over the note, the counter attendant turned white. My doctor had written, 'This unfortunate woman is being extensively treated for a terminal case of metastatic breast cancer.' "

I was as taken aback as the ticket agent. It was hard to credit that this woman, so young and alive, had been undergoing surgery, radiation, and chemotherapy for over a year to combat a malignancy that had spread beyond her breasts and invaded many areas of her bones. As I probed deeper into her medical history, Barbara began to reveal in bits and pieces her present frame of mind, which was extraordinarily peaceful.

"You see, I have been spending twenty years in a drive toward success. As a young woman I set up certain totally artificial goals for myself. I wanted it all: a beautiful house, adoring husband and children, and financial independence by age forty so that I could quit working and enjoy my family. These goals were set in my mind before I was out of college, and I never lost sight of them.

"I finished law school and launched myself twenty-five hours a day into achieving what I wanted. By last year, it was all within my grasp. I do have the house, husband, and children, and at my legal practice I have risen to full partner. Then I was diagnosed with breast cancer. Mentally, I knew that I had been told something terrible, but within a few days I found that I was falling into an extremely strange mood. I began to feel very happy and contented."

I agreed that this was quite an unpredictable reaction.

"I have always believed that you get what you wish for in life," she explained. "And I asked myself why I had gotten breast cancer. Was there a secret wish at work? For many people that is a scary question, full of guilt and denial, but for me it was quite reasonable to ask. And you know what the answer was?"

I told her I was very curious to find out.

"Cancer allowed me to achieve my final goal," she said with a note of triumph in her voice. "I had wanted to retire at forty, and now here I am, on a full disability pension. I am a woman of leisure at last."

"You don't seem to think that you've paid a very high price for achieving financial security," I said. I couldn't help but suspect that Barbara's amazing self-possession must be masking fears she couldn't confront.

"Let me finish," she replied excitedly. "Soon after my original diagnosis my oncologist came to see me in the hospital looking extremely upset. He said, 'I'm very, very sorry to have to tell you this, Barbara, but the malignancy has spread to several other areas in your body. In my professional opinion, you are now a terminal case.'

"Without any hesitation I replied, 'Well, if I am a terminal case, so are you, doctor, and so is everyone around me.' He was shocked. But as I saw it, if he lived thirty or forty years longer than me, that made no real difference. Dying is inevitable; it is a natural part of life, and what I had realized, what gave me such peace of mind, was that dying can be an adventure.

"When I quit worrying about my inflated and totally artificial goals, goals that had weighed me down for my entire adult life, the experience of liberation was also a kind of death —and yet it was the greatest thing that ever happened to me. More and more I began to realize that 'dying' every day would be an ideal way to live, because every morning would be new. How can life ever be new unless you learn to die?"

"Yes, yes," I murmured, holding myself back from saying, "How can life ever be new unless you learn to *live*?" But I could feel exactly what Barbara meant. She was escaping the threat of death by "dying" to her old habits and false values. Having "died," she discovered that new life rushed in to fill the vacuum. The great Bengali poet Rabindranath Tagore gave a beautiful image for this: "When old words die out on the tongue, new melodies spring forth from the heart."

Even though Barbara may be harboring buried feelings of threat that she has not really resolved, I am happy to report that her "death" has been as life-giving as she hoped. Her oncologist informed me that she is now responding extraordinarily well to treatment. The pockets of metastasis have started to shrink, and her side effects remain well within the acceptable range.

Despite Barbara's sense of jubilant conversion, I have to insist that something has gone awry here. Disease is no way to solve the core issues of life. We are weakest when sick, least able to summon the resources that are needed for real transformation. The beauty of Barbara's conversion experience does not automatically cancel the suffering that went with it. Nor does it settle the crucial issue of whether suffering was needed in the first place. An age-old belief says that suffering is inevitable, deeply human, and even a grace. Barbara felt that she had learned from her pain, and took pride in that. "I'd rather live six months with this cancer," she told me at one point, "than seven years the way I was."

Under the circumstances, she had little other choice than to feel this way; the alternative was to be crushed by the forces set against her. But whatever meaning people feel can be derived from their personal suffering, to live without pain would, I believe, be even more meaningful, even more human. People have to be transformed *before* the crisis. If not, they may find themselves with not enough time to enjoy the life that suddenly seems so worthwhile.

Chaos in the Heart

Having got this far in my observations, I was obliged to take my thoughts outside medicine, even outside the expanded boundaries of mind-body medicine. Only in a very limited sense are any doctors I know willing to approach their patients as fully human. "Mind-body medicine" is a nebulous label for a field that is still searching for its proper methods and values. What mainly holds it together is one key insight, that thoughts and feelings cannot be rigidly compartmentalized from the physical effects they create. Medical science was not being true to reality until it conceded that illness is connected to a person's emotions, beliefs, and expectations. (Perhaps I shouldn't be glib about medical science having made the concession. The newsletter of the American Medical Association queried AMA members in 1990 and found that only ten percent "believed" in the mind-body connection. A cardiologist friend of mine thrust the article at me and grumbled, "How do the other 90 percent think they wiggle their toes?")

Having made its big breakthrough, mind-body medicine has not gone on to uncover the answer to why people hurt. Instead, we find ourselves staring into even deeper confusion. This confusion has to do with the nature of life itself, and therefore it is extremely hard to express. In childhood we all asked our parents pressing meaningful questions: "Who am I? What will happen to me when I die? Why do things turn out the way they do?" Few, if any, parents provided answers that were good enough to settle the disturbing fears that lie behind such questions, so we stopped asking them. But they continue to linger inside us, burning more intensely than ever. Having reached adulthood ourselves, we tend to dismiss these as "ultimate questions," a label that makes them sound very abstract. Actually, they are the most primary questions, and as long as they remain unresolved, the hole that they leave creates much of the misery we struggle with—physical illness, emotional malaise, a pervasive sense of restlessness, and a nagging lack of happiness.

I find it revealing that the most secure people I know, materially as well as psychologically, are fascinated by the homeless. They are not merely concerned or distressed; they see specters of themselves in the most hopeless outsiders on the street. They feel that they, too, could be dispossessed at any moment. This fear is a very real one if you consider that the home they are afraid to lose is basically inside themselves. It is their center, which is so uncertain that they wonder whether it ever really existed.

Intellectually, the same mixture of fascination and fear has tinged a young branch of physics called chaos theory, which goes far beyond the neat, stable mathematical models of Newton or even Einstein into the domain of constant change, where instability is the rule. Chaos is the absence of predictable patterns and connections. Swirling water, puffs of smoke, and dancing dust motes in a beam of sunlight exemplify chaos. They are all unpredictable, random phenomena; if patterns seem to emerge inside them, these dissolve as quickly as they are created. To a nonscientist, the behavior of chaos sounds disturbing and all too human. Colliding dust motes translate into the lonely crowd; swirling smoke translates into personal relationships that cannot hold for long before vanishing into thin air.

In purely rational terms, physics has long been intrigued by the fact that the universe, which in many respects functions like a well-knit machine, lacks the wires, pulleys, and rods that hold a machine together. The primordial stars were flung apart from each other at the moment of the Big Bang, when they were unformed, fiery gases, and the flinging has continued ever since. Where are the connections, the principles of order? Why do field daisies and bats' wings and the planetary crust hold together so precisely when the whole machine—the cosmos—seems to have its parts strewn in every direction?

Chaos theory tries to unriddle the deeper orderliness that might underlie nature's ceaseless play of creation and destruction. In that sense, it is an optimistic science, because every new layer of orderliness comes as a reassurance, at least to the lay person, that nature makes sense. On the other hand, why won't this orderliness hold still? Because that is not how nature apparently works. For every layer of order, there is another layer that collapses into disorder. An exploding nova is sheer chaos, yet its individual atoms are models of orderliness. A human skin cell performs its myriad biological functions with such astonishing orderliness that medicine just barely knows its secrets, but after three weeks, when the skin cell dies, it disintegrates into chaos. Nature seems unwilling to demonstrate that either order or disorder is finally preeminent.

Physicists are sometimes scornful of the popular images their theories give rise to, yet lay people have been deeply affected to learn that nothing in nature can stand firm against the ravages of change. The most fearsome diseases left to be cured, including cancer, seem to be rooted in the *probability* that DNA will make a mistake. Under normal conditions, DNA is self-correcting; that is, it knows how to repair itself when it is damaged, how to dismantle aberrant genetic material, how to nullify even the most drastic errors to preserve the delicate balance of normal life functions.

But since each of our 50 trillion cells contains a complete set of 3 billion genetic bits, perfection in this area is impossible. An unknown number of mistakes slip by (probably millions of them per year); some of these aberrations run out of control, and the result can become a wildly proliferating cancer. Diabetes, arthritis, and heart disease are all hypothesized to have a genetic component as well. The triggering mechanism would be different for each of them, and all are unlike cancer, but the underlying uncertainty is just as dreadful.

It is not only disease that creates a sense of groundlessness. The body itself is not a fixed package of atoms and molecules—it is a process, or rather billions of simultaneous processes being coordinated together. I once watched with fascination as a beekeeper reached into a swarm of bees and, by gently enfolding the queen in his hands, moved the whole hive, a living globe of insects suspended in midair. What was he moving? There was no solid mass, but only an image of hovering, darting, ever-changing life, which had centered itself around a focal point. The swarm exists as an outcome of bee behavior. It is an illusion of shape behind which the reality is pure change.

Such are we, too. We are a swarm of molecules hovering around a center, but with diminishing confidence. The old queen, the soul, has decamped, and the new queen seems reluctant to hatch from her cell. The great difference between us and a swarm of bees is that we find it hard to attribute reality to the unseen center that holds us together. It is obvious that one does, for otherwise we would be flung apart into chaos. But a queen looks like any other bee, only larger, while we cannot hope to find a lump of cells that contains what we consider to be central to us—love, hope, trust, and belief.

Chaos may provide compelling science, but it is no way to live. The lack of meaning hurts too much. The great scientific explorers who marched into the heart of nature, intent on dismantling the nucleus of hydrogen atoms and measuring the farthest horizons of space-time, overlooked that for every marching in there is a marching out. To get somewhere you have to leave somewhere. This means that the deeper one explores into nature "out there," the greater the danger that our own human nature, the reality "in here" that we live with privately, gets abandoned.

We are deep into that danger at the present moment. Freud made a strong point about the mixed blessings of material progress when he was musing about the telephone, an invention that came into general use during his youth. It was undoubtedly true that thanks to the telephone, he could talk to his daughter far away in another city. However, if there were no telephones, Freud said, she might not have moved away. This is not to imply that machines are evil, however, or intrinsically antihuman. It is just that the technological march forward needs to be balanced in such a way that the antihuman backlash does not occur.

I don't want to dwell on this backlash, except to give one indelible example. A journal article in the May 1986 issue of *Pediatrics* appraised the medical benefits of "tactile/kinesthetic stimulation on preterm neonates." Doctors at the University of Miami medical school divided into two groups forty premature babies—"preterm neonates" in medical jargon— who had been delivered after an average of only thirty-one weeks of pregnancy, not quite eight months.

One group was given normal treatment in the hospital's intensive care unit for neonates. The other was scheduled for fifteen minutes of special attention, in which someone reached in through the portholes of their sealed cribs to stroke them and gently wiggle their arms and legs—this was their "tactile/kinesthetic stimulation," which was repeated three times a day.

The results of such a simple addition to the usual hospital routine were striking. Although fed on demand with the same formula, the stroked babies gained 47 percent more weight every day than the control group; they were more alert and started to act like normally delivered babies sooner. Finally, they left the hospital a week ahead of schedule, allowing the authors of the study to note a savings of $3,000 per infant in the final bill.

Here, the contrast between life and antilife seems almost too obvious to point out. Scientific medicine has reached the stage where it is not respectable to call stroking by its right name—much less love and affection. Stroking has to go by the Orwellian "tactile/kinesthetic stimulation." It is even more Orwellian to perform controlled experiments to see if babies need loving attention, meted out in doses like cough syrup or iodine.

My deepest emotions, however, are aroused by the group of babies who were *not* stroked. When I think of them lying alone in their closed Lucite cribs (called "isolettes"), stranded in the weird ICU environment that numbs adult patients and frequently induces psychotic breaks, my heart cries out in protest. Not just premature babies but everyone suffers when our belief in truth falters. We lose the words for basic values, and then the possibility arises that we may lose the values themselves.

Personal Reality

Over and over, we are pulled back to the world "in here," which our culture has not properly understood in so many ways. When I was a young doctor, I often found myself surprised by how two patients with identical diagnoses could react so differently to their illness. After all, a diagnosis is meant to be an impersonal tag for a clinically defined disease entity. But it is rarely that simple.

I recently heard from one cancer patient whose disease had metastasized to her bones, causing intense pain. This woman also happened to be mired in a bad marriage, and one day, utterly weary of the constant conflict with her husband, she decided once and for all that their relationship had come to an end. The day after she asked him for a separation, her bone pain inexplicably disappeared. "Suddenly the phrase 'weary to the bone' came to mind," she says, "and I saw in a flash that my disease was my body's way of expressing the same concept." Having released some of her bottled-up weariness, this woman relieved herself of the pain that was its literal double. Now she wonders, as do I, if the cancer itself will be forced to retreat. Was her entire illness just a metaphor?

Our culture chooses to believe that disease is basically

created on the material level. After you inhale it, an asbestos fiber can lodge in the smallest crevices of your lung tissue, and over time there is a definite small probability that it can cause a specific form of lung cancer. But by the same token, cancer rates have been found to increase among newly widowed men. Grief, too, lodges deep inside a person, and even though a molecule of asbestos from "out there" is not at all like a grief-stricken mood "in here," at some deep level of the self, they can be identical. We nourish our bodies with every impulse of trust and love, we poison them with distrust and hate.

Physically, you and I may have very similar hearts; if you inject enough potassium chloride into our veins, both of us will suffer cardiac arrest. But our experiences are completely individual. We have walked through different gardens and knelt at different graves. Your sad memories make you heart-weary or heartsick, while I am perfectly immune to them. Likewise, the joyful images that gladden our hearts may closely resemble each other, but your memories have a personal flavor that I cannot taste.

"Reality" is a word that we generally apply in the most impersonal sense. The trees, sky, clouds, buildings, and social institutions that define what is real seem to exist without much regard for our personal thoughts and feelings. Yet the neat division between the inner and outer world, between "me" and things "out there," is not accurate. Everything a person experiences must pass through a mental filter before it registers as real, which means that we are constantly engaged in *making* reality.

Let me return to Robert, with whom I discussed these ideas at length. In one of our later meetings, I asked him, "Have you ever had the experience of waking up at night, usually about two or three in the morning, feeling very afraid? Do you know that feeling, call it cold dread, free-floating anxiety, or whatever you will?" I didn't wait for his answer—we both knew it already.

"The next time it occurs, you might be able to notice something very curious. Almost the instant that you awaken with this sensation of dread, your mind finds something, usually a sound, to be afraid of. The drip of a faucet, the wind in the trees, the ticking of the clock: any innocuous everyday sound can suddenly seem absolutely horrifying.

"You have caught yourself in the act of giving a personal flavor to things by projecting yourself onto them. How does this happen? The mind does not naturally dwell in abstractions. It prefers concreteness. So when an impulse of fear arises, the mind attaches it to something tangible. This is a kind of automatic reflex that keeps going of its own accord because there is always something—losing one's money, failure at work, dying of a dreaded disease—that we accept as a genuine cause for anxiety. If you wake up feeling dread about having cancer, it seems so reasonable that you miss the essential point: cancer is not scaring you, the mind's reflex is.

"Next time, stay on the lookout and watch this amorphous fear as it gropes for something to hang on to. You may notice, as you lie there in bed, that your mind races from one pretext to another, like a beggar being turned away from several houses, before a good excuse takes it in. Your initial focus might be on the rattle of a windowpane. Just at the instant the mind is about to grab this pretext, it will say, 'What am I doing being afraid of the wind? For God's sake, I have cancer, and that's something to really worry about.' "

Despite himself, Robert had to smile.

"You see," I went on, "sitting here you catch on to the ridiculous element in all this. Why does the mind need to indulge in this habit? For security—like a climber pulling himself hand over hand up a rope, the mind pulls itself along from one minute to the next by identifying with sights, sounds, tastes, smells, textures, and above all, memories.

"In this way life remains continuous, but the conditioned mind leaves little room for anything new. Once you start seeing that your most cherished thoughts may just be reflexes, the urge to break free cannot help but arise. Rather than being so convinced by the stimuli of pain and pleasure, you will begin to see the possibility of a new perspective."

"But it's not the worrying that scares me," Robert objected, "it's my disease."

"The worrying grows from your viewpoint," I insisted, "not from your disease. Your inner awareness has primary importance in the reality you are experiencing." Robert continued to look doubtful. "Two people can ride the same roller coaster," I pointed out. "One is terrified, and his body is flooded with stress hormones, causing his immune response to plummet. The other loves roller coasters, and he produces a flood of chemicals, such as interferon and interleukin, that strengthen his immune system. Same input, opposite results, all because of a different point of view."

I waited to let this sink in and then said, "What I want to propose to you is that it is possible to achieve the freedom to have any viewpoint you choose and therefore any reality. To be the maker of your reality is in fact your basic viewpoint, although it may be nearly impossible for you to see that now. Once you return to this basic viewpoint, however, you will no longer see yourself as a passive victim of life—you stand at the very center of life and have the power to renew it at every moment."

"This is beginning to sound very mystical," Robert said hesitantly.

"Not once you actually have the experience," I replied. "Who am I talking to now? If I were talking only to a collection of habits and memories, you would be a totally predictable quantity, but you aren't. The old scenes and events that have piled up inside you are not you; you are their arranger and overseer. You give every iota of sense data its meaning, and without you, everything would lapse into chaos."

This brings us to what Robert was pleading for—a way out of his deep-seated hurt. Frustration and pain are trapped inside us by conditioning that tells us they are inescapable; therefore, to heal the pain, you have to go beyond the conditioning. We are all beset by limitations. The mind is structured around the impressions held inside it, and trying to deny or escape them is futile. Every day, a person thinks approximately 50,000 different thoughts, or so someone has calculated—a bewildering cascade of wildly mixed and conflicting impulses. In and of itself, this turmoil can be extremely painful. We feel true love and true hatred for the people closest to us, with seemingly no possibility of finally sorting one from the other. The most destructive emotions—doubt, fear, guilt, shame, and loneliness—roam the mind at will, beyond our conscious control. It is truer to say that they control us.

But this prison has an air of illusion about it once you realize that you built it and locked yourself inside. Having erected the barriers it feels trapped by, the mind should be able to take them down. From that viewpoint, it becomes every person's choice to take responsibility for his own inner reality. On one side, the old conditioning tells us that we will hurt worse if we try to break free. On the other, the impulse toward freedom is urging us to discover that all limitations are at bottom false. What makes this impulse so hard to obey is that it is shrouded in pain.

In the presence of pain, people flinch, as though drawing back from enemy attack. But pain is basically a signal of where healing should begin. My purpose, then, is to calm people's fears and let them realize that a healed life is the most natural way to live. Once a person has even a little courage to confront his old conditioning, he will find that turning inward starts to dissolve that conditioning. Presently, the prospect of turning inward is extremely intimidating to most people, but it is the only way the mind can conquer its built-in resistances. There is no cure from the outside. The lack of meaning we presently endure will only become worse, and in time humanity might get too sick of itself to recover.

Better Brain Pictures?

So far, I have painted a grim picture, of people who hurt without knowing the cause and seek relief without ultimately finding it. But that perspective is much too limited, for if we look at matters differently, the situation changes completely. If you turn the telescope around, nature is nothing if not healing. Stars explode, but they are also constantly created; cells die but they also divide and produce offspring to carry DNA onward (and upward: for all my sorrows, I greatly prefer being human to being an amoeba or even the most attractive chimp).

In this light, life shows itself as a miracle of renewal. All the order that dissolves into chaos comes back as another kind of order. All the life that surrenders to death is continually being reborn. The dance of sunlight on the sea, the lush greenness of alpine valleys, the simple goodness of children, the frail hands of an old woman that retain their grace despite the scars of age—all these things exist independently of our moods, waiting to be acknowledged for the joy they in fact contain. When patients go through a conversion experience, what changes is their viewpoint about these matters, not reality itself.

Once we realize that nature contains healing and destruction entwined together, the suspicion arises that all the misery people are feeling is basically self-inflicted. We see the clouds instead of the rainbow and blame them for the depression they cause. I have come to think that this is a valid way of looking at the problem, but in the same breath I must admit that I share the resistance that people feel when they are asked to perceive a brighter reality. Their mind violently rejects any suggestion that its pain, so intense and uncontrollable, has been self-induced. Yet all pain comes to us through the mind-body connection. It only stands to reason that the connection works both ways. If you have proof that certain brain chemicals make people feel a sense of well-being, the ones that make them feel depressed, sick, and hopeless cannot be denied.

The catch-22 is that the brains that need the most healing are entrenched in wrong brain chemistry to begin with. Because it is conditioned to see the world as sad and hopeless, a depressed brain will react to any idea, including its own healing, as more cause for depression. We may invoke the inner healer as if it were a thing, like a dose of penicillin, but it is abstract, a child of words and memories. It elusively abides in the private world that each one of us builds inside himself, changing shape from person to person and minute to minute.

And so the matter might stand—the brain's picture of reality is ruled by its chemistry—except that we now have drugs that can drastically alter that chemistry, which means that they can fundamentally alter our picture of the world. A depressed person swallows a pill, and suddenly other people appear friendlier and less threatening; situations seem less hopeless; colors look brighter, sounds become more vivid. Such a dramatic transformation does not always occur, but the field of mind-altering drugs has expanded so rapidly that for the first time, science may be able to hand us our desired reality in a bottle.

Peter Kramer, a psychiatrist in private practice in Providence, Rhode Island, recounts the case of a woman who saw him several years ago in a state of chronic depression. She was a well-placed executive, so hardworking and intent on the details of her job that she had almost no time for socializing. Her personal life, when she gave it any attention, was wrapped up in a hopeless long-term affair with a married man. If any new men tried to come near, she gave off signals that kept them at arm's length.

Kramer was not asked to treat this woman, who was making progress in therapy with an outside psychologist; he was simply needed to prescribe medication for her, which he did in the form of a conventional antidepressant. The drug seemed to help. There was a marked decline in her symptoms; she slept and ate better; she had fewer crying jags than before. Still, no one would have said that this woman led a normal life. Kramer marked her case down as a partial remission and continued to hope that something more could be done for her.

Two years later a new antidepressant called Prozac—the trade name for the chemical fluoxetine—came on the market, accompanied by remarkable stories about its effectiveness. Structurally, Prozac is not a radical departure from other drugs in the class called tricyclics, but it is more specific. It helps normalize the action of a brain chemical called serotonin, one of the basic messenger molecules, or neurotransmitters, by which one neuron communicates with another.

Kramer decided to place his patient on Prozac for a trial period, and a dramatic transformation occurred. After at first becoming frenzied and euphoric, the woman settled down into a state that was just a bit more energized and optimistic than before. This slight shift was enough to turn her life around. She became more flexible at her work. She stopped giving off hostile signals and began treating men in a less businesslike manner. As a result, her social life took off. "Three dates a weekend!" she exclaimed as she walked into Kramer's office. "I must be wearing a sign on my forehead." She outgrew her old friends, who basically related to her on the level of her depression, and found new friends who were as lively as she.

It was a classic example of changing someone's reality by changing his brain chemistry, and Kramer had very mixed feelings. "The patient's judgment remained good, the slight extra pep did not seem to endanger her daily functioning—quite the opposite in her view—but I was left uneasy. I saw the medication as having given my patient a personal style that came from outside her." Kramer could only articulate his uneasiness by saying that Prozac had somehow impacted this woman's "character," but that is an amorphous kind of judgment. Was it part of her character to suffer? If so, can't we toss out a little character to allow her to suffer less?

Other psychiatrists stand by the pharmacy door with worried expressions on their faces, but clearly we have reached a turning point. The day may come when being clinically depressed will no longer be a prerequisite for taking such drugs. A prominent New York physician commented, "The fact is, we're all depressed. The whole world is depressed. I don't know a human being who isn't." Are we supposed to prescribe Prozac to the whole world?

In fact, the main reason we have not been handing people reality in a bottle is largely tactical. Most mind-altering drugs are highly toxic, habit-forming, or have other unacceptable side effects. Amphetamines may give a sense of heightened alertness, concentration, and creative intensity, but they also induce paranoia. Valium and related tranquilizers erase low-level anxiety but are addictive. LSD and a wide variety of other hallucinogens deliver visionary experiences, sometimes of a very high order, but they so wildly distort perception that few people can walk around under their influence and still remain normal. In all these cases, feeling good comes with the high penalty of also having to feel very bad.

In his old age the French philosopher Jean-Paul Sartre admitted that he had written his last book under the influence of amphetamines. Even though he realized that he was destroying his brain and shortening his life, he preferred the added brilliance that the drug imparted. In America, where physicians keep a tighter hold upon dangerous drugs, Sartre would not have been allowed to make such a decision; the doctor who denied him amphetamines would take responsibility for losing a book but saving a life. Can we deny anyone his extra measure of genius once there is no price to pay?

Now that the toxicity of mind-altering drugs is being reduced, the picture emerges more clearly. A brighter, more alert brain is an obvious advantage in life; in order to deny it to people, we have to have a very good reason. Prozac is said to alter the sense of self so subtly that some patients have to set an alarm clock to remember to take it. Otherwise, they forget that the happy, energized person they have turned into was not originally there.

Although they may have ethical objections today, it is likely that doctors will gradually give way, eventually supplying chemical brain enhancement more or less on demand. The only justifiable reason I can think of for denying people a happier brain picture is that they might be missing something better. What is better than happiness and creativity? The answer is *true* happiness and creativity, the kind that will not go away if you forget to set the timer.

Instead of viewing the brain as a series of chemical relays that can be brightened or dimmed like a TV monitor, we should explore much more deeply its role as a creator. If we are all co-creators of reality, then our goal in life is not just to be bright, alert, or imaginative, but to shape existence itself. If the brain could do that, then it would achieve real meaningfulness, far beyond the chemical boost of a mind-altering pill.

What really matters is not things "out there," no matter how cheerful you can make them look, but the experiencer sitting inside ourselves. Without the experiencer there is no light, no sound, no touch, smell, or taste. To create these things is each person's private brand of magic, so spellbinding that it is all we can do to remember that we are the magician and not just the audience.

This book carries the subtitle "Discovering the Power to Fulfill Your Dreams." Such a premise cannot be fulfilled until people are taught to master the forces that now shape their personal reality. It has taken me a long time to think through and articulate what such mastery means. It does not mean manipulating one's psychology or rising to superhuman heights of willpower. Both avenues have failed to change our situation. We live in a culture dedicated to the belief that you have to work to survive and the harder you work, the more you will be rewarded. That assumption makes it nearly impossible to see that certain things require no work and yet bring enormous rewards. Healing is one such thing. You cannot make it happen, and yet it happens. And when healing is deep enough, it solves much worse problems than physical illness. The search for meaning is brought to an end, and nature's immense ability to purify and restore balance asserts itself once more.

It hurts inside when pressure is put on us, even the pressure to heal. As soon as the pressure is removed, the mind begins to heal by itself. This is not an experience many people immediately accept. They prefer to struggle against their pain, fighting off grief, depression, and fear, despite the overwhelming evidence that if these emotions ever resolve themselves, it is of their own accord. Struggle only slows down the process and makes it more painful.

Complete healing depends upon your ability to stop struggling. I will explain more fully what this means in the following chapters. They have been arranged to present the principal stages that take a person away from conditioning toward freedom. As each barrier falls, a new possibility opens up in its place. Reading a book cannot make you free or heal a deep hurt or restore meaning to your existence, but it can provide the understanding of what is holding you back. Understanding and experience are the two legs of healing, marching side by side. Thus the self that was crippled by fear discovers, without strain or pressure, the repressed power of truth that has been denied for so long.

2

❧❧❧❧❧❧❧❧❧❧

The Lens of Perception

One time a man died because of something I said to him. He was an emergency patient I'll call Arthur Elliott, a lawyer in his thirties who showed up at the emergency room outside Boston after midnight, alone and dressed in rumpled pajamas. Visibly frightened, Mr. Elliott announced at the nurses' station that he had just been waked up from a sound sleep by a sudden, excruciating pain in the middle of his chest. He had waited, hardly daring to breathe. After a few minutes the pain receded, but he leapt out of bed and headed for the nearest hospital.

The young ER doctor on duty that night quickly performed an examination but found nothing amiss. Having ascertained that Mr. Elliott had no prior history of heart disease, he told him that the pain might have been caused by a cramp in his chest muscles.

"But it was like being stabbed!" Mr. Elliott protested.

The ER doctor reassured him that a heart attack typically begins with a dull, squeezing pain, not a sharp stab. Nor did Mr. Elliott have any dizziness, nausea, sudden weakness, or loss of breath—signs that a heart attack might be in progress. Mr. Elliott was advised to return in the morning when a complete battery of tests could be run.

25

He reluctantly went home, but within an hour the stabbing chest pain struck again. He frantically rushed back to the ER, and as the senior physician on call, I was waked up and asked to see him. In passing, the ER doctor mentioned that Mr. Elliott was "sort of belligerent."

The man I confronted in the examining room appeared pale and anxious. He jumped back as soon as I laid my stethoscope against his chest.

"Relax, now," I said gently. "This is probably nothing we have to worry about."

"We?" he shot back, nailing me with a glare. "I'm the one who could die here."

Without replying, I bent down to listen to his heart. It sounded a little fast but otherwise normal. To make sure, I had Mr. Elliott hooked up for an EKG reading; it too showed no evident abnormalities. Nevertheless, I decided to admit him to the hospital for observation, largely because he was displaying so much emotional agitation.

The next morning, after a new EKG was run, I had ambiguous news. "I asked some of our cardiologists to take a look at both of your EKGs, and there is a very slight change since last night. It could indicate that your heart muscle suffered minor damage during your two episodes of pain."

I was about to say that Mr. Elliott did not appear to be in imminent danger. A healthy heart is quite capable of compensating for such small injuries. Some wounds simply heal, others are sealed off and the heart operates around them. But before I could inform him of this, he exploded. His eyes popped with rage, and he lashed out violently.

"This is outrageous! You don't give a damn about me. For all you care I could have dropped dead, but you're not getting away with it. I'll take you for everything you've got!" He was practically incoherent with fury, but it was clear enough that he intended to slap me with a massive malpractice suit on the spot, and the entire ER staff in the bargain. To make good on his threat, he grabbed the bedside telephone and began calling up his legal colleagues, growing more and more agitated in the process. I pleaded with him to try and calm down. As his blood pressure skyrocketed, we administered the strongest antihypertensives and tranquilizers on hand. Nothing helped. He had spun out of control into a world of his own.

An hour later, still ranting on the phone, he felt the stabbing chest pains return again, this time with such violence that he collapsed. The nurse who found him detected no pulse. In two minutes a cardiac unit arrived on the scene with a crash cart and electric paddles, but all attempts at resuscitation were fruitless.

My immediate reaction, once I knew that we had lost him, was total bewilderment. Of course, it is upsetting for any patient to hear that he has had a possible heart attack. Yet a phrase that seemed gentle to me—"minor damage to your heart"—became catastrophic when Mr. Elliott took it in. It set off a chain reaction that nobody could control, least of all he.

Whenever a sudden death occurs inside a hospital, a detailed autopsy is performed. In this case the cause of death was pronounced as myocardial rupture—a necrotic, or dead, part of the heart muscle had torn open, presumably as the result of a violent spasm of the coronary arteries, with fatal results.

The necrotic tissue was not scarred over, which implied that the damage to the heart had occurred recently. However, there was no way of determining if his two bouts of pain had created any of this injury. According to the autopsy, Mr. Elliott's coronary arteries were clean. We already knew that he did not smoke or have high blood pressure, two primary risks for a heart attack. The heart muscle exhibited no intrinsic defect, such as a damaged valve, and there were no signs of an infection.

In other words, he was as safe as one could reasonably hope to be—until his heart decided to rip itself apart.

It had never occurred to me that a word could kill. Physically, a word is just a faint sound, so to call it the cause of heart failure is absurd, unless you are willing to radically expand your belief system. I have read that New Guinea islanders can fell a tree by standing in a ring and shouting at it at the top of their voices. They depart, and when they return in a few weeks, the tree has toppled of its own accord. The Old Testament records that Joshua won the battle of Jericho by commanding his troops to blast their rams' horns until the

city's walls tumbled down. Thinking about Mr. Elliott, I began
to believe that a similar wonder had overtaken him.

One reason that a very faint stimulus might kill someone
is that the human heart already harnesses more than enough
power to destroy itself. Although no larger than a man's
clenched fist, the heart does enough work in a day to raise a
one-ton weight to the height of a five-story office building. Or-
dinarily, this enormous power is disciplined for good. Yet
seen at close range, the gentlest beat of the heart is poised on
the very edge of violence—the heart literally tries to jump out
of the chest cavity with every beat it takes, being stopped only
when its pointed end, or apex, strikes abruptly against the
inside of the chest wall.

Fortunately, built into everyone's body is a formidable
array of safety features. Nature safeguards our hearts against
self-destruction particularly well, beginning in the tiny region
of the brain called the hypothalamus. Though barely bigger
than the tip of one's little finger, the hypothalamus carefully
regulates dozens of bodily functions, including blood pressure
and heartbeat. In addition, one of the ten cranial nerves, the
vagus, is responsible for slowing down a racing heart and
bringing it back to normal. The heart is protected internally
by its own independent pacemaker cells and a built-in electrical system, just in case the brain becomes incapacitated by
disease or trauma. Yet, elaborate as it is, in Mr. Elliott's case
this fail-safe machinery did break down, battered by the nothing of a thought.

Seeing Yourself in the World

The coroner's precise and objective phrase, "Cause of
death: myocardial rupture," did not even begin to hint at how
this disaster happened. It only put a conventional label on the
outcome. If the report had read, "Cause of death: distorted
perception of the situation," we would have come closer to the
truth.

A camera records an event by taking in light signals and
turning them into a literal image, but this is not at all how our
senses operate—we *perceive*, which means that we add mean-

ing to every signal coming our way. It does not matter to a camera if a bus is painted yellow, but when we see it, we know children are aboard and certain precautions must be taken. Perception is the first and most important step in turning the raw data of the universe into reality. Seeing the world is far from the passive act it appears to be, for when we look at something, we see it colored by our own set of unique experiences.

If I am looking at the dawn and feel depressed, my mood seeps into the dawn, making it look sad and lonely. If I am joyful, the same dawn reflects my joy back at me. This fusing of "me" and things "out there" is what makes the lens of perception magical. Just by listening, looking, smelling, tasting, and feeling, I turn the world into *my* world.

Nor is there any limit to how much sense we can read into the data we are interpreting. It is entirely possible to have a love-hate relationship with a string of random numbers, as a Harvard psychology team once proved. They asked students to play a gambling game with a partner. The rules of the game were simple: "You and your partner will be given two buttons to push, marked 1 and 0," the experimenters said. "If you both press 0, you will both be given nothing. If you both press 1, you will both be given one dollar. However, if you press 0 while your partner presses 1, you will win two dollars, and he will get nothing."

The point of this game, they said, was to see if people will cooperate to gain a small reward rather than trying to outwit each other in hopes of getting more. The students were told they would be in separate rooms so that they could not see their partners—this was to prevent them from signaling or showing their feelings as the game went on. The game commenced, and after the allotted time each student emerged. "On the basis of this game," they were asked, "can you tell what kind of a person your partner is?"

"He's very devious!" came the typical reply. "At first I pressed 1 all the time so we both could benefit, but he got greedy, and after only a few moves he would press 0, just when I least expected it. So I started pressing 0, too."

"But then you both got nothing," the experimenters pointed out.

"What could I do?" the students said. "He was trying to cheat me. I had to teach him a lesson."

Every subject had a tale to tell, of treachery and greed, of brief lapses back into cooperation, followed by a streak of vengeful behavior or sheer irrationality. You may have guessed by now that there was in fact no partner. Each student was playing against a sequence of random 0s and 1s spouted by a computer. No one caught on to the trick, however; instead, each player emerged with a full-blown psychological portrait of a partner whose behavior was everything from "sadistic" to "brilliantly manipulative."

This raises a disturbing question: if my perception is just a bundle of random experiences in response to a basically random world, how real am I? Perhaps my full-blown personality has no fixed core at all. I may just be a collection of accumulated habits and tastes, a walking interpretation that likes spinach, dislikes okra, feels attracted to jazz, repelled by Wagnerian opera, and so on.

There is no doubt that we all have built ourselves up from the merest wisps of experience that come our way. Mr. Elliott was given no more than a wisp and he died of it. What I said to him was not earthshaking, but it didn't have to be. It only had to be one wisp too many. The words "minor damage to your heart" seemed to propel him into a chaotic private reality. In truth he was already in it chin-deep. The violence of his reaction depended on the pent-up violence that was seething in his self.

The self's hidden anger and pain often escape notice even when they are building up enormous pressure to be expressed. Holding negative feelings back, as most of us do, causes inner reality to become warped, because no matter how hard the mind pushes this energy down, its presence is constantly felt.

I was in the midst of examining a young woman who had been diagnosed a few months earlier as having lung cancer. I was asking her about her childhood illnesses when she suddenly blurted out, quite defiantly, "Whatever you tell me to do, don't tell me to give up smoking."

"Why not?" I asked, taken aback.

The woman replied, "Because the type of lung cancer I have isn't related to smoking."

Since she had oat-cell carcinoma, her statement was technically correct; this disease is not the squamous-cell carcinoma linked to cigarettes. Before I could tell her that I didn't care whether she smoked or not—under the circumstances, this was the least of her problems—she added, "Life's not worth living if you can't enjoy it, and smoking is what I enjoy."

Something snapped in me that is not supposed to snap when a doctor talks to a seriously ill patient. "You enjoy not tasting your food?" I asked, "not being able to smell the flowers anymore, having a constant reek on your breath, half-numbed fingertips, and blood pressure climbing so high that it is potentially as dangerous as cancer?" As soon as my outburst ended I felt ashamed, but I was deeply frustrated at the same time. How do people "enjoy" things that they know perfectly well are bad for them?

On the verge of tears, she had an answer: "Don't dictate to me. I know what I like." She was throwing her self, her indisputable right to be "I," in my face. Just the way she leaned on the word "I" made me cringe—it was like an appeal to a court of last resort. This lost self had suffered so much, had made such bad mistakes, and was going to enter into an inescapably grim future. Yet what else could she cling to? "I" was her anchor to reality, and no one willingly surrenders that, unless he is so desperate that his mind must unmoor itself and undertake what Freud called "the perilous journey of psychosis."

The self has a troubling way of acting against its own interests, of twisting good into bad and bad into good. It seems to be human nature for the mind to divide itself into one region that is conscious and another that is unconscious, to subdivide both regions into many smaller layers, and finally to create thousands of compartments within each layer. Like an ambitious king who builds his palace too fast to actually enter each room, our minds have lost track of their own labyrinths, secret chambers, and ghost-filled attics.

Certain compartments, moreover, hold things that are clearly too painful to express or even confront. We seal them off in order to avoid conflicts that would be unbearable. Like a baby smothered in swaddling clothes, our perception of reality gets covered by layers of experience, until "I" becomes quite confused about who "me" really is.

No Light Without the Eye

Up to this point I have done everything I can to make perception seem highly personal, changeable, illusory, arbitrary, and untrustworthy. To a researcher in the field, this is a strange stance, for the overwhelming trend in recent years has been to "explain" perception in terms of the senses, to make it much less psychological and much more mechanical. Thus, for the sense of sight we learn that a human eye has about 125 million rods and 7 million cones implanted on the surface of the retina. Rods are responsible for night vision, cones for day vision. No one knows why we have nearly twenty times more receptors for moonlight than for sunlight, but that is the case.

These specialized receptors are direct extensions of the brain, and each reacts to only a narrow wavelength of light. When a photon strikes a retinal cell, it creates a chemical change that in turn sparks an electrical spike that is sent to the visual cortex in the back of the head via the optic nerve, a bundle of 800,000 neural fibers wrapped into a single cable. During the early stages of visual processing, the brain keeps the images from each eye separate; only at the very end are they merged to create a three-dimensional object. Even then, there is no picture of the world in your brain. The image of a tree, for example, is decoded purely into electrical data. However, the visual cortex is definitely a map that marks certain aspects of the tree. The parts of the visual image that run from top to bottom and left to right are registered by brain cells that also are arranged top to bottom and left to right.

The mechanics of eyesight are so well understood by now that they can be imitated artificially: robot eyes have been developed that can detect light and send it to be stored and decoded by a computer. In some cases, robot vision is sophisticated enough to interpret color, texture, and shape, follow moving objects, and distinguish near-far perspective much as our own eyes do. The only problem with this impressive cracking of the visual code is that the *experience* of seeing has been entirely missed. Robot eyes are never bored by what they look at, or enthralled by beauty. They do not prefer crimson to scarlet, or vice versa. They do not relish the softness of the shadows in Titian's paintings or the stark melodrama in Caravaggio's. None of the qualities of light that really matter, in a human, personal sense, can be translated into mechanical terms.

The mother of a friend of mine has grown old, and as sometimes happens, she is becoming bald. The wispy blue hair on top of her head distresses this once-beautiful woman, and when she was nearly eighty, she finally resigned herself to wearing a wig. My friend wanted to cheer his mother up, so he invited her to a party where many distinguished guests would be present. The company was sparkling, and his mother seemed greatly impressed.

"Weren't those people fascinating?" he asked afterward.

"Remarkable," she murmured, "and did you see how much hair they had?"

All of us see the world just this subjectively. When we walk into a room, we see what is important to us, screening out what is indifferent. We also see much that is invisible—that person over there is an old lover, another a renowned bore; that vase is worth a fortune (where did they get the money?), that painting looks like a fake. A map of the brain's visual cortex can never tell you the first thing about the subtle connotations that light reveals to the eye, just as the diagram of a piano can tell you nothing about how music enchants the ear.

The only reason a robot eye can even pretend to "see" is that it was built by humans. Every part was designed to approximate what a person knows to look for. If we could not see backgrounds as different from foregrounds, for example, no robot eye would be built to sense such a distinction, and no software would take it into account. Even if a robot eye could perfectly duplicate a human eye, including the visual cortex, it would still be blind. The light filling the world is *my* light.

This truth struck home while I was reading *The Magic Lantern,* the autobiography of the great Swedish film director

Ingmar Bergman. Bergman gave up filmmaking before he was seventy years old, a situation he has made peace with, despite many moments of intense regret. "Most of all," he says, "I miss working with Sven Nyquist [his longtime cameraman], perhaps because we are both utterly captivated by the problems of light, the gentle, dangerous, dreamlike, living, dead, clear, misty, hot, violent, bare, sudden, dark, springlike, falling, straight, slanting, sensual, subdued, limited, poisonous, calming, pale light. Light."

Following the curve of this singing, elegiac sentence, I can see all those qualities in light as well. All of us can, because without us, light would not have them. It would have no brightness, no color, no tone whatsoever. Without *my* eye (or yours), there is nothing to see, not even blackness. Photons would bounce randomly, unintelligibly through the void, never defining anything, never becoming light. In interstellar space, light is invisible; when it strikes an object, it bounces back on a new track, but it does not become any more visible. The sun is not radiant, nor the stars. At best, they would be "hot spots" of energy emission, but even that term depends on our sense of temperature.

By itself, nothing "out there" has any definition without a perceiver. When scientists claim to have deciphered the mechanics of vision, all they have done is found a map, which must not be mistaken for reality. A map of Tahiti is meaningless until you realize that it is supposed to match a certain island whose mountains, coasts, and rivers have been experienced by humans. We do not put on the map the air currents or prime nesting sites that would be noticed by birds, even though these belong to the real Tahiti as much as the features we look for.

The map is not the territory. Everyone has seen photographs of what the world looks like through the multiple eye of a bee, spider, or fly. Each of these insects sees through more than one lens, and the photographs therefore present a cluster of eight or ten or twenty images, generally of a flower, and we are to suppose that the insect brain sees the flower that way.

These composites, however, do not really capture the actual experience of insect eyesight—they only indicate what a human being might see if he looked through several camera lenses at the same time. In reality, the eye of a horsefly is divided into 20,000 separate eye-cell clusters. Each one responds either to a very specific wavelength of light or to certain chemicals floating in the air. As a result, the picture of the world processed by a horsefly's nervous system is inconceivable to us (what does it mean to "see" a chemical in the air, anyway?).

A porpoise's brain is almost as large as a human one, but 80 percent of it is devoted to processing sounds. Porpoises, whales, and dolphins have remarkable hearing; some species are able to detect one another's "songs" through miles of water. The map of a porpoise's ear will tell me what kind of eardrum it has, and if I look at the minute hair cells inside the ear, I will see relatives of the cells in my inner ear. All this similarity of structure is misleading, however, because the porpoise's experience is not understandable by the human mind, no matter how good the map.

Even to use the word "hearing" is suspect. Hearing to a porpoise is a kind of sonar, like a bat's, that brings back three-dimensional images closer to sights than sounds. A porpoise can "hear" how large a shark is and in what direction it is moving. Actually, I shouldn't even venture this crude guess; for all I know, a porpoise can "hear" that it is summer, that the sun is low on the horizon, that a grouper is gray, or that Mars is tilted on its axis.

Looking at Sounds

If all perception is personal, where do the "real" sights, sounds, smells, tastes, and textures begin? We trust our eyes to see "real" photons and our ears to hear "real" vibrations in the air, but it is easy to show that this trust rests upon a very shaky foundation. In his penetrating book on the world of the deaf, *Seeing Voices,* neurologist Oliver Sacks tells the strange tale of David Wright, an Englishman who thought he could hear until he "saw" that he was deaf.

Wright had lost his hearing gradually in early childhood and was not stone deaf until the age of seven. Since he had been born with normal hearing, the young Wright had already mastered speech and was used to hearing people talk. This made it hard for him to detect that he was being shut out of the hearing world: "From the very first my eyes had unconsciously begun to translate motion into sound. My mother spent most of the day beside me and I understood everything she said. Why not? Without knowing it I had been reading her mouth all my life." In other words, when his mother spoke, Wright found himself unable to tell that her voice was not real, since like the rest of us, he "heard" it. "It was an illusion that persisted even after I knew it was an illusion," he recalls. "My father, my cousins, everyone I had known retained phantasmal voices."

Wright's brain instantly and automatically turned the sight of moving lips into sounds. These "projections of habit and memory," as he called them, lasted until he left the hospital where it had been finally determined that his hearing loss was total and irreversible. Then the turning point came: "One day I was talking to my cousin and he, in a moment of inspiration, covered his mouth with his hands as he spoke. Silence! Once and for all I understood that what I could not see, I could not hear."

Why, then, don't we all see voices, instead of restricting ourselves to the same worn rut of hearing? Many deaf people do "hear" the wind in the trees when they see the branches swaying. Some junction point in their minds converts a visual signal into an auditory one. Many blind people can likewise "see" faces by feeling them with their hands. A mental junction point has taken the signals of touch and converted them to sight. Presumably our brains could do the same thing, but we prefer to let habit and memory take over. We see through our eyes and feel through our fingers because we have been conditioned to do so. Is that statement so incredible?

In *Walden*, Thoreau records that sometimes he lingered after nightfall at a friend's house in Concord and would have to tramp back to his hut on Walden Pond without a lantern. Even if there was no moon and the woods looked pitch black, he would "see" his way perfectly, without stumbling, and after several miles would arrive unerringly at his doorstep.

There is also the case of Meyer Schneider, an Israeli, born

blind, who managed to recover a remarkable degree of sight through self-devised eye exercises. (He currently teaches these to a wide following from his home base in San Francisco.) Although his vision has been measured as 20/70, ophthalmologists who examine the interior of Schneider's eye see the same defective parts that he has always had.

The whole notion that we have exactly five senses is completely arbitrary to begin with. Under the sense of touch, for example, we include our response to heat, texture, pressure, the placement of our limbs, the weight of our bodies, and pain —all are things we "feel." When the nervous system is intact, we may be said to have as many as seventeen senses, according to researchers on perception. We do not give names to most of these, and some are still disputable. Everyone seems to be able to detect pheromones, for example, the distinctive chemicals the body gives off when a person is afraid or sexually aroused, and the pineal gland in everyone's brain changes its hormonal output by sensing the yearly cycle of the sun. But only selected individuals count among their senses ESP or the ability to see auras of light around other people.

Perception, we must conclude, is infinitely flexible, serving the mind in any way the mind chooses. We create new worlds inside our private universe, worlds that the five senses then confirm as real. Outer reality can even be turned off by a mere flick of the wrist. A psychiatrist friend of mine told me about being called on an emergency in downtown Boston. A car had stopped at a red light and had not moved when the light turned green. A policeman arrived and found the driver motionless at the wheel. He was apparently the victim of a heart attack. However, the ambulance attendants who showed up within minutes saw that the driver was alive but catatonic. He registered no response to light, sound, or touch, even though his pupils continued to dilate if a flashlight was shone at them. He sat like a statue, his hands gripped to the wheel, and had to be pried from the car by force.

When my psychiatrist friend saw the man, it was clear that he had become totally withdrawn. He had no history of mental disease (although that does not rule out the possibility that he was a "walking schizophrenic," of which there are many). For reasons of his own, he had just decided to stop, and in one instant his entire perceptive machinery shut down. No one knows why some people decide one day to make the world disappear. It is their prerogative, and once they exercise it, no one outside the mental bubble holds any importance.

Perhaps the difference between five and seventeen senses is not all that significant, since any sense is just a channel for the real business of the mind, which is to sort out, interpret, and finally create reality. A newborn baby feels completely fused with his mother, and with all objects. Even though his skin contains working nerves and his eye a working retina, these mechanical parts are not enough to tell a baby that he is an individual. The touch and sight of anything "out there" feels like "me" touching and seeing myself.

Getting out of this homogeneous soup of "me-ness" is the baby's main intellectual task during the first months of life. All of us have accomplished the task, except for a few. There are some people, for example, who were autistic in childhood and still experience flashes of feeling that they have blended back into the soup of me-ness; they feel the touch of a wall when they look at it. The fusing experience may be blissful for an infant, but for an adult it is disorienting and, if it persists, terrifying.

Once a sense has been chosen for a particular function, the things it sees, touches, or hears become "real," but billions of stimuli have to be excluded during the selection process. When you look at another person you do not pick up the infrared wavelengths he emanates, the electrical field around him, the lines of magnetism that loop away from him and back again, the shudder of the ground when he walks—all are signals that do not fit our conventional senses, even though we probably do respond to them unconsciously.

Snakes, bats, and insects depend on these signals and therefore inhabit a world that overlaps ours while remaining quite different. I particularly like to imagine the world as seen by a chameleon, whose right and left eyes rotate independently in their sockets. A beam of light hitting a table would be a double beam to a chameleon. Two chairs could never be a foot apart, or any fixed distance, since with the swivel of an eye, the chameleon can make them as far apart as he wants.

Someone once vigorously challenged me on this point. "If I had a chameleon's eyes," he said, "I might see that door as two feet to the left, but that's not where it is in reality. If I tried to walk through the door I saw, I would bump into the wall."

"But think about it," I replied, "that just means you trust your sense of touch more than your sense of sight. The world may look very convincing, but that does not answer the deeper question: why should you trust any of your senses at all?"

Many Realities

If each person is constantly creating his own inner experience, placing innumerable interpretations on the raw data that the senses provide, that is strong grounds for not denying anyone his personal version of reality. A generation ago, the ruling assumption was that one reality—hard, scientific, materialistic—would do for all. Now we have to learn to cope with the state of many realities.

The story is told of a British anthropologist who undertook a field trip to India. One evening he crept through the jungle and caught sight of a strange scene. An old holy man was dancing ecstatically in the forest. He ran up and embraced the trees; he laughed when the leaves stirred and bathed his face in the moonlight with an expression of delirious joy. The anthropologist watched this display in fascination until he couldn't contain himself.

"Pardon me," he said, stepping from the bushes, "but what makes you dance out here, alone in the jungle?"

The holy man looked bewildered and replied, "Pardon me, but what makes you think I'm alone?"

Both questions are mutually unanswerable, because they depend on unique world views. The holy man sees himself surrounded in the forest by nature spirits, while the anthropologist sees wood and chlorophyll. The two realities overlap and yet do not come alive for each other.

I am especially drawn to such stories because my own life

has been dominated by conflicting and sometimes contradictory realities. In my Indian childhood, which was spent in the family of a military doctor, I saw a regimental band of Punjabis marching on the parade ground in turbans while playing Highland flings on their bagpipes. At my birthday parties the children sat wide-eyed, hands on their mouths, while a snake charmer performed for us, yet my favorite present was a model train from England complete with tiny station houses marked "Wembley" and "Paddington."

My school was St. Columba's in New Delhi, which was run along strict English lines by Catholic brothers. During games period, Brother McNamara would drag me off, pull down my pants, and wallop me every time I bowled outside the left wicket—cricket was a matter of life and death at St. Columba's. On graduation day he took me into his office and said, "Christ died to redeem you from eternal damnation. That is the point of your education here. What are you going to do about it?"

Could I tell him that a swami lived next door to our house who subsisted on the fifty rupees a month my mother, a devout Hindu, gave him? (Not that he needed much, since he sat in deep *samadhi*, hardly breathing or moving, for seven days at a time.) Or should I have told him how thrilled my mother was when she came back from a pilgrimage to a holy cave in north India? As she was kneeling at the mouth of the cave, she opened her eyes and found that Lord Shiva was giving her his blessing in the form of a rearing cobra two feet away.

My sense of reality continued to veer unsteadily from one world to the next. When I flew to Sri Lanka to take the exam that would entitle me to practice medicine in America, I spent the morning at a temple built around Buddha's tooth and listened to ethereal wind chimes tuned thousands of years ago to be pleasing to the *devas*, or angels. That afternoon I sat through an exam crammed with metabolic pathways and basic biochemistry. The American consulate was anxious to import only those foreign doctors who knew English well, so I also had to pass a language test that contained the memorable question, "A heavyweight boxer is A) A man who lifts heavy boxes, B) A kind of sportsman, C) A large man shaped like a box."

If you ask who is the "real" me, I would have to answer, "All of them." The triumph of the self is that it can create something entirely new and individual on the face of the earth. My inner self contains Brother McNamara, my mother, the swami next door, Shiva in the form of a cobra, my cricket team, and a toy station marked "Wembley." These images have been digested and turned into me; newer images, including everything I saw, heard, touched, tasted, and smelled today, are turning into me at this moment. Every time I bring one of these aspects of myself into view, I am also launching a display of unique physical reactions. Each new thought may cause only a slight shift inside my physiology, but "slight" still amounts to millions of neuronal signals in the brain, giving rise to billions of other cellular events that occur in the blink of an eye. In a very real sense, a new thought turns me into a new person.

The same holds true for everyone. An old man reliving a cherished boyhood memory can suddenly glow with youth. The effect, although temporary, can often be strikingly convincing—his wrinkles soften, his skin looks fresh, his eyes sparkle with life. The boy is still inside him, yearning to cross the threshold of time. You can see the powerful regret when the child has to turn back and the mask of old age wearily returns.

The depth and intensity of such changes is hard to fathom at times. I was fascinated by a first-person account given by a woman parishioner concerning the French priest Père Jean Lamy, who died in 1931 at the age of seventy-eight. An extremely devout and saintly man, Père Lamy was giving a rapturous sermon when this woman saw, uncannily, the complete emergence of a young man from inside the old:

> He stopped and looked upward. His face became translucent, like a block of alabaster lit from within. Old as he was, I saw him go young and handsome, like a man of thirty. I saw his wrinkles disappear. There was no sparkling light about his head but an inward light which made his face transparent, without dimness, without shadows about either the nose or the eyes. That lasted five or six seconds, perhaps

more—I don't know. He was looking lightly into the air in front of him. Imperceptibly all became normal again, and he went on talking as before.

This magical moment, which was seconded by another eyewitness, falls into a pattern of inner illuminations exhibited by saints and holy men in all times and traditions. Avoiding for the present the spiritual content of the event, I am struck by how effortlessly the body's hard mask can melt with a shift of awareness.

To fully come to terms with the power of awareness, we have to surrender the idea that its activity is confined to our mental bubble. Almost every primitive society believes that looking at an object requires the mind to shoot forth through the eyes. Instead of explaining vision by saying that light comes in, they say that sight is going out. Thus a skilled hunter can mesmerize game by stalking it with his eyes, and a shaman can heal or harm people by the power of his gaze.

In both cases, the glance is behaving as a carrier wave, transmitting mental intention out into the world and placing it upon whatever is being observed. Instead of understanding visual perception as a *taking in* of reality, this viewpoint, which was shared by Aristotle and the entire ancient world, says that perception *confers* reality. The same holds true for the other senses. Sound goes out with a power that is more than its physical vibrations, which is why New Guinea tribesmen can shout down a tree or the trumpet blasts of the Israelites topple city walls.

Modern people scoff at such things, reducing them to the level of superstitions like the "evil eye." We feel confident in our knowledge that light waves enter the eye and sound waves the ear. Surprisingly, this does not finally settle the question, because it is the flow of attention, not photons or air molecules, that transmits the powers we are talking about.

We have seen how the body can live or die on the basis of mental interpretations. The age-old idea that our minds can interact with the world needs to be more closely examined. Otherwise, we will not be able to tell if we have turned our backs on superstition or overlooked a dormant power that might be awakened from its long sleep.

3

⌇⌇⌇⌇⌇⌇⌇⌇⌇⌇⌇⌇⌇

Magical Thinking

There was a time when I lived outside the reach of magic. I was a new resident in Boston, working sixteen-hour shifts at the veteran's hospital. I barely had a free hour to be with my wife and was lucky when I got home to spend three sweet minutes with our baby daughter, who went to bed almost the instant I walked in the door. My salary was meager, five hundred dollars a month, and when our tiny apartment began to close in on us, I decided that I had better work harder. I began to moonlight. Instead of pointing the battered VW toward Jamaica Plain at night, I drove the long road to an emergency room in the suburbs, where I stayed on duty until dawn.

Another doctor worked with me, a seasoned trauma surgeon named Karl. We were comrades in exhaustion, and to avoid complete collapse we took turns catnapping. One of us curled up on a gurney in the back corridor while the other propped his eyes open at the nurses' station.

No one could call such a life magical; the word would have had no meaning for me. Life was difficult, and at times—as when I had to perform a cesarean upon a woman who had just been murdered—life was crushing. I worked without Karl that night, with a young Irish nurse beside me. We didn't have time to take the stretcher upstairs to an operating room but had to stand there in the door of the ER. The eeriness of the situation made both our hands shake. The baby came out within two minutes after the mother died. We waited tensely. It was breathing, then it wriggled.

"The pretty thing's all right," the nurse whispered. She gently cradled the infant to take it away to an incubator. I saw her smiling, but at the same time she couldn't stop the tears from rolling down her cheeks. Joy was coming in on the heels of sorrow. *When were things ever different?* I thought. The world is a mill wheel, impartially grinding out birth and death. A doctor dances on the edge of the wheel, trying to keep one jig-step ahead of death so that birth might have a better chance.

My assumption that things happen randomly in nature, without any regard for human feelings or hopes, was buttressed by a lifetime of experience, not just one disturbing incident. However, a strange coincidence started to unfurl that challenged my beliefs, making me wonder if the mind is not in some way helping to fashion events—this is the beginning of what I mean by magic.

The coincidence started with something quite mundane and seemingly innocuous: Karl developed a cough. You couldn't be surprised, because he was a heavy smoker, even on the job. He had the wracking, rasping cough that needs two packs a day to really ripen. One night I confronted him and asked why in the world he didn't go and have a chest X ray, just in case. "Because if I see cancer on it," he said seriously, "it will scare me to death." The look on his face told me to leave it alone.

Karl's cough eventually got so bad, however, that it was clearly interfering with his work. He bowed to my pleading and went for the X ray. When we held the film up in front of the viewing screen, a gray shadow as round as a penny could be seen in the lower lobe of his left lung.

"My God," Karl blurted out, "I do have cancer." I told him we had no conclusive proof, but within a few days he turned out to be right. A week went by and he coughed up blood for the first time. After three weeks he was panting and short of breath. They gave him heavy radiation, but he responded poorly, and within two months my friend Karl died.

He was gone with shocking swiftness, and in the aftermath I tried to be fatalistic. Karl had succumbed to epidermoidal lung cancer, a disease whose mortality rate approaches 100 percent. It was reasonable to tell oneself that his chances had been statistically very slim, but then I happened to run across one of Karl's old X rays, taken five years before. Curious, I held it up next to the new one and shivered. You could hardly tell them apart—the same lesion, a gray shadow as round as a penny, was visible in the earlier picture. It looked a bit smaller and more vaguely defined, which was why it had avoided firm diagnosis.

Karl's body had lived with this little round shadow for five years. How could he suddenly die of it in a matter of two months? Did he actually scare himself to death, as he had predicted? Conventional medicine would answer with a thundering "No!"—the mechanics of malignant tumors are just that, mechanical. They work according to the set laws of physics, chemistry, and biology, not according to the whim of a patient's mind. You don't die of a disease just because you are afraid of it. And yet one had to wonder.

Puzzled by Magic

A fear is just a negative kind of wish. If fears can come true, so can wishes in general. But neither one is supposed to. In fact, when a psychiatrist sits down to interview a patient who might be going insane, one of the chief symptoms he looks for is called "magical thinking." The hallmark of magical thinking is the person's firm belief that he can control reality with his mind. Stoplights do not turn from red to green automatically—he wills them to. His thoughts make people move toward him or away from him. If he shuts his eyes and wishes hard enough, he can even make a psychiatrist disappear.

The fact that a thought comes true does not necessarily make it magical. People have sudden premonitions not to take a certain flight and later read in the newspaper that the flight crashed. These things happen, and once the moment of wonder passes, they are usually dismissed from our minds. However, what if a causal connection is at work? Perhaps unseen powers warned those travelers in order to save their lives. Now we are flirting with magic.

The next step could lead to mental disturbance. There are paranoid schizophrenics who can no longer draw the line between their mind and God's. Such a person will begin to hold himself responsible for world events—without his personal intervention, earthquakes might topple the Empire State Building or nuclear missiles come flying across the Arctic Circle. Some paranoiacs drive themselves to stay awake around the clock, keeping watch like fretful mothers beside the cradle, so strong is their belief that reality will disappear, vaporizing like a dream, unless they fix their minds on it.

However, that is only one aspect of a mystery that has puzzled humankind for thousands of years. Can we in fact influence reality with our thoughts? A pure mystic immediately says yes to this question; a pure rationalist just as quickly says no. Most people, however, find themselves intrigued and confused. No one has ever proved that thinking magically has to be wrong, and in some cases there is no other way to explain why things happen the way they do.

There is, for example, the rare phenomenon in which terminally afflicted patients suddenly intuit that, despite all the odds, they are going to recover. This sudden shift in awareness cannot be predicted by either the patient or his doctor—it seems to strike with the fickleness of lightning. A striking example (which came to me via Dr. Yujiro Ikemi, Japan's leading researcher on spontaneous remissions) is the terminal cancer patient whose tumor, often massive in size, suddenly disappears, and as it does, or just before, the patient *knows it.* At one moment he is subject to uncontrollable mood swings, like any other patient confronting death. All at once despair gives way, not to hope, but to a calm, almost unearthly knowingness. "This tumor is going away" becomes as natural a belief as "This cold is going away." The shift in awareness has made something happen in the body, or has given a signal that it has already happened. Nobody really knows which.

Let us accept that this may be magical thinking, not in the disturbed sense, but as a potentially valid power of the mind. Clearly nature has gone to great pains to keep this power hidden. One could spend a lifetime not knowing that it exists, were it not for those people who are too innocent or too mad to keep their inner world a secret.

One way to approach magical thinking may be to set aside the mind-body connection, at least for the moment, and concentrate on the magical thinker's own idea of what he is doing. I would propose that he operates differently from most people, according to a principle called "self-referral." Self-referral means that I gauge reality not by externals but by internals, by my own feelings and intuitions. If I am living according to this principle, there is no mystery when a shift in awareness causes a change in my body, because *all* reality begins with such a shift and keeps on changing as I do.

Things appear to be happening to me, but in fact I am participating in each and every event. If I were alert enough, I would see my thoughts radiating like light from a candle or a star. Thoughts surge up from their invisible source and lap against the world like waves against the shore. They strike everything in my vicinity—oak trees, clouds, skyscrapers, other people, even the most random atoms and bits of atoms. These things are basically reflections seen in the mirror of my awareness. And the mirror is vast—my thoughts roll on as far as the edge of the universe, beginning at a finite source but spreading out to infinity.

The opposite of self-referral is object-referral, which means giving primary importance to externals instead of to myself. A person whose thinking is based on object-referral automatically assumes that his mind has no influence over things in the outside world. A thought is a subjective event that ricochets around inside a mental bubble, never able to break out. For all practical purposes, this means that object-referral awareness is mercilessly dominated by things. Compared to the ghost of a thought, the hard, solid objects of this world seem much more real and therefore much more powerful. This is the position almost all of us find ourselves in.

Even if you cannot imagine a reality centered entirely on yourself, however, another person could be living that wa⸴

very successfully. A friend of mine was traveling in Kashmir and brought back the following tale:

"Holy men are a common sight in Srinagar, the capital of Kashmir, because of its proximity to the Himalayas. One day I saw a holy man making his way down the street. He was an old ascetic with a long beard, but very tall and vigorous looking. He was dressed in a saffron robe, and by his side he carried a three-pronged staff called a *trishul*, or Shiva's trident. The god Shiva is looked upon by many ascetics in India as their patron.

"As this imposing figure neared me, he was suddenly accosted by a gang of jeering boys. They were rough, and in a minute their taunts turned to shoves. They pulled the old ascetic around, while he showed not the slightest irritation. One of the boys stole his trident and ran away with it. Still the old man walked on, smiling as if nothing had happened. That stick was all he had. No doubt it had been ceremonially presented to him by his guru decades ago, and all his possessions were in the cotton bag that was tied around its neck.

"All at once another boy dashed up and grabbed the trident back. He ran up behind the ascetic, and just as he was holding out the stick, the old man, who couldn't see the boy behind him, gracefully reached backward to receive it. He was still walking straight ahead at the time and didn't even turn his head. It was as if hand and stick were fated to meet again, or had never been separated. Then he disappeared.

"I walked on, absorbed in my thoughts. How could the old man have remained so unperturbed? Did he know that the stick would come back to him? At the next block, I looked up, and there he was, crossing my path again. He gravely turned his eyes in my direction and gave me a slow, conspiratorial wink. I didn't even realize that he knew I had been watching. Then in English he said, 'May I buy you a cup of tea?' The words sounded faintly ludicrous, but immediately I felt drawn into his seamless, unshakable reality, and I marveled at its security."

What this story tells me is that the self and the world do not have to be separate entities. The whole incident was not necessarily a contest between an old man and a gang of boys; it was a diverting play within the old man's awareness that took on outward shape. He stood at the center of the event, certain of its outcome, and his hand found the stick again because it was meant to. Some people see more of this magic than the rest of us. As Robert Frost wrote in one of his shortest poems: "We dance round in a ring and suppose, / But the Secret sits in the middle and knows." My friend went and had tea with the holy man, but he found it hard to get any more words out of him. The ascetic had exhibited enough of the Secret for one day.

People who learn to live on the basis of self-referral need not lose sight of the objective world; even the most austere ascetics require food, water, and shelter. Also, we should not hastily assume that worldly pleasures are the enemy of the self. It is just a matter of reorienting one's perspective, seeing the self as primary and outward things as secondary. Unfortunately, to someone who defines himself through outside objects, the prospect of trusting in himself as the linchpin of reality can be quite disturbing. For every desirable word in our vocabulary like self-reliant, self-motivated, and self-sufficient, our object-referral culture has found an undesirable one: self-centered, introverted, withdrawn, narcissistic, solipsistic, egocentric.

Although subjectivity is supposed to be changeable and untrustworthy, it seems no less treacherous to rely psychologically upon exterior objects. I remember a fable I used to hear in India: Once there was a poor villager who possessed only two things of any value—his son, who was sixteen, and a handsome gray pony. The villager loved these two above all else in creation. One day the pony vanished and could not be found. The villager was plunged into deep dejection. No one could lift his spirits until three days later, when the pony returned, followed by a handsome black Arabian stallion. Overjoyed, the man embraced the pony and quickly bridled the stallion.

His son eagerly asked if he could ride the wild horse, and since he could deny him nothing, the father consented. An hour later, news came that the boy had been badly thrown while riding on the beach. He was carried home in a litter, bruised and battered, his right leg shattered in two places. At the sight of his injured son, the father's happiness again turned to utter sorrow.

He sat in front of his hut wailing, when a contingent of the king's soldiers swept by. War was imminent, and their duty was to drag off conscripts from the village. They ruthlessly seized every eligible son, but when they came to this man's house, the soldiers saw that his son was maimed, and they left him behind. The father's tears again turned to joy, and he gave fervent thanks to heaven for the tragedy he had bewailed the moment before.

What's peculiar about this fable is that it has no ending, and that is its moral. The rise and fall of the villager's spirits goes on and on, bound to the fate of a boy and a pony. In real life, people have more than two things they cherish, but the result is the same. So long as our happiness depends upon objects "out there," we are their prisoner. We have given our freedom away to things.

Sad Love Stories

Although medicine is not yet prepared to admit that self-referral plays the major part in either the onset or the cure of disease, a large number of patients are very open to the possibility. They instinctively refer to the feelings that surround their illness. If there is a great deal of denial or self-blame present, their feelings will usually be turbulent and therefore misleading. But they can also be startlingly clear, giving the patient a truer understanding of his situation than anyone could objectively supply from the outside.

In this regard, there is a fascinating account from the popular writer Michael Crichton, who was trained as a doctor at Harvard Medical School twenty-five years ago. In his book of autobiographical sketches, *Travels*, Crichton remembers the months he spent on the cardiac ward of a Boston teaching hospital. It is routine for third- and fourth-year students to rotate briefly through all the major medical specializations. Crichton had no intention of pursuing cardiology, but he had a simple, quite novel insight during this particular rotation:

what if heart disease was not the same for every patient but had some kind of personal meaning for each one?

What prompted Crichton to speculate along these lines were some famous pathology findings made in the early fifties. During the Korean War autopsies were routinely performed on young soldiers who had been killed in battle, and doctors were surprised to find that the arteries of more than 70 percent showed advanced stages of atherosclerosis; these young arteries were already building up fatty plaques, cutting oxygen off from the heart, and moving inexorably in the direction of a heart attack.

Yet if men as young as seventeen already had this disease, Crichton wondered, why did a typical coronary occur much later, typically in a man's forties or fifties? "You had to assume that all these patients had been walking around with clogged arteries since they were teenagers," Crichton writes. "A heart attack could happen anytime. Why had they waited twenty or thirty years to develop a heart attack? Why had the heart attack happened this year and not next, this week and not last week?"

To answer his questions, he decided to learn something about the feelings the cardiac patients had about their disease. The direct approach seemed to be the best, so Crichton went on the ward and asked his patients point-blank, "Why did you have a heart attack?" He realized that his inquiries might set off unforeseeable reactions.

"My question also implied that the patients had some choice in the matter, and therefore some control over their disease. I feared they might respond with anger. So I started with the most easygoing patient on the ward, a man in his forties who had had a mild attack.

"Why did you have a heart attack?"

"You really want to know?"

"Yes, I do."

"I got a promotion. The company wants me to move to Cincinnati. But my wife doesn't want to go. She has all her family here in Boston, and she doesn't want to go with me. That's why."

The man said this completely calmly, without any sign of

anger. When Crichton went on to question the rest of the ward, every other patient had a similar answer:

"My wife is talking about leaving me."

"My son won't go to law school."

"I didn't get the raise."

"My wife wants another baby and I don't think we can afford it."

Not one person lacked an answer, yet not one mentioned arteriosclerosis as the cause of his heart attack, nor the standard risk factors, such as a high-fat diet, hypertension, lack of exercise, and smoking. In the late 1960s, the mind-body connection was considered not quite legitimate, and Crichton was perplexed by his patients' perspective. Looking back, he writes, "What I was seeing was that their explanations made sense from the standpoint of the whole organism, as a kind of physical acting-out. These patients were telling me stories of events that had affected their hearts in a metaphysical sense. They were telling me love stories. Sad love stories, which had pained their hearts. Their wives and families and bosses didn't care for them. Their hearts were attacked. And pretty soon, their hearts were *literally* attacked."

This insightful account does not "prove" anything new about heart disease. Yet Crichton can be credited with anticipating a key mind-body concept, now widely accepted, that our feelings do not live in a separate world from our cells. It is the precise timing of these heart attacks, however, which was controlled by the victim but also completely unforeseen by him, that gives Crichton's story its unique fascination. His patients knew what they had done only after they did it. This blind spot opens up a new aspect of the mystery. We see the body acting out the mind's dramas, yet we have not yet spied the director who decides which scene comes next. That is because the mind has decided to deny a part of itself.

A Space Beyond Reason

Because magic seems so foreign to it, the rational part of our minds is generally quite fearful of the nonrational part.

The very word "magic" has a sinister overtone to most of us, equated with all that is dark, dangerous, uncanny, and wild. But the threat has been greatly exaggerated. We spend much of our lives in the space beyond reason. If I say "I love you," the sound waves from my voice bounce against your eardrum, setting up a vibration that the inner ear turns into an electric signal. This impulse is passed along the neurons to the brain's speech center, and you look pleased.

Reason knows all about this journey, except for the last step, which is the most important. Why are you pleased that I love you? Why do those electrical impulses in the brain have a meaning? If I say a different sentence, "You have terminal cancer," the same physical impulses carry my voice to your brain's speech center, but now you are devastated. Scientifically, the signals are all but identical, yet the results they produce could hardly be more different. An EEG cannot decipher the meaningfulness of brain activity; the squiggles on the readout have nothing to say about what distinguishes love from hate, joy from sorrow, inspiration from tedium. The output generated by swamis deeply immersed in bliss creates patterns that closely resemble epileptic attacks; the voltage generated by the nervous system of a poet is not necessarily less than that from a psychopath.

Meaning slips through the fingers of science, which provides any person who is interested in meaning with a good reason to take magic seriously. The materialistic bias of science leads it to shun things that cannot be directly contacted by the senses. Yet nature has reserved a huge region set apart for things that cannot be seen, touched, or weighed. If you have ever observed a flock of swallows flying at dusk, you have seen them wheel and turn together, veering off at impossible tangents in the blink of an eye. How does each bird know to turn at the precise instant the others do? Scientists have established that there is no bird acting as leader—the impulse is somehow shared by every bird at once. The magic lies in each one but also in between, over, and around them. It is fluid and invisible, like the air, but more so.

A similar mystery exists if I happen to think a word at random—"archipelago." In order for me to think this word, millions of brain cells have to fire in a precise pattern at the exact same instant. One isolated cell doesn't dream up the word and then pass it along. It appears everywhere at once. For that matter, where was "archipelago" hiding when I wasn't thinking it? The location of mental space is as elusive as the space outside the universe.

Mental space is so inconceivable that one could easily claim that it is entirely magical. Computers can be programmed to play chess at the grandmaster level, but unlike real grandmasters, they do not grow tired, have brilliant inspirations, throw tantrums, exult in victory, or sulk in defeat. One grandmaster went mad and refused to play in tournaments unless a pineapple sundae was placed next to the board. Such a thing is inconceivable to a computer's mimicked intelligence, but it is all too human. This is what it means to have a mind. If a computer became the greatest chess player in history, humans would still have all the fun.

Magical thinking, then, presents itself not as a deviation from reason but as a way of probing past it into a space that is more alive and meaningful. It is just as natural to us as rationality, and perhaps more so. At birth a baby is totally self-centered; therefore it comes as no surprise that we started out in life thinking magically all the time. On the day you were born, you began to look around the world that was born with you. Soon a peculiar flying object appeared in your field of vision. Soft and rather doughy in appearance, it floated randomly before your eyes, sometimes visible, sometimes darting out of sight.

You did not relate to this object until the day came when you made a momentous discovery. Spurred by an intense desire for the breast or the bottle, you had an impulse to reach out. When you acted on this untested impulse, the apparatus that fastened onto the breast was this same object—and now you understood. The entity dangling in front of your eyes was yours to command; you acquired a hand.

The most complex motor skills, such as playing the violin or performing gymnastics, develop from the same basis. A desire reaches out into some unknown region and comes back with a report: it finds out what is possible and what is not. Using this information, the mind slightly changes its attitude, and when the next report comes back, the news has changed.

Now more is possible, or less—the new finger position on the bridge of the violin allows better flexibility or it doesn't. In either case, the mind has become renewed.

The ability of the mind to extend its influence seems limitless, even when impossible obstacles confront it. In his last book, *Wisdom, Madness, and Folly,* the renowned Scottish psychiatrist R. D. Laing recounts the following remarkable story about Jacqueline du Pré, the celebrated British cellist who died in her forties of multiple sclerosis.

Tragically, du Pré was stricken by the disease when she was twenty-eight and her musical career ended very quickly, as she soon lost her ability to coordinate her two arms. A year passed during which she had no contact with the cello.

One morning, however, she awoke to find that she was completely, inexplicably cured. Not just her muscular coordination but her musical abilities had returned intact. She rushed to a studio and recorded beautiful performances of music by Chopin and Franck that, needless to say, she had not been able to practice for a year. Her remission lasted four days, at the end of which she returned to her former helpless state.

It is hard to deny that for these four days, du Pré was *totally* free of her disease, and yet that makes no sense medically. Multiple sclerosis causes progressive organic damage to the nervous system; the fatty sheath covering each nerve cell, called myelin, becomes destroyed in patches that are randomly scattered throughout the brain and spinal cord. For some patients the degenerative process takes up to fifty years, while others are incapacitated within a few weeks or months of onset.

Du Pré was already at the point where her damaged neurons were physically dysfunctional. How did she recover? How did a nervous system that could not move an arm one day suddenly regain mastery over the incredibly precise and delicate motions involved in playing the cello? She did not think herself better, nor did courage and willpower seem to play a new part. Somehow she transcended her illness so completely that reality simply changed.

As a capstone to this tale, Laing records that he helped a patient create the same magical effect, although only for a moment. The patient was a man in his late thirties who had been confined to a wheelchair for some time. He "definitely presented the clinical picture of someone with well-established multiple sclerosis," Laing writes. "Just to see what would happen, I hypnotized him and told him to get up out of his wheelchair and walk. He did—for a few steps. He would have fallen if he had not been supported and helped back to his chair.

"He might still be walking now," Laing believes, "if I (and he) had not lost nerve after those first three or four steps—he had not been supposed to be able to walk for over a year." This argument implies that for a moment Laing allowed his patient to enter a space where his MS did not exist. The ravaged neurons either acted like healthy ones or failed to count in some wholly mysterious way. Either notion comes down to the same thing: the paralysis depended, to what extent we do not know, on the patient's state of awareness.

This conclusion would outrage a hard scientist, but we would all be paralyzed if thoughts did not have an invisible animating force. This is poignantly evident in cases of autism. Autism, which is derived from Latin roots meaning "self-centered" or "independent," is a rare infant disorder that was first diagnosed as late as 1943; it strikes fewer than 1 baby in 10,000, affecting four times more boys than girls. Its cause is still debated. The older, psychological theories blamed the child's "refrigerator mother," but these have given way to biological theories that hypothesize a chemical imbalance or perhaps a physical lesion in the child's brain.

Whatever the cause, an autistic child displays almost no response to the outside world and other people. If he is placed in a swing and pushed back and forth, he may appear to be slightly engaged in the experience, but as soon as he is left to swing himself, he lapses into apathy. If a ball is thrown at him, he will not lift up his hands either to catch it or to fend it off. Much of his spare time may be spent in repetitive, mechanical movements called "twiddling." Somehow, the spark of desire has become lost in the dark, winding maze of self-absorption.

It can sometimes be tricked into returning. I once watched a videotape of autistic children who at three or four years of age had not yet learned to walk. Withdrawn in their sealed-off worlds, they could stand up only if given a prop to lean against. Otherwise, they immediately fell down and did not try to get up again. To help these children, an ingenious contrivance was devised.

First, two chairs were set up ten feet apart with a strong rope connecting them. Each child was coaxed to hold on to the rope and walk a few steps. After a while, this task was mastered, and the child could make it from one chair to the next without falling. The next time, a slightly thinner rope was substituted for the thick one. Again the child leaned on the rope and made it from one chair to the other. On each successive day a slightly thinner rope was substituted, but the child noticed no difference. Finally, he was walking "supported" by only a flimsy piece of string.

Then came the stroke of brilliance. To release the children from the mechanical routine of walking from one chair to the next, the experimenters handed each of them a piece of string to carry around in his hand. Feeling secure that he still had his support to lean on, the child could now walk freely. That moment of letting go has magic in it. Seeing these newly liberated children roaming their playroom for the first time, I wondered how many small gaps separate me from freedom, gaps that seem like huge, impassable gulfs because I do not have a piece of string to use as a bridge.

Bridging Two Worlds

So far, my defense of magical thinking has not strayed far outside the tightly enclosed domain of the brain and the body it controls. Yet people do at times believe that their thoughts influence events completely beyond the reach of nerve signals. The study of parapsychology has staked out a shaky sort of credibility here. Most people have had premonitions that come true, but as we noted before, magical thinking goes beyond ESP and precognition by apparently causing people or things "out there" to move according to one's will.

Since there is such fear and prejudice surrounding it, this

is the final kind of magic that I would like to demystify. To have another person enact a thought you have had does not mean that he must be an automaton or that you have encroached upon his free will. These are reflex fears that spring to mind, reinforced by the "rational" belief that each person occupies a completely isolated portion of space and time.

Let us suppose for just a moment that this is a prejudice. If you hold a small horseshoe magnet in your hand, its charge is extremely tiny and apparently isolated. But the magnet would have no charge without the earth's immense magnetic field; there is an invisible connection between the two, and beyond. The earth could not be magnetized without the magnetic field of the sun, the sun depends for its fields of force on the galaxy, and so on, expanding to infinity. The final result is that the magnet in your hand is woven into the scheme of the entire universe.

The evolutionary sequence leading from the Big Bang to my mind is just as continuous as that which leads to the horseshoe magnet. Although each thought in my mind is tiny, it emerges from the trillions of potential thoughts a person might have, and they depend on millions of years of human evolution leading up to the present structure of the brain. Evolution in turn depends on the unfoldment of the entire universe since the moment of the Big Bang. Therefore, a single thought may be seen as a small outcropping in a universal field.

The crucial difference, of course, is that the electromagnetic field can be measured for millions of light years, while no one has proven that the cosmos has a mind. We prefer to believe that intelligence arrived late on the scene, at the last minute of the eleventh hour in the known life of the universe, and our intelligence is a special outgrowth in that extremely isolated occurrence. Indeed, aside from a handful of evolutionary biologists, science gets along very well without having to confront the thorny issue of where and how intelligence began.

We are facing the issue here because magical thinking seems to exhibit many of the characteristics of a field. The universe's electromagnetic field is invisible, all-pervasive, and capable of responding to the slightest change within itself. As the earth's magnetic pole shifts, every compass on the planet follows it; in return, if you take a compass out of your pocket, the earth's magnetic field is affected by a minuscule amount. In short, no part of the field can move without moving the whole.

If we transpose this understanding onto the mind, it would mean that each of our thoughts affects all other minds, not because we are exercising psychic powers, but because every mind is a small outcropping in the field. This is a sweeping paradigm that I am introducing here, and I have every intention of pursuing its many ramifications. Yet if we ignore the huge questions that loom up before us, the idea of belonging to one interwoven intelligence is the logical conclusion of the argument that reality "in here" is connected to reality "out there." For what is more likely to connect the two than intelligence?

If a person's mind is engaging in a creative give-and-take with the world—as we concluded when we looked at perception—there must be some sort of common ground. It may sound absurd to claim that anyone's mind can affect a boulder or a tree, but inside our brains, mental activity is constantly altering the structure of brain chemicals. These chemicals are made of molecules and atoms, as are boulders and trees. Just because a carbon atom resides in the gray matter of your brain does not bring it any closer to the mind than if the atom resided in a tree. There is still the impassable gulf between mind and matter to contend with.

Magical thinking provides us with evidence that we are bridging that gulf all the time. Actually, this linear image is far too static, since fields are continually pulsating with life. It is much closer to the truth to say that mind and matter join in a dance, moving instinctively together, aware without speaking of where their next step will fall. To bring this metaphor to life, I can present Sheila, an Englishwoman in her mid-fifties who was profoundly affected by one magical thought.

Thirty years ago, as a young girl fresh out of convent school, Sheila conceived a child out of wedlock. Her family, who were devout Catholics, could not accept this pregnancy. Sheila herself realized that she was not ready to raise a child alone, and although she was distraught about giving up her baby, she decided to carry it to term and allow the adoption agencies to find the infant a home. As she told me in a remarkable letter:

"I watched my baby being born, in the mirror they placed at the foot of my bed. I remember my sense of wonder, excitement, and achievement when this beautiful tiny boy appeared. I remember as well the sense of loss that came from having no one to share these feelings with.

"The moment my baby was born, we both started to cry. I held him close to my heart, trying to comfort the two of us and to feel his heart beating in unison with mine. For six days I bottle-fed him while the slow, relentless adoption procedures took over our lives. I wasn't counseled, other than to be told that I was 'a poor dear' who should forget what had happened, go out, and start all over again. A deep sense of grief settled into my soul."

A suitable family had been found for her infant son, and Sheila agreed not to interfere in his growing-up years or even to make her existence known. In return, she asked that he keep the name she had given him, which was Simon. For twenty years she kept her promise, although the separation became harder rather than easier for her to bear as time went on. She was never able to have another child, fearing to repeat the intense trauma of her first birthing experience.

Finally, when Simon turned twenty-one, Sheila decided to return to England from her home abroad and ask for a meeting with him. Since she did not know the whereabouts of the adoptive family, she hired a detective agency to make an investigation. In the meantime she retreated to stay with old friends in Oxford. At this point an event took place that lifts Sheila's story to a new sphere.

"To pass the time, I took long walks among the dreaming spires of Oxford. I found myself captivated by the medieval air of the town. One afternoon, after visiting Christ Church College, I walked through the meadows down to the riverbank. An Oxford eight rowing crew was practicing nearby.

"All at once, an eerie feeling crept up my spine. For no reason my adrenaline started pumping, my palms grew sweaty and my mouth dry. My mind became very alert, and I heard the word 'Simon' ringing in my ears. I rushed back to my friends' house, stunned. I lay on the sofa in front of the fire, feeling very cold, shaken, and confused. Somehow I knew that my son was a student at Oxford and that I had seen him rowing on the river that afternoon!

"A second wave of insight came over me, and I said aloud, 'I know something that I shouldn't know. He is studying medicine. Simon is following in his grandmother's footsteps.' [Sheila's mother was a practicing internist.] I had no idea where this state of heightened awareness came from."

Her friends hastened to borrow a college roster, and as she had intuited, it contained a listing for her son. Sheila was troubled at her uncanny knowledge, but since she had no idea what to do next, she did nothing. The detective agency called with a report verifying other details of her intuition; they were amazed that she knew them already.

Our conventional study of human psychology cannot explain this occurrence, yet there is no doubt in my mind that Sheila "magnetized" this event, drawing to herself the lost child she had fiercely longed to regain. It was as if all her pent-up frustration could no longer be held back. It had to break free, and to do that, it broke down the artificial barrier between inner and outer reality.

There is another detail of Sheila's story that provokes in me a sense of both awe and gratitude. As it turned out, her uncanny insights did not lead to a happy reunion with Simon. His adoptive family put strong pressure on him to reject the sudden appearance of this unwanted woman in their life. It took another nine years before mother and son found the mutual courage to meet and accept each other.

Their emotional reunion took place in 1989, when Simon, now a practicing physician in Oxford, invited his mother to visit him. Despite her trepidation, Sheila's most cherished hope was realized—she was accepted for who she was, on her own terms, and welcomed as a member of Simon's family. Soon after she arrived at his home, her son suggested that they go for a walk through the woods near his old college. By chance he picked the same riverbank where Sheila had seen the rowing team years before. She told him about her intuition, and he listened mesmerized.

"It's true," he said in a halting voice, "I *was* rowing that day, and I remember looking up to see a woman standing alone on the riverbank. I felt the hair rise on the back of my neck. My spine tingled, and I became very agitated. She seemed to be watching me. Then the thought flashed into my head, 'She is your mother.'"

Sheila and Simon fell silent. It was impossible for them to comprehend how they had been brought together, but they felt that something supernatural had occurred. "We walked to the chapel at Merton College," Sheila said. "Simon took off my gloves and gently held my hands while we prayed in gratitude. 'I'm embarrassed,' he whispered. 'It's like being on a first date.' I laughed, and tears trickled down our cheeks, softly and silently. They seemed to wash away the pain in my heart, leaving only love and forgiveness. I wasn't sure who or what was being forgiven, but at that moment I felt free of my old anger and loneliness."

Sheila's tale is extraordinary, but I think it illustrates a much wider phenomenon. The world "in here" is meant to flow into and merge with the one "out there," and if we oppose this flow, we only postpone the day when the mind reaches out to restore the natural scheme of things. This must be happening, in both small and large ways, much more often than we notice or care to admit. One is led to believe that magical thinking is an act of healing, and the most magical minds are therefore the healthiest.

4

︽︽︽︽︽︽︽︽︽︽︽

Bending the Arrow of Time

$\mathbf{A}$s ill fortune would have it, the two worst days in Malcolm's life came back to back. On Monday his brother was jogging in the park, as he did every morning, when another runner saw him suddenly collapse onto the path. The man rushed to help, but Malcolm's brother was already dead, the victim of a massive heart attack. He was fifty years old, seven years younger than Malcolm, and he had no previous history of heart disease.

On Tuesday, the wife of Malcolm's best friend, who was a local pediatrician in his late forties, called up weeping incoherently. Her husband was driving home from the hospital that afternoon when he slumped over the wheel of his car. He, too, had been struck with a fatal heart attack without anyone suspecting that he had heart disease.

These two losses affected Malcolm deeply. Numbed and shaken, he began to dwell moodily on the uncertainty of life. By week's end, he decided to consult a doctor about his own heart. His cardiologist ran an EKG, which proved normal, but since his brother's heart attack might point to a family predisposition, Malcolm was asked to take a treadmill test. He performed extremely well, taking his heartbeat up to 180 without suffering pain, nor were there indications of any distortions in his heartbeat. "Stop worrying," his cardiologist reassured him, "you have the heart of a twenty-year-old."

The next day, however, Malcolm was sitting at a red light in morning traffic, continuing to obsess over the two deaths that had left such a gaping hole in his life. He missed the light turning green. Suddenly he found himself at the head of three lanes of angrily honking cars trying to zoom around him. Confused and disoriented, he took a few seconds to regain his composure, and as he shifted into gear, he noticed a funny sensation in the middle of his chest—he couldn't tell whether it was pain or pressure, but it made him feel momentarily dizzy.

Malcolm decided to consult another cardiologist, who spotted some potential irregularities in the way the first tread-mill test had been conducted. "Why don't you have another stress test?" he advised. "Just to make sure." Malcolm showed up early at the testing laboratory and was told that he would have to wait for the patient in front of him. He sat down and peered in through the lab window to see a fit-looking man in running shorts walking briskly on the treadmill. As if in a silent movie, the man opened his mouth without emitting a sound, clutched spasmodically at his chest, and fell to the floor. The nurse hustled Malcolm away. In a few minutes he learned that the man had died of a coronary. His own test was postponed for another week.

Malcolm feared that he was being followed by a curse. Greatly distressed, he returned home and for the first time began to notice definite twinges of pain in the area of his breastbone. He immediately reported this symptom to his new cardiologist. "Look," the doctor said, "no treadmill test is all that reliable. If you really want to be sure about your heart, let's do an angiogram." An angiogram, which allows the heart to be observed on a monitor while the coronary arteries are illuminated with an injection of dye, is considered the gold standard for assessing coronary heart disease.

The test was run, and if Malcolm had feared the worst, it now came true. Two of his coronary arteries were 85 percent blocked, causing blood flow to his heart to be dangerously restricted. His chest pain suddenly increased in intensity and frequency. It began to show the profile of typical angina, coming on whenever he exerted himself physically. Alarmed, his cardiologist put him on nitroglycerine pills to control the attacks. All next week Malcolm stayed home from work, but to combat his dejection, he decided to finish some home repairs, which required climbing a ladder and setting in some heavy window sashes.

On his next visit to the doctor, he mentioned that he had been doing this work without any chest discomfort. His cardiologist looked aghast. "You can't do that kind of thing! Don't you realize that with coronary arteries as blocked as yours, you could suffer a heart attack at any moment?"

Upon hearing these words, Malcolm felt squeezing chest pain that left him breathless—it was his first attack of unstable angina, a late and very serious symptom of heart disease. It is called "unstable" because the bouts of pain start coming unpredictably, with or without physical exertion. His cardiologist felt that they had no choice but to operate. Malcolm underwent a double bypass graft that Friday. It was less than a month after the two fatal heart attacks that had sent him into a tailspin.

Nor was this the end. When I saw him four months later, Malcolm's newly grafted coronary vessels were still open, but his chest pain had not abated. Today he still exhibits all the classic signs of unstable angina. He has to avoid even the least stress and therefore has been forced into early retirement. Since a stroll to the refrigerator is now enough to trigger a burst of chest pain, he is almost completely housebound. Presumably his high anxiety level triggers his attacks, either by causing spasms of the coronary arteries or by creating psychosomatic pain.

"What do you think caused all this?" I asked him.

"I lie awake thinking about it," he said mournfully. "Did I do this to myself, or am I just incredibly unlucky? No one's given me any kind of acceptable explanation. Let's call it a mystery and leave it at that."

Time and the Perceiver

If Malcolm's condition had taken forty years to develop instead of four weeks, there would be no mystery. We would just say that he grew old. Coronary artery disease afflicts so many old people that it was long considered a normal part of the aging process, and even now, when heart disease is known to be preventable and therefore is not, strictly speaking, normal, it remains the leading cause of mortality among the elderly. Historically, medicine has not been able to hunt down the cause of aging or even describe it well, but by definition getting old is something that takes a long time to happen. A heart that ages in a month is acting in a fashion that is highly abnormal, even bizarre.

There is more than a hint that Malcolm somehow generated the series of events that victimized him, although his consciousness did not recognize the fact. To begin with, explaining his case as the product of random chance is not convincing. The timing and orchestration of events following the death of his brother is just too perfect. They unfold like a well-crafted play, with rising dramatic tension and a swift, gripping denouement. Malcolm has no knowledge of how he might have done all this. To hasten the aging process implies the ability to control it, but that implies control over time itself, which is clearly impossible—or so we assume.

If we step outside the limited world view of science, explanations do exist. First we can challenge the basic assumption that time is objective. The clocks we depend upon to tell us the time appear to tick their hours and minutes independent of our influence, and daily events appear to be jumbled up with no rhyme or reason; but from another viewpoint, all this is only the conventional treatment of time which all of us happen to share. We have made a collective agreement that time has certain unalterable features: it moves forward, it is measured by clocks, it is uniform everywhere, it waits for no man.

Yet this agreement is not ironclad, and at certain moments time turns inexplicably flexible. Recently a Swiss friend of mine, also a physician, read me a curious and moving newspaper story about a coal mine disaster in Germany. A small group of miners were trapped underground after a massive cave-in. They realized that the air in the mine shaft would last only a limited number of hours. As it turned out, just one of the group was wearing a wristwatch, and he began to announce the time while the men anxiously awaited rescue. To sustain hope in the others, he did not announce the right time, however; he called out one hour whenever two hours had passed. Six days later, a rescue team found the trapped miners; astonishingly, they were all still alive with one exception —the man who wore the watch.

In essence, the man with the watch fooled the others into breaking their agreement about what constitutes real time. Tragically, he could not fool himself. Can it be that time will wait for one man and overtake another, depending on what each one expects? In the spring of 1990, sociologists from the University of California at San Diego reported that Chinese mortality dropped by 35 percent the week before the Harvest Moon Festival, one of the most auspicious days in the Chinese calendar, and one where special importance is given to elders. When the festival ended, death rates climbed again, and by a week later they were 34 percent higher than normal. This implies that people who are near death can postpone their passing in order to savor a day that is special to them.

A similar swing has been found with Jewish mortality just before and after Passover (by contrast, non-Jewish control groups showed no such effect, maintaining the same death rates throughout). Finally, cardiologists have pondered the fact that heart-attack rates are higher at 9 A.M. on Monday morning than at any other time of the week. This is not exactly a randomly chosen hour. For many people, going back to work after the weekend is a return to harsher realities. Have some of them found the drastic escape route of suffering a heart attack instead of punching the time clock one time too many?

These examples are limited to biological time, the hidden clock in our cells. To see truly comprehensive mastery of time, one must turn to dreams. Dream time lacks any fixed sequence or logic altogether. It can go backward or forward, speed up or slow down, come to a halt or simply disappear—

many dream events are frozen in a kind of no-time without beginning or end. Flying through the clouds, being caught in a riptide, or running down the street pursued by a phantom villain are dream events that can seem to last either an instant or an eternity, as if time has fled the scene.

When we wake up to the world of reliable clocks, time resumes its creeping pace, but that proves little about its real nature. Suppose a man is sitting in a room idly looking out the window. Morning, noon, and evening go by; he passively stares at people as they parade before him and watches the events taking place on the street. The same man could go to sleep at night and witness the exact same people and events in a dream, but now morning, noon, and evening occupy only two minutes of his sleep. Like the rest of his dream, time was created by his brain. In what way is waking time any different? The same brain cells process the passage of time in both cases; therefore, waking time and dream time could both be self-created.

If so, then time itself is only a personal perception, liable to the same fluctuations as a mood, reverie, fantasy, or any passing thought. Psychologists already recognize that time contains a strong personal element. All of us exercise some ability to manipulate time according to our whims. If I am languishing in a dentist's waiting room, my unhappiness makes time drag. To speed it up, I need only go somewhere else—to an Indian restaurant perhaps—where I can enjoy myself again. If I turn to something I find deeply enjoyable, time will start to fly. The difference between slow, dragging time and swift, fleeting time resides in my perception of the situation. As long as I am free to move from the dentist to the restaurant, I have personal control over how time feels.

But if I am forced by a sense of duty to remain at the dentist's, then I have no choice but to experience the creeping kind of time that is offered there. This sort of compulsion has trapped all of us. We stay in the same time-frame day after day because we think we have to, or ought to. But this is only an agreement we made somewhere along the line—we have even forgotten when. Anyone can break free and reassert his ability to control time.

Time Travelers

One of the main themes of the world's spiritual traditions is the falseness of time, and one of the aims of enlightened teachers is to break the spell of time that limits the minds of their followers. A master in India once said to his disciples, "You have enclosed yourself in the prison of time and space, squeezing your experience into the span of a lifetime and the volume of a body. It is because of this self-imposed illusion that all your conflicts arise: life and death, pain and pleasure, hope and fear. To end these problems, you must first end the illusion."

"But how is that done?" a disciple asked.

The master replied, "You are caught in this world like fish in a net. But all nets have holes. Find one, escape through it, and you will see what reality actually is."

Apparently the net of time is full of just such holes. It appears to be objectively real but in fact may be no more than a notion fostered in our minds. The great sage Shankara, who towers over the whole tradition of Indian philosophy, once wrote, "People grow old and die because they see other people grow old and die." I remember, on first reading this sentence ten years ago, feeling a mixture of disbelief and wonder. If Shankara is right, then aging is not a fixed biological process; it is just a bundle of perceptions we have picked up, taken into our bodies, and given physical shape.

There is a revealing, although heartless, biology experiment in which a rat is thrown into a tank of water. Rats are not adept swimmers, and the animal will thrash around, trying vainly to climb out of the tank, only to slip back down from the glass walls. After a few minutes the animal is totally exhausted, on the verge of drowning. The experimenter then pulls it out and allows it to rest.

The procedure is repeated over the following days, and within a short time, usually less than three weeks, the rat will have undergone dramatic changes. The pressure of so much daily stress will have aged its tissues enormously. If the experiment is kept up, the rat will die of "old age" in a month; on dissection, its heart, liver, lungs, and other organs will be as

dark, tough, and fibrous as those of a rat that lived a normal
life span of two years or more.

In essence, the experimenters sped up time and forced the
rat to absorb it into its body. The discolored, exhausted tissues
that resulted were like bits of frozen time given material expression by the aging process. The same process happens in
human beings, although we absorb time more complexly, according to our own personal values. Unlike experimental rats,
we can choose to live with more or less stress; more impor-
tantly, we can interpret time differently and therefore cause it
to change. Misusing this privilege creates untold suffering. I
am not thinking just of people who place themselves in desperately stressful situations, although millions do. The deeper
ignorance is that we do not realize that time does not have to
be frozen inside us.

Shankara's seemingly strange idea that we grow old because we watch others grow old may well be true. Partial vali-
dation has already come from an ingenious study the Harvard
psychology department ran in the late Seventies. The Harvard
team, headed by Professor Ellen Langer, did not actually set
out with Shankara's dictum in mind; they were testing
whether aging is an irreversible process, as is widely accepted.
The National Institute on Aging takes the official stand that
there is no reliable method, through drugs, diet, exercise, or
mental techniques, to restore lost youth. Although a large
body of research backs up this position, Langer's team had its
doubts; they suspected that aging might be a creation of the
mind that the mind can undo.

To test this possibility, they first placed a newspaper ad in
a Boston daily asking for men seventy-five and older who
would be willing to go on a week's vacation, all expenses paid.
A group of suitable volunteers was chosen, placed in a van,
and whisked off to a luxurious retreat on ten acres of secluded
woodland in the New England countryside.

When they arrived at this isolated setting, the men were
met with a duplicate of daily life as it existed twenty years
earlier. Instead of magazines from 1979, the reading tables
held issues of *Life* and the *Saturday Evening Post* from 1959.
The radio played music from that year, and group discussions
centered on the politics and celebrities of the era. A taped

address from President Eisenhower was played, followed by the film *Anatomy of a Murder*, which won the Academy Award in 1959. Besides these props, every effort was made to center each person on how he felt, looked, talked, and acted when he was twenty years younger.

The group had to speak exclusively in the present tense, as if 1959 were today ("Do you think Castro will become a puppet of Khrushchev's?"), and their references to family, friends, and jobs could not go beyond that year. Their middle-aged children were still at home or just going to college; their careers were in full swing. Each person had submitted a picture of himself taken twenty years before; these were used to introduce each one to the group.

While this week of make-believe went on, a control group of men over seventy-five also talked about the events of 1959, but using the past tense instead of the present. Castro, Mickey Mantle, Eisenhower, and Marilyn Monroe were allowed to have their real futures. The radio played 1979 music, the magazines carried the latest news, and the films were current releases.

Before, during, and after the retreat, Langer measured each man for signs of aging. For members of the 1959 group, to a remarkable extent these measurements actually went backward in time over the one-week period. The men began to improve in memory and manual dexterity. They were more active and self-sufficient (instead of waiting to be helped, they took their food and cleared their tables by themselves).

Some such changes might be expected in any older person enjoying himself on vacation. However, traits that are definitely considered irreversible signs of aging also started to turn around. Independent judges looked at before-and-after pictures of the men and rated them three years younger in appearance. Hand measurements showed that their fingers had actually lengthened and gained back some of the flexibility in their joints. The group could sit taller in their chairs, had a stronger hand grip, and could even see and hear better. The control group also exhibited some of these changes but to a smaller degree, and in some measures, such as manual dexterity and finger length, they had even declined over the week.

In her intriguing book, *Mindfulness*, Langer attributes

some of these reversals to the fact that the men were given more control over their lives than they enjoyed at home. They were treated like anyone in his mid-fifties, who would naturally carry his own suitcase or select his own food for dinner. Their opinions were valued in group discussions, and it was assumed that they were mentally vigorous, an assumption probably not made about them in everyday life. In this way they moved from a mindless existence to one that is "mindful," Langer's term for living with alertness, openness to new ideas, and mental vigor. But why did the group who lived in 1959 do so much better than the 1979 group? It is quite plausible that they improved because of what they saw. In a neat twist on Shankara's dictum, *not* seeing other people grow old seems to prevent us from growing old ourselves.

Langer's men were like time travelers of a special sort, who went back to the past by going back inside themselves. We tend to think that time is outside us, but in this instance, it was just as much inside, packaged as memory. To remember is to take your body time traveling, even though you do not leave your chair. For example, if I remember being scared in a dark alley when I was six, my heart starts to thump like a six-year-old's again. The mind can also project the body forward in time. I have seen twenty-year-old women, on being told that they have cancer, age before my eyes, becoming as worn as someone who has battled the disease for years.

In each case, the mind manages to be in two places at once, both traveling in time and staying in the present. The old men who went back to 1959 were also firmly fixed in 1979 —they read old magazines, but the same rain fell on them as on the other citizens of Boston that week. The illusion of fixed time was thus partly dissolved. One could go further. If I lost all my prior conditioning of seeing others age, perhaps I could remain a twenty-year-old permanently, although I would still walk around experiencing the ordinary passage of time as other people do. I would then have taken "my time" under control.

Why not speak of "my time" and "your time"? A clock on the shelf mindlessly taps out its seconds and minutes, but our inner clock possesses as much intelligence as the brain that houses it. After years of searching, physiologists in the last decade have pinpointed the biological clock that governs all the rhythmical functions of the body, such as waking, sleeping, eating, thirst, body temperature, blood pressure, growth, and the ebb and flow of numerous hormones.

A tiny core of cells in the hypothalamus, called the suprachiasmatic nucleus, regulates all these wheels within wheels, orchestrating rhythms as long as the twenty-eight-day menstrual cycle and as short as the three-hour burst of growth hormone. Even the chemical reactions inside individual cells, which take place thousands of times per second, must obey the body's master clock.

To use the word "clock" here is deceptive, because we can dictate the flow of time within ourselves, breaking free of any mechanical ticktock. We wake, sleep, eat, and breathe at will, overriding the preset cycles for these functions. Some women seem to be able to reset their ovulation cycle, delaying their periods under times of stress (they may not realize that they have made this choice, but their bodies apparently are responding to a specific brain signal triggered by the woman's emotions). In more extreme cases, women suffering from multiple personalities—the syndrome made famous by Eve and Sybil—can have a period for each personality, separated by several days or weeks each month. A woman with three personalities and three menstrual cycles does not have three separate clocks inside; instead, she has better control over time than we generally acknowledge.

To have so much freedom of choice can play havoc with rhythms that should not be thrown off—jet lag temporarily disrupts our major sleep-wake cycle, pulling dozens of smaller cycles along with it. Yet the very fact that time and mind can blend into one another points to the possibility of total freedom, an escape from mindless clocks into a reality where every second is alive.

The Arrow of Time

The concept of personal time would strike a physicist as a fantasy. To him, space-time is fundamental to existence, and time is governed by laws that do not bend because the mind wants them to. Physicists use the phrase "the arrow of time" to indicate that events move forward in the ordained manner and cannot be reversed. Stephen Hawking among others has used the example of knocking a glass off the table. When the glass strikes the floor, it shatters into a hundred pieces, and once shattered, it will never regroup itself into a whole glass. By the same law, ice cubes melt in a glass of tea and do not reform; junkyard wrecks rust into chaotic heaps, with no chance that they will suddenly turn back into new cars.

On paper you can put a broken glass back together again by carefully computing the energy exchanges that sent each shattered fragment off into space. A whole glass could then be conjured up by reversing each tangent. As pure mathematics, a whole glass is just a smashed glass with the equations turned around, and you can alternate one version with the other endlessly.

But the arrow of time forbids such easy shuffling in the real world. The instant the smash occurs, time carries the glass away, never to return it whole again. If this is indeed the law, it would only be wise to resign yourself to it, to bow to time as heat, light, all moving bodies, and all forms of energy in the universe do. But personal time, "my time," is not at all like that. Instead of shooting off in one direction, it moves forward when I worry about the future and backward when I remember the past. "Time is not just a road," the novelist John Fowles has written. "It is also a room." We call the room memory, a space where one can sit and be surrounded by heaps of things past.

Personal time can also be dead or alive. Several decades ago a team of archaeologists unearthed a clay vessel of wheat grains buried in an Egyptian pyramid. The grains were planted and watered, and within a few days they sprouted, amazingly, after two thousand years of dormancy. If you can imagine seeing this event from the wheat grain's viewpoint, it must have been very much like waking up. Time was dead while the seeds were dormant, causing no change or decay. That twenty centuries had passed was no different from one season, since the intervening time had no life in it. It was dead time, or sleeping time, wrapped up inside the seed, waiting for the touch of life.

The location of this wrapped-up time is the wheat's DNA, which has also stored time for us, in the form of our own genetic memory. You could not survive a cold or any other disease if your thymus gland did not store up the memory of antibodies that learned to combat viruses and bacteria millions of years ago. Your immune system is an encyclopedia of every disease ancestral man caught; thousands of generations died from fevers and plagues so that you may live.

Science has yet to recognize that DNA has a magical side, yet imagine that you are standing in an empty room with a spiral staircase directly in front of you. It is a wooden staircase, the kind once standard in old colonial houses and churches. As you are admiring its perfect carpentry, a strange thing happens. The staircase slowly rotates and splits in two, right up the middle, as if a zipper had opened it up from bottom to top. The two halves stand apart, facing each other.

Now you notice something that had escaped your eye before. The staircases are surrounded by a swirling cloud of sawdust. The sawdust cloud appears to be formless, but currents and eddies begin to form in it, and then, inexplicably, the cloud gradually rebuilds the half-staircases, adding new steps, banisters, and posts, until you behold before you two complete staircases, identical in every respect to the original.

DNA behaves in exactly this uncanny fashion. Every time you need to make a new cell (a need that crops up millions of times per minute), a molecule of DNA has to split itself in half. It does this exactly like the dream staircase: first the original double spiral divides down the middle, leaving the cell temporarily with no intact DNA. Then out of a formless, swirling bath of biochemicals, the DNA rebuilds each half of itself to form two replicas of the original molecule.

What is so astonishing about this process is not its complexity—although in every cell, 3 billion genetic bits get replaced with perfect precision. The truly astonishing part is that all this rebuilding is done by *things*. A DNA molecule, like a wooden staircase, is just a thing. It is built of quite ordinary hydrogen, carbon, oxygen, and nitrogen molecules, which themselves are just smaller things. Similar molecules make up a lump of sugar, a drop of oil, a clump of peat moss. None of them can perform the actions we just witnessed. How is it, then, that stubborn, inert molecules learned to build a staircase many million times more complicated than any constructed by human hands?

The answer is that DNA is not really a thing; it is a living memory residing in a thing. The memory is not intrinsic to the component carbon, hydrogen, or oxygen atoms. If it were, then a sugar cube would be alive, too. DNA is basically a material mask behind which one finds a rich but abstract awareness.

Consider DNA's mastery over time. To a human being, a film running at twenty-four frames per second is a movie, because our brains register its flashing images as continuous motion. That is pure illusion to a horsefly, whose eye is quick enough to catch the black spaces projected between each frame—the fly's brain sees a slide show of still pictures going by. A snail, on the other hand, being able to see only one new image every four seconds, misses three-quarters of the film; it sees only a hodgepodge of jerky pictures (if you moved fast enough, you would have time to surreptitiously pluck a rose from underneath a snail's nose and it would think the flower had disappeared into thin air). In each creature, DNA has adopted a different configuration, which brought with it a different style of consciousness suited to that creature and in turn a different mode of time.

DNA is like a switching station between eternity and all the forms of life that partake of time. DNA chops the endless continuum of time into neat slices according to a species' unique awareness and the specific life span allotted to it. Human time, horsefly time, snail time—each framework is completely different from the rest. What is even more impressive, DNA can exert control forward in time or backward. The fact that we all grow third molars, for example, is a bit of our inheritance that DNA fetches from the past. DNA has to go into the future, however, to know that this tooth will not appear except as the final addition to our adult teeth after age twelve.

The same speck of DNA deposited in the womb knows how to perform millions of actions that will not be needed for years or even decades to come. Our genes know how to fuse an infant's loosely joined skull bones and at the same time how to compensate for lost calcium in a seventy-year-old femur. The blending of time and life goes far beyond what a human brain can imagine. It has been estimated that 6 trillion chemical reactions take place in the body every second. The same speck of DNA controls them all, rarely mistiming a single one, no matter how distant in time and space.

If these teeming reactions remained the same from moment to moment, a cell biologist might one day give a complete explanation of how DNA masterminds the flow of life. However, there is a fourth dimension, wherein each cell obeys its own destiny: a skin cell survives one month while a neuron, motivated by the same genetic strand, endures a lifetime. It is unimaginable how our genes coordinate lifelines so vastly different. Some small patch of nowhere and no-time has been woven into the texture of our genes, a place where we can perch, as a fisherman perches on a riverbank to cast his line into the current. From that timeless position, you are old before you are young, bald before you sprout baby hair, expiring on your deathbed before you draw in your first breath.

The Self Beyond Time

Since DNA has such manifest mastery over time, we must share in it. If so, Malcolm's mystery is pointing to its own solution. He was unchaining himself from the arrow of time, abandoning time's straight line like a train jumping the tracks. He plunged into the unknown with all its perils. Even so, he came closer to the truth than most of us, for time actually is much more like a vast unknown country than a railroad track.

If you look at the whole landscape of time, the straight-line boundaries disappear, and what is left is eternity, the timeless. In their own ways, every spiritual tradition has tried to persuade man that the timeless is more real than any experience to be had in time. Nevertheless, we still find ourselves stranded in the flow of time, both physically and mentally. One has to look hard for escapees, and in this century, they are not necessarily men of faith.

Erwin Schrödinger, who was among the most influential theorists in the early decades of quantum physics, made the conceptual leap that most of us cannot: "Inconceivable as it seems to ordinary reason, you—and all other conscious beings as such—are all in all. Hence this life of yours which you are living is not merely a piece of the entire universe, but is, in a certain sense, the *whole*." To the isolated ego, this is an unfathomable statement. How can a person be the whole, which means everything that exists, and still remain what he seems to be, an individual being with separate ideas and memories?

Even though our world is time bound, there are many clues to indicate that we are tuned to the larger reality of "all in all." A prominent Japanese neuroscientist, Dr. Tadanobu Tsunoda, has spent fourteen years testing the functions of the left and right sides of the brain. In all of us there is a switching mechanism, located in the brain stem, that enables us to shift dominance to our left cerebral hemisphere when we are engaged in speech, calculation, and logic, and to our right hemisphere for music, recognizing shapes, drawing analogies, or engaging in anything that stirs our emotions. (We are speaking of a temporary shift here, not the permanent left- or right-brain dominance that has been publicized in recent years.)

Tsunoda devised a new way of mapping this switching mechanism, based on the delayed feedback of sounds, very much like watching the brain of a person who is hearing the sound of his own voice as he speaks. Many delicate aspects of the brain's shift from left to right were uncovered, but the most remarkable was this: It was found that people's brain dominance switched when they were played a sound whose frequency was a multiple of their age (e.g., a multiple of forty vibrations per second in the case of a forty-year-old). Even stranger is the observation, verified with thirty subjects in Japan, that a lasting shift in dominance also occurs on one's birthday. For a varying length of time, right-brain people become left-brain and vice versa. The phenomenon occurred in more than half the subjects tested, and for some it occurred three years in a row.

Confronted with these enigmas, Tsunoda speculates that our brains must somehow be tuned in to the earth's revolution around the sun, to the phases of the moon, or other cosmic clocks. "The link with cosmic activity suggests that there is a miniature cosmos in the human brain," he writes. "Yet we have lost our ability to perceive this microcosm within ourselves in the hustle and bustle of civilization." In the West we might consider this conclusion rather a far leap, considering the slimness of the data, but the ancient Indian sages declared,

> *As is the macrocosm, so is the microcosm,*
> *As is the atom, so is the universe,*
> *As is the human mind, so is the cosmic mind.*

In other words, you cannot stand anywhere in the universe that is outside yourself. As Schrödinger said, "You are a part of an infinite, eternal being. . . . Thus you can throw yourself flat on the ground, stretched out upon Mother Earth, with the certain conviction that you are one with her and she with you. You are as firmly established, as invulnerable as she, —indeed, a thousand times firmer and more invulnerable." This affirmation was not made out of mystical reverence. Schrödinger took seriously the proposition that the feeling of self, of "I am," must be primary in the universe. It is more invulnerable than the earth because the earth endures only by being a lump of matter, which time continually wears away. I, on the other hand, wake up with a refreshed sense of life every day, grounded in the certainty that I exist.

How did this feeling of "I am" come about? Apparently it exists in the very nature of life. Currently, most people are not able to accept that there is actually life in everything "out there." This blindness sets our culture apart from the main tradition of humankind. The same stream of life once flowed through the whole world, emanating from the gods or God. That unimaginable force created galaxies and at the same time preserved the most fragile mountain flower. All around us life gushed forth and met itself coming back, curving in joy onto itself and leaping in jubilation at its own infinite strength. We were part of this stream too. We issued from it, and our destiny was riding its crest.

Now all that has become very vague and quizzical. We equate life with DNA molecules, ignoring the fact that a person's DNA is just as intact the second after he dies as the second before. Sometimes after a hard November frost I walk in the tall grass near my home and find a grasshopper lifelessly clinging to a withered stalk. I pick up the cold shell, examine it, and think, "Something once lived in this. Now it has gone, I don't know where. I am holding on to a husk, and very soon its molecules will also disappear, returning back to earth. What made them alive once and then took their life away?"

In my puzzlement, I cannot help but see myself as the best judge of what life is. I have questions and an unlooked-for gift, a summer in the grass, in which to ask them. So time exists, as far as I am concerned, for me to race against time. I already foresee that my molecules will return to the earth, too. But unlike the grasshopper, I may be able to consciously defeat this threat, by knowing how to get beyond it. In its broadest and deepest sense, that is what the "meaning of life" is—the sum total of what each person has learned about his own life, and the chance to keep it. Other ages may have known the answers to this mystery, or people then may have simply settled for a ready-made answer, dictated by faith.

The final, "hard" proof that mind exists in nature is not anything I am waiting for. The proof may never come, since it is our mind conducting the search, and the mind is notorious for changing the rules. Meaning is where you see it, and how. You can look under a microscope at the flashing dots on a color television screen and see them as random scintillations in a phosphorescent chemical base, or you can back away and see that the same scintillations form a picture. One perspective detects orderliness and meaning, the product of mind; the other does not. The difference between the two resides solely in the perspective, not the thing itself.

If you glance outside your window and recognize the trees, sky, and clouds as part of yourself, your perception is not automatically true or false. Perhaps you are having a schizophrenic hallucination; perhaps you are experiencing the deepest insight of the ancient Indian sages, *Aham Brahmasmi*—I am Brahman, the all in all. The gamut of meaning contained in such an experience runs from the absurd to the sacred. The point is that the same mind-stuff contains all meanings. When we touch a new level of consciousness, a new world is created.

To find oneself living in an age of doubt is not such a curse. There is a kind of reverence in undertaking the quest for truth, even before the first scrap has been found. "Desire for wisdom!" Albert Schweitzer once wrote. "Explore everything around you, penetrate to the furthest limits of human knowledge, and always you will come up with something inexplicable in the end. It is called life."

The inexplicable thing that escaped out of the grasshopper's shell is repeated in my own life, and if I look at the data collected from the edge of the universe, I still read the same mystery there. What this means is that my search for truth is just life looking for itself. Nature is a mirror; the seer is the seen. That may be the very clue that brings the mystery to an end. I once heard about a spiritual exercise that an Indian master asked his disciples to perform:

"Hold up your thumb and forefinger together. Do you feel that the thumb is touching the finger, or is the finger touching the thumb? It can be either way, can't it? In one case the thumb is the experiencer, in the other it is the experienced.

"Now ask yourself, 'Who is it that switches from experiencer to experienced?' Being in control of the operation, you must be beyond it. You are larger than the experiencer, larger than any set of experiences. Whatever you are, you will only find yourself beyond the things you now know."

Perhaps not everyone will find this lesson as earth shattering as I do. It tells me that my individual mind and body, which place such obvious limitations upon me today, cannot be the whole story. What is the mind but the experiencer, the knower? What is the body but the experienced, the known? If I can switch my attention from one to the other, then there must be a "me" that is not trapped in the dualism of mind or body. This "me" is not to be discovered by simple means. I cannot look at it, because it is in my eye; I cannot hear it, because it is in my ear; I cannot touch it, because it is in my finger. So what is left? Only the voice inside that whispers, "Go beyond." By following that whisper I may lose myself in unknown country. On the other hand, I may step outside the boundary of time itself. Then I will discover, once and for all, whether time is my real home, or eternity.

Part Two

~~~~~~~~~~~~~~~~~~

Beyond Boundaries

5

꙰꙰꙰꙰꙰꙰꙰꙰꙰꙰꙰

A Mirage of Molecules

As a boy growing up in New Delhi, I wondered at the wild contrast between my two grandfathers. One was a man of action, a soldier who was born the son of a small-scale rajah in the dry hills of the Northwest Territory. "Rajah," or prince, is rather a grand title, too high-flown to capture those fiercely independent tribal chieftains, whose people were the most warlike in India. When British soldiers were sent to force his allegiance to the Crown, my great-grandfather rashly decided to fire on them. His tiny forces were quickly defeated.

Our family legends hold that the rebellious village had only a single antiquated cannon to fight with. The old gun futilely thundered away, and when the foreigners finally marched in, the dead were sprawled beside it, my great-grandfather among them. The sins of the father were not visited upon the son. The British graciously presented my grandfather with the pension that would have been offered to the rajah, along with a life commission as a sergeant in the British army.

This was a signal honor at the time. Grandfather relished regimental life, and it molded every detail of his character. He greeted my birth by climbing onto the roof of his villa in Lahore, firing a smart volley of rifle shots into the air, and blowing a triumphant blast on his bugle. Having satisfactorily alerted (and terrified) the neighbors, he descended to calmly resume his breakfast.

My other grandfather, on my mother's side, was a man of peace. His life had been molded by foreign influence, too, but in an entirely different way. When the Singer sewing machine was introduced to India at the turn of the century, he became the company's sales representative, traveling throughout the country to tout this miraculous machine that could do the work of three women. He quickly amassed a sizable sum of money and retired before he was fifty, spending the rest of his life in meditation and spiritual inquiry. At the announcement of my birth, he unobtrusively took his way from his house on Babar Road in New Delhi to a back street in the old city, where he distributed alms to the poor.

This grandfather passed hours in the company of yogis, swamis, and other holy men, or simply with his old cronies, who constantly talked of "the Mysterious One." If a friend found a Queen Victoria gold rupee in the street, they would smilingly shake their heads and murmur, as if sharing a private joke, "Oh, it's the Mysterious One again." If a young mother lost her first child, that, too, was a whim of the Mysterious One, and in fact no unusual incident, large or small, went by without invoking this unseen and unseeable person. I had no idea whom they were referring to, although there was a mixture of the inscrutable, the unpredictable, and the divinely playful in his character.

Few ten-year-old boys, even in India, can be said to have a contemplative bent, and I was no exception. It did not occur to me that these old men in their white jackets and peaked caps, sitting on our veranda half the day without exchanging six words, could be investigating anything very worthwhile. This grandfather died without letting me into his world. Instead, most of my life has been dominated by my army grandfather. Medicine is suited to action and is almost military in its disciplined training, its attention to defense, its rallies and last-ditch stands against the enemy, and not least of all, in the violence often done to the human body in the name of doing it good.

To most physicians, the most fearful prospect is not a case

that cannot be cured but one where the doctor is helpless to act. Even an incurable disease has treatments, working toward the day when one of them will prove effective. Without this "anything is better than nothing" attitude, we would not have most of the cures that do exist. But what about the times when doing nothing *is* the cure? In those moments the Mysterious One begins to make his presence felt.

In his brilliant book of essays on surgery, *Mortal Lessons*, Richard Selzer recalls one patient of his, a short-order cook named Joe Riker, who always showed up for his weekly appointments wearing a fedora. Beneath the hat was hidden a terrible secret: In the middle of his head a tumor had progressively worked its way through the skin, the skull bones, and the three tough outer layers of the brain, leaving a gaping hole. Through it, the actual moist tissue of the brain could now be seen. Selzer's reaction to this disturbing sight was not horror but urgent compassion:

> I would gaze then upon Joe Riker and marvel. How dignified he was, as though the tumor . . . had given him a grace that a lifetime of good health had not bestowed.
>
> "Joe," I say, "let's get rid of it. Cut out the bad part, put in a metal plate, and you're cured." And I wait.
>
> "No operation," says Joe. I try again.
>
> "What do you mean, 'no operation'? You're going to get meningitis. Any day now. And die. That thing is going to get to your brain."
>
> I think of it devouring the man's dreams and memories. I wonder where they are. The surgeon knows all the parts of the brain, but he does not know his patient's dreams and memories. . . .
>
> "No operation," says Joe.
>
> "You give me a headache," I say. And we smile, not because the joke is funny anymore, but because we have got something between us, like a secret.

Week after week, for six months, Selzer had no choice but to apply fresh dressings and set the next weekly appointment, always for Thursday at four o'clock. Then one day Joe missed his appointment and did not return. After a month, Selzer drove to the diner in New Haven where Joe worked and found him behind the counter, still wearing his fedora. When he demanded to examine him, Joe nervously refused, but he agreed to meet Selzer at his office that Thursday. He showed up late for his appointment.

> "Take off your hat," I say, and he knows by my voice that I am not happy. He does, though, raise it straight up with both hands the way he always does, and I see . . . that the wound has healed. Where once there had been a bitten-out excavation . . . there is now a fragile bridge of shiny new skin.
> "What happened?" I manage.
> "You mean that?" He points to the top of his head. "Oh well," he says, "the wife's sister, she went to France, and brought me a bottle of water from Lourdes. I've been washing it out with that for a month."
> "Holy water?" I say.
> "Yeah," says Joe. "Holy water."

Off and on after that, Selzer would see Joe at the diner, looking completely ordinary, not at all like "a fleshy garden of miracles," as Selzer dubbed him. There seemed to be no change at all in Joe's shuffling walk or his matter-of-fact manner. "Perhaps the only change is just the sly wink with which he greets me, as though to signal that we have shared something furtive. Could such a man, I think as I sip my coffee, could such a man have felt the brush of wings?"

The Mask of Maya

In his own very different words, Selzer is posing the same question as my spiritual grandfather: Is there a mysterious force that brushes us at times, lifting ordinary life above the laws that seem to bind it? "What is to one man a coincidence is to another a miracle," Selzer writes. "It was one or the other of those I saw last spring." But isn't there a third alternative? The body might be a mask, an appearance of reality suited to the five senses, which *usually* follows the well-known set of physical laws, but is also free to change. If this is so, then the strange events that occasionally crop up would not really be miracles but glimpses behind the mask, or small windows into a corridor of reality that is usually sealed off.

If I use the phrase "the body is an illusion," I am demoting this structure of skin and bones from the fixed, predictable, solid status it seems to have in time and space, but I am not implying that we should give up on it, treating it as indifferently as the illusory patterns that a swirl of cigarette smoke makes in the air. The body is precious to us, all the more so *because* it is not fixed and predictable.

We have a wide choice about how to react to the illusion. It can be made into something deceptive, unreal, and unreliable. But I could also regard it as something marvelous, enchanting, and surprising, like the illusions of Houdini. Certainly I am free to choose this second interpretation. That is what my spiritual grandfather did when he approached the even greater illusion of life as a whole: for him, the Mysterious One was not a deceiver. He was the all-powerful animating force that makes things happen, sometimes according to the rules but not always. After all, they are *His* rules.

In the Indian tradition, the formal term for this omnipotent force is *Maya*. Maya is a Sanskrit word that means "illusion" or "delusion," but much more besides. The eminent mythologist Joseph Campbell has traced the shades of meaning contained in this word. Maya comes from the root verb *ma*, "to measure out, to form, to build," denoting the ability of the gods to change form, to make worlds, to assume masks and disguises.

Maya also means "magic," a show of illusions. In warfare it can mean camouflage or deceptive tactics. Finally, when used by philosophers, Maya denotes the delusion of thinking that you are seeing reality when in fact you are only seeing a layer of trick effects superimposed upon the *real* reality.

True to its deceptive nature, Maya is full of paradoxes. First of all, it is everywhere, even though it doesn't exist. It is often compared to a desert mirage, yet unlike a mirage, Maya does not merely float "out there." The Mysterious One is nowhere if not in each person. Finally, Maya is not so omnipotent that we cannot control it—and that is the key point. Maya is fearful or diverting, all-powerful or completely impotent, depending on your perspective. If cancer is just Maya, then its frightening appearance is a bogeyman, to be dispelled by anyone who sees through it. The fearful illusion becomes a wonderful show if only you can manipulate it.

Maya would be a worthless or degrading trick if we could not pierce its mask. Who wants to be told that he is too ignorant to see the real reality? In the case of a doctor, one is almost forced to pierce the mask of Maya, because so many patients, like Joe Riker, keep throwing our ignorance back into our faces. My own patient, Mr. Elliott, at least had a slim objective reason—the bad news about his heart—that he could blow up out of all proportion. But I cannot really convince myself that this reason is good enough. Somewhere deep inside, each of us knows that the rules that hold life together are provisional, and we can decide, with barely a wisp of a reason, to stop abiding by them. A secret decision maker can awake in panic and anger, roaring, "I made this body, I control it, and I will do with it what I will!"

Maya does not generally shift this violently. The body has been set up to operate like a well-behaved machine. Yet to claim that the body is literally a machine is to express a subjective decision, not an objective fact. One time I was asked to speak in front of a small audience of Boston doctors, and the physician who introduced me, a pathologist, began genially, "I'm sure we will all find the views of mind-body medicine intriguing, but I must declare that I am a scientist, and until I can see it under my microscope, I cannot believe that a thing is real."

"I'm embarrassed to begin," I responded, "because I was going to try to prove that what you can see under your microscope has no reality at all. I don't want to put you out of a job."

"Go ahead," he said amiably, "I don't think you can prove that, and besides, I secretly want to be a psychiatrist anyway."

Everybody laughed, but I wonder if he grasped that I was

serious. If you exclude every part of a human being that can be viewed under a microscope, nothing remains for the scientist to hold on to. Every atom inside us is more than 99.999 percent empty space, and the "solid" particles whizzing around are themselves just compact bundles of energy vibrations. As you sift through this solid-looking, convincing body, you only have to go so far before you wind up with a handful of nothing. Yet this nothing is not really a void but a womb. With incredible fertility, our inner space gives birth to "love and hate, joy and sorrow, misery and happiness, pleasure and pain, right and wrong, purpose, meaning, hope, courage, despair, God, heaven and hell, grace, sin, salvation, damnation, enlightenment, wisdom, compassion, evil, envy, malice, generosity, camaraderie, and everything, in fact, that makes life worth living." That is quite an impressive list of things for scientists to exclude from reality. (R. D. Laing made up the list, but then he *is* a psychiatrist.)

Scientists defend objective facts by saying, "I can see and touch this thing; it has measurable dimensions; it follows objective laws that mathematics can describe to the nth power." This sort of reasoning does not prove much. If I go to a movie, I can walk right up to the screen and count the stitches on the actors' clothes. If I take a diagnostic look, I can find signs of disease in their appearance, and with the proper microscope, I could probably examine the skin cells on the celluloid image. None of that makes the image real. Our bodies occupy three dimensions instead of the two occupied by a movie, which means that I can go deeper into the image I see and touch, but that doesn't make it any more real, either.

What makes the body more real than a movie is Maya. Above all else, Maya is convincing. If it were not, we would all see through it, and yet the next layer of reality would be Maya as well. The process doesn't ever have to end. As long as you want "proof" that the sensory world is real, Maya is deep enough to have all the layers you want: organs give way to tissues, tissues to cells, cells to molecules, and on to atoms, protons, electrons, quarks, and finally—nothing.

Intellectually, we all know that empty space is all there is at the bottom of things, but to keep everyday life going, we agree to certain conventions. "Objective" science is the keeper of these ad hoc rules and performs an extremely valuable task so long as it remembers that rules are made to be broken. For example, in the midst of this machine we call a body, nothing is more orderly and reliable than the heart. Its complex workings have challenged brilliant medical minds for four hundred years, ever since William Harvey discovered the circulation of the blood. But like every other part of the body, the heart is just empty space when you get down to it. The "real" heart is not this tough bundle of twitching muscles that beats 3 billion times before it expires but the organizing power that pulls it together, that creates a thing out of nothingness.

Dr. Harvey's Metaphor

Historically, the heart played a key role in turning the body into a machine. As early as 1616 Harvey wrote a simple sentence in his notebook: "The movement of the blood is constantly in a circle, and is brought about by the beat of the heart." No one had ever expressed such a daring thought before (at least not in the West; ancient texts from India give credence to the claim that Ayurvedic physicians had already discovered blood circulation centuries earlier). Harvey's bold assertion flew in the face of the greatest medical authority of the ancient world, the Greek physician Galen, whose words had remained law for fourteen centuries.

In Galen's view—and therefore the view of every educated physician in Europe—the heart helped the lungs to bring *pneuma* into the body; this was the Greek term for the invisible vital force that kept living creatures alive. Galen held that the blood did not circulate. Rather, there were two kinds of blood, one in the arteries, the other in the veins, which ebbed back and forth like the tides. Blood of either kind was produced by the liver; it then oozed out to every other part of the body and in some unexplained way got consumed, never to return to its source.

Since their culture was revolted by the thought of dissecting corpses, the fathers of Greek medicine gave scant attention to the anatomy of the heart. Observing the living heart was out of the question, and in any case, its beat went by too fast to be accurately described, taking barely a second in a human being and far less time in smaller animals. This led medieval churchmen to state definitively that only God could know the actual workings of the heart.

Doctors had of course seen blood spurt from cut arteries and noted the difference between the bright red of arterial blood and the dark bluish red of venous blood. They had also detected the pulse, but it was thought to be the independent throbbing of the arteries themselves. In one way or another all these details were fitted into Galen's scheme.

Harvey was a short, intense, black-haired man and a fervent experimentalist. He paid fishermen to bring him live shrimp from the estuaries of the Thames so that he could peer into their transparent bodies and watch their blood move. He visited butchers and looked into the carcasses of animals as they died, because only then did their heartbeats slow down enough to be observable. He thrust his hands into the steaming cavities of expiring dogs and pigs to squeeze their arteries and veins; in this way he could personally validate that the arterial blood flowed away from the heart and the venous blood back toward it.

Yet what Harvey supplied was not just new observations but a new metaphor for the heart. He took the ineffable source of our tender emotions, the seat of love, the mystery knowable only by the divine mind, and reduced it to the status of a pump. This was not the first time that the metaphor of the machine had been applied to the human body, but it established such a deep mind-set that medicine still has not recovered.

Very few people seem to realize that Harvey was not handing down pure truth. A metaphor is a symbol, a verbal play that substitutes an imaginative word for a literal one. In metaphor, the woman you love can be a rose, the sun, the moon and the stars—all images that express your feelings better than the naked statement "My love is a woman." Calling the body a machine is a particularly powerful metaphor because "machine" is not a poetic word—it is hard, solid, literal. A machine is a thing of matter, not of fancy.

Doctors are great believers in matter. Training to become a doctor reinforces this bias again and again, from that moment in medical school when you first touch a dissecting scalpel to a cadaver's gray skin. As an initiation rite, the first cut through human skin is at once adventurous, furtive, shocking, and very convincing, much too convincing to shake off easily in the years to come. Alone in our society, physicians are trusted to violate the body's sacred interior, to reach in and roughly handle its tissues and organs. This experience is more potent than any chart in *Gray's Anatomy* can remotely suggest. The opening of the brain, for example, is an awesome event even to the most practiced neurosurgeon. In large part, the awe comes from actually setting eyes on the moist, vulnerable gray matter that hides under the skull's armor, touching it, and manipulating it with utmost care.

Yet unlike the Greeks, we are no longer handicapped by feeling too much awe in the presence of the body. The machine is there to be tinkered with. Dr. Michael DeBakey, the renowned Houston cardiologist, begins his authoritative textbook, *The Living Heart,* with these words: "The organs of the body might be likened to a series of working engines. For example, the heart, which is linked to all of them, is a two-stage stroke pump. The liver and intestines refine the fuels used by the body's engines. The kidneys, lungs, bowels, and liver are sanitation units, disposing of potential pollutants, wastes or the ashes left after fuel is consumed."

Proceeding to the lungs (bellows for the furnace), the nervous system (a network of telephone lines), and the veins and arteries (fuel pipelines), DeBakey elaborates his image of carefully linked up machinery, all at the service of one great machine, the body itself. The whole scheme is eminently useful in a world that wants newer and better artificial valves, bypass grafts, and synthetic arteries. The problem with assuming that the heart is a machine, however, is that it may predestine you to live like a machine, too. Metaphors can be very convincing to the mind, and once the mind is convinced, reality gets stuck, like a river frozen in winter and unable to flow.

Seeing the heart as a pump, we expect it to behave like the pump at a well or a gas station. It wears itself out; its parts become damaged or defective; in time its usefulness is gone. But if you are not spellbound by the metaphor, it is self-evident that the heart is not a pump. It grows, for one thing: your heart weighed less than two ounces when you were born and took more than a decade to reach its final weight of just over a pound. The heart can alter its rhythm and stroke volume as your activity or moods change, self-regulate its timing, and repair damage inflicted by minor heart attacks. What pump does any of that?

Then there are the feelings associated with the heart. Something in my chest aches with pain, soars with joy, turns hard as flint when it feels distrust, and melts as softly with tenderness as a snowflake in the sun.

"Granted, the heart is more than a machine," you may reply, "but be practical. Surely the day must come when the heart, like any other pump, does wear out?" We cannot be so sure of that. Twenty-five years ago, the heart was thought to lose function steadily with age, to grow stiffer and more fibrous, eroding its ability to pump as much blood with each stroke. Then pictures came back from faraway places like the Caucasus region of the Soviet Union showing ninety-year-olds who could perform prodigious physical activity.

Western doctors witnessed these people as they climbed steep hillsides, leaped into mountain streams for their morning bath, and did many other things that should not be possible for old pumps. Medical examination revealed that these remarkable hearts were often years younger biologically than they should have been, but even when disease and deterioration was present, the person had not been deterred from leading an active life. To compensate for the impairments of old age, the heart thickened its walls, learned to pump a different style of stroke, and generally operated at full strength.

To ignore all these facts would be an ironical legacy from Harvey, given his deep-dyed respect for fact. Modern doctors consider themselves just as dedicated to truthful investigation as their great predecessor, and yet they have not given all the facts equal weight. Some facts have been rudely shut out simply because they do not fit the machine metaphor.

Indian yogis have been observed under controlled conditions to slow down their hearts at will, to the point that *no* blood flow reaches the heart muscle. By Western standards, such a feat is not only baffling, it is inconsistent with the maintenance of life. A stopped heart can survive without oxygen for up to fifteen minutes; brain cells are irreversibly damaged without oxygen after only four minutes. This sets the critical time limit that cardiac units are racing against in their frantic emergency efforts. Some yogic subjects have virtually halted blood flow for hours, however, and spent days with their hearts barely fluttering. If medicine is pledged to be an objective science, such demonstrations should topple our whole conception of what the body actually is. Unfortunately, metaphors die hard.

Phantoms

Nothing forces you to try and break through Maya's mask. As long as you accept the physical world at face value, your compliance keeps the machinery running. Rocks remain hard and solid, the wind blows, water makes things wet, and fire burns. Maya is very obliging. At a certain point, however, the mirage of molecules is not real enough to be satisfying. The illusion starts to dissolve—we have seen many instances of that by now—and then the search begins for the true reality hidden under the trick effects.

I do not have to recover "miraculously" from a brain tumor to begin this search. Just to observe that I am not a handful of empty space is a good enough beginning. Something must hold me together, a kind of glue or magnetic pole that keeps my molecules from flying apart. What is this glue? How do I manage to organize myself around a stable, meaningful core?

One clue, strangely enough, lies in the experience of amputees who continue to feel that their lost fingers, toes, arms, and legs are still present. Oliver Sacks has written evocatively of these "phantom" limbs, as neurology calls them. Phantoms are observed frequently in the aftermath of amputation and can persist for days, weeks, or years. Their appearance can be disquieting, to say the least.

Dr. Sacks describes one patient, a sailor, who lost an index finger in an accident at sea. At the time of injury, the finger was rigidly extended, and the phantom that appeared in its place retained the same position. The man had the distinct sensation that he was forever pointing his finger in the air. This feeling was so lifelike that he could hardly touch his hand to his face to shave without fearing that he would poke an eye out. Other patients have phantoms that bring pain, itching, and various other uncomfortable sensations, bordering on the bizarre—one man reported that his phantom leg regularly suffered severe cramps at night, complete with curled toes and knotted calf muscles.

Phantoms often possess the uncanny ability to change size. Thus a leg may seem eight feet long at one minute and only two inches long the next. Phantoms are not simply deceptive, though. Anyone who has worked with disabled patients soon discovers that without a phantom, learning to use an artificial limb is made much more difficult. Walking steadily on a prosthetic leg is a matter of integrating it into your existing body image. As long as the prosthesis is dead weight, this integration will never be completely natural. But the phantom leg can mold itself to the false leg, giving the feeling that it is alive.

Even when it proves useful, a phantom is not always cooperative. Sacks mentions one patient who would wake up some mornings to find that his lower leg, a phantom, was not there. In its place would be a vacuum, nothingness devoid of any sense of existence. (Of course there *was* only air below his knee to begin with, but on these mornings it was "dead" air.) To bring his phantom back to life, the patient would vigorously slap his thigh five or six times like a baby's bottom until the phantom woke up and extended itself. Then he could fit on his prosthesis and walk.

What so intrigues me about phantoms is that all of us have one—we just happen to call it our body. Being basically an inert lump, the body is as dead as a false limb. Its sugars have no more feeling than a gum drop; its proteins are no more sensitive than a pinto bean. Through the nervous system, which infiltrates every fiber of the body, we have learned to project ourselves into this inert lump, fitting it on the way an amputee fits on his prosthesis. When a foot or hand goes to sleep, we can feel what a dead weight it really is. "Going to sleep" is a temporary paralysis that results when the nerves have been crushed, usually under the weight of our torsos when we inadvertently roll over in bed or sit with one leg curled up under us too long.

Many other people besides amputees rely on misguided phantoms. A young woman afflicted with anorexia looks in the mirror and is confronted with a thin, almost skeletal image. The body she has starved through her eating disorder is there before her eyes. But inside she has a contrary image of herself as too fat (or rather, not thin enough), and this visual phantom rules her mind. She "sees" a fat person in the mirror, just as an amputee "feels" that he has a two-inch or eight-foot leg.

Whatever the phantom tells you is real becomes real. I "know" that my leg is three feet long, that my body weighs 150 pounds, that I am sitting upright and am awake, but to believe these things is to take them on trust, for my phantom could be tricking me. The nature of the mind is to crave continuity, to bridge one thought with another, to give our actions consistent motives and look for consistency in others.

To get some idea of how much it takes to organize a continuous reality, we can consider the plight of schizophrenics, whose brains process the world so poorly that what emerges as speech is a chaotic, jumbled outpouring called "word salad." In David Noonan's penetrating book, *Neuro-*, there is a vivid account of the kind of "loose association" that cannot hold logic together when schizophrenia strikes. One patient says, "My last teacher in that subject was Professor A. He was a man with black eyes. There are also blue and gray eyes and other sorts too. I have heard it said that snakes have green eyes. All people have eyes."

Seemingly overwhelmed by thoughts and sensations, the mind of a schizophrenic can no longer form any ordered or logical statements from the swirl of impressions generated inside and out. Another patient was asked to comment on the energy crisis. "They're destroying too many cattle and oil just to make soap," he replied. "If we need soap when you can jump into a pool of water and then when you go to buy your gasoline, my folks always thought they should, get pop but the best thing to get, is motor oil and money. May as well go in there and trade in some, pop cans and, uh, tires, and tractors to grup, car garages, so they can pull cars away from wrecks, is what I believed in."

It is clear that this patient understood the question he was being asked, but he could not sort out the images, memories, and concepts that it brought to mind. They all became mixed into a salad that is quite crazy but hints poignantly at the lost days when the world made sense. The resulting verbal garble reminds me that my own words are glued together in a very mysterious way by a consciousness I take for granted. I do not have to go through any mental struggles to make sense when I speak—it just happens or it doesn't.

Without this deceptively automatic continuity, life would turn into "life salad." Yet there is a seeming paradox here. How can one maintain continuity and still be open to unexpected things, to the ever-changing flow of events and the lightning flash of revelation? My choice plays the key role in whether I accept the world as it is or alter it to suit my desires. Maya and I have been very good about abiding by our agreement to keep the world predictable. Yet—who knows?—I may decide to break the agreement tomorrow. Or a minute from now. Reality is always open to revision.

Waking from the Spell

Milton Erickson, a great pioneer in the therapeutic use of hypnosis, was once giving a lecture-demonstration to an audience of medical students. He asked for a volunteer to join him on the platform. A young man came forward, took a seat facing the audience, and placed his hands on his knees as Erickson requested. Then Erickson asked him, "Would you be willing to continue to see your hands on your knees?" The student said that he would. While he was talking, Erickson silently gestured to a colleague, who walked up on the other side of the young man and raised his right arm in the air. The arm stayed there.

"How many hands do you have?" Erickson asked.

"Two, of course," the young man answered.

"I'd like you to count them as I point to them," Erickson said.

"All right," the young man replied, a patronizing note in his voice. Erickson pointed to the hand resting on the left knee, and the young man counted, "One." He pointed to the right knee, where there was no hand, and the young man said, "Two." He then pointed out the hand dangling in midair. The student became hopelessly confused.

"How do you explain that other hand?" asked Erickson.

"I don't know," said the young man. "I guess I should be in a circus."

You may have guessed by now that the volunteer was already under hypnosis. The astonishing part of the story is that he was not hypnotized beforehand. Erickson was such a master of his art that he induced a trance merely by asking the question, "Would you be willing to continue to see your hands on your knees?" That suggestion is exactly what the student carried out when he "saw" a hand on his right knee.

And what about me? Everything I see around me right now is just as precarious as that third hand. I have a "sense of reality" that I trust, not because it is real, but because my trust makes it real. A hypnotist can, with the slightest twist of my attention, make me believe that there are six people in a room instead of two dozen, or that a foul-tasting concoction brewed up by a local pharmacist is the most delicious glass of dry sherry. Both of these were done to R. D. Laing by a hypnotist friend in Glasgow.

Commenting on the dry sherry episode, Laing bewails, "How could one's sense of *taste,* such an intimate sense, be so readily deceived? I could not believe my *taste!* This was not merely interesting. It was profoundly disquieting. It baffled me. It *scared* me." High emotions are aroused when we feel ourselves swaying over a bottomless gorge. As Laing quite logically asks, "What is the *real* taste of anything? In what sense are any phenomena really real?" This is the very question that teased the old men gathered on our veranda on Babar Road. Laing is more dismayed. "How far is the whole feeling and fabric of our ordinary, everyday world socially programmed, an induced fiction, in which we are all enmeshed?" he asks. The only ones to escape the net are "a few whose conditioning has not 'taken,' or has broken down, or who have awakened from the spell—a motley crew of geniuses, psychotics, and sages."

Exactly—the only way out of Maya is to wake up from its spell, to join the few who are not utterly enchanted. In our culture, the spell has become respectable as "hard" science, but that does not make it truer. The advantage of seeing through Maya is that the scientific spell, although it has given us this convenient modern life with its jets and computers, CAT scans and carrot juicers, has not done away with fear, violence, hatred, and suffering. Those have been programmed into Maya, too. They come with this dream when you agree to be its dreamer.

Every once in a while, I meet someone who already belongs to the motley crew whose conditioning did not "take." They are not necessarily psychotics, geniuses, or sages; they are just people who cannot be convinced as easily as the rest of us. Invariably, our encounters shake my dream a little. I walk away aching to see what they see and to be what they are. But there is also happiness and even hilarity when we realize what is happening. For a moment, we have looked across the illusion to find that we are equals. "Who knows?" their eyes seem to say. "Maybe you will wake up next."

I am thinking particularly of Harold, an old man who appeared, when I first met him, to be completely ordinary, although at seventy-five, his body was in evident decline. His daughter brought him to see me because she was worried about the prospect that Harold was rapidly going into severe kidney failure, a serious and even life-threatening prospect that many older people face.

While the three of us sat in my office, she talked anxiously about what steps we could take, including putting her father on dialysis. Harold, however, settled into his chair and looked unconcerned. When I looked at his blood tests, I immediately saw why his daughter was upset. Harold's BUN, or blood urea nitrogen, was near 90; a normal level is around 10. Another indicator called creatinine was also extremely elevated.

Everyone collects nitrogenous wastes in his blood as the

residue of protein breakdown in the cells. This waste is toxic
in any large amount and would quickly become lethal if the
body did not have a way of constantly disposing of it through
the kidneys. When a doctor sees a high BUN or creatinine
level, it indicates serious if indefinite kidney problems. Harold was very close to the point where dialysis is automatically
called for. That was what his family doctor had insisted upon,
but Harold had refused.

Harold should have been in considerable discomfort, but
when I ran down the typical symptoms of kidney failure—
nausea, dizziness, weakness, and loss of appetite—he said that
he felt fine, maybe a little tired. I must have looked disbelieving, because before I could question him again, he said, "This
isn't a new problem, you know."

"Oh?" I said. "When did you first find out about it?"

"About forty-five years ago," he answered, giving me a
mischievous look.

A man who had lived with chronic renal failure for forty-
five years would be plagued by a host of symptoms, not to
mention permanent damage to the bones, eyes, lungs, and
blood vessels, among many other possible sites, including the
kidneys themselves. But Harold insisted that he had first
heard about his problem during World War II when an army
doctor told him that his blood tests qualified him for immediate medical discharge. He was told point-blank that with his
elevated BUN levels, he had no more than five years to live.

Harold exhibited no symptoms then, and since there was
no effective treatment for chronic renal failure, he took his
discharge and went away. Five years later he returned to see
his army doctor, only to learn that the doctor had died.

"It bothered me that he wasn't around anymore, since he
knew my case," Harold said, "so I went home without seeing
anybody else." It was the mid-Fifties before he sought out another kidney specialist. This doctor panicked when he saw
Harold's BUN levels and told him that he had very little time
to live—his only hope was that a new technology then in its
first stages of development, kidney dialysis, might be perfected in time to save him. Harold went away again and bided
his time.

"I thought the kidney machine was going to be the answer, so I kept a lookout for it," he said. About ten years later, he read in the papers that dialysis had come into practical use. He returned to the kidney specialist, only to find that the second doctor had now died. Harold's counts continued to get gradually worse, and five years ago, when he applied for health insurance, a third specialist told him that he was so sick he should either go for regular dialysis or consider a kidney transplant.

"That really shook my daughter," he said. "And I kept thinking that I should do something, so last month I called the doctor back. His nurse told me he had just died of a heart attack."

The three of us sat there for a second, but what could we say? We all burst out laughing at the same time. "I mean, if I have outlived three kidney specialists," Harold said, bewildered by his good fortune, "I think I should just stay away from doctors altogether. It would be much safer for them."

I had to agree.

6

꩜꩜꩜꩜꩜꩜꩜꩜꩜

Thread to Freedom

"I'm not afraid. I realize that deciding to have this surgery means that I'm taking a big risk. I might be fed on a tube for the rest of my life. It doesn't matter, just so we do something. I've never felt fear at the prospect of death. I just wanted to reassure you about that."

It was a very unconvincing speech. As Lou was delivering it, I watched his darting eyes and the uncontrollable tremor in his hands. He tried not to notice how much his true feelings were coming through. Perhaps he really didn't notice.

How could we defuse some of this pent-up fear, I wondered. It was not an easy task, considering how swiftly the catastrophe had fallen.

Two months before, there had been no signs of trouble, unless having a life that is too perfect is a sign of trouble. Lou was an American living in Spain on a private income and following his passion, which was art history. When he began to feel ill, the symptoms were almost trivial. His Spanish-born wife always served wine at dinner, but Lou began to notice that just one glass of the local red wine was enough to give him a sudden attack of nausea and diarrhea.

He complained to an internist in Madrid, who reassured Lou that he probably had a transient intestinal virus. When the problem persisted, however, the doctor decided to run some diagnostic tests. A CAT scan detected a suspicious mass about five centimeters long at the head of the pancreas. A needle biopsy was taken, and in a few hours the hospital lab sent back grim news. The mass was adenocarcinoma, a deadly cancer of the pancreas.

Even now, when he had only a fifty-fifty chance of surviving for six months, Lou was still free of pain. His body showed no sign of cachexia, the wasting away of tissues typical of the end stage of cancer. If he hadn't been so conscientious about investigating his bouts of indigestion, Lou might still have considered himself healthy.

"It's bizarre waking up every morning feeling so good," he said. "Just as I start to think about whether to play tennis or sort through some drawings, I remember that I am a terminal case, and then I can't work up the energy to do anything." A shadow crossed his face. "If only I could hold on to that first moment."

More than usual, I felt a personal need to help. Lou had flown back to America for treatment, but the standard interventions with surgery and radiation were grim affairs. The pancreas is the body's chief source of digestive enzymes; once it is removed, the patient loses almost all of his ability to digest food. Replacement enzymes can be provided, but as yet they are feeble substitutes for the body's natural processes.

When I was training in endocrinology, I spent a rotation on the oncology wards at Boston's Baptist Hospital, doing workups for a famous pancreatic surgeon who was a prominent attending physician. His patients lay in bed looking horrible—moribund, cachectic, yellow with jaundice. Since they would never again be able to eat properly after their surgeries, these patients spent weeks hooked up to IV tubes being fed entirely on drip. In the end, after the expenditure of enormous effort and care, the vast majority survived barely a few months.

My first priority was to save Lou from that grim scenario. I was not his primary-care physician; he had been referred to me because his doctor had read a book of mine and felt that a mind-body approach might help ease Lou's massive anxiety. However, I couldn't help feeling that Lou was as anxious about his treatment as about his disease. I advised him to consider not having surgery. With it, his life expectancy might be prolonged slightly, at least according to the statistical tables, but his own comfort needed to be weighed in the balance. Did he want to go through so much misery for such a small gain? Lou listened carefully but was not persuaded by my arguments.

"My instincts tell me not to have an operation," he said, "but what if I am dying six months from now after doing nothing? It would be so cruel to my wife, and I would feel too guilty hurting her that way."

After much soul-searching, he agreed to a compromise. Instead of having the entire pancreas removed, he would undergo a limited procedure that leaves most of the organ intact. He would then still be able to eat normally in the weeks to come. As the operation loomed nearer, however, Lou's moods started swinging drastically. Sometimes he came into my office acting confident, even ebullient, about his chances; more often he was somber and depressed. His normal self, with its normal relationship to the body, had collapsed in confusion. Nothing was properly connected anymore. His body was no longer his; it was a strange, fearful object. He wanted to distance himself from this thing, but he was becoming more and more mesmerized by it. Stare at a monster long enough and you become the monster—that adage was coming true for Lou.

One day I asked him to close his eyes and sit quietly. As he did, I said, "For the moment, let's take time off from talking or thinking about your case. Just be yourself. Don't identify your mind with any particular problem; don't do anything." I paused, and we both sat in silence.

"Do you notice any pain?" I asked.

"No," he murmured.

"Good," I said. "Now just sit comfortably appreciating whatever comes to mind. If you have a strong thought, even a gripping one, just let it go by. You'll find that it's not hard to do." Another pause, and then, "Did you feel any impulse of fear or anxiety?"

He nodded.

"Don't mind that," I said. "It's just a passing cloud. What I want you to notice is that there are spaces between your thoughts, like patches of blue between the clouds. When you notice such a space, just give a nod." He closed his eyes again, and after a moment, he slowly nodded. We continued the exercise for a few more minutes.

"Do you feel anxious now?" I asked. Lou shook his head, and I asked him to open his eyes. He had a rather surprised look on his face.

"You see, it's not so hard to stop being a cancer patient," I said. "I wanted you to sit quietly for a moment in order to experience, if only vaguely, the state of inner silence. Thoughts come and go in this silence. But when a thought isn't present and there is also no impulse of fear, no strong memory or temptation to act, the mind is just by itself, being itself. At that exact second, there is a choice to have the next thought or emotion. Now ask yourself, who faces that choice?"

"I don't know," Lou said, somewhat baffled. "No one has ever put it to me in quite those terms."

"To project a movie requires a screen," I said. "The images move and play on the screen; vivid emotions and high drama are enacted. Despite all that, the screen itself isn't engaged. It's not part of the movie, is it?"

"No," he said doubtfully.

"The difference between the mind and a movie screen is that we do become engaged in the movie, because it's *our* life. The screen inside us becomes so soaked in compelling personal images that the sense of there being a screen—an unchanging, unaffected part of the mind—is lost."

We both realized how new this all sounded. One's inner sense of "me" is built up of images from the past, all the fears, hopes, wishes, dreams, loves, and disappointments one calls "mine." However, if you strip all of these images away, something of "me" is still left: the decision maker, the screen, the silent witness.

"I can't find that untouched core for you," I said earnestly. "It has to be encountered directly. One clue I have given you, though. The thoughts and feelings that flow by, like clouds against the sky, are distractions. The real you is the sky beyond. Every time you manage to witness that clear, open

space, you will find a place that is safe, because it never had
cancer to begin with. Here you come face to face with yourself—the witnessed is also the one who is doing the witnessing."

The Thread of Yoga

The belief that the self has an untouchable core plays a
crucial part in modern psychology, particularly in the setting
of psychotherapy. In therapy, a patient will at best undergo
superficial change as long as he confronts only the superficial
layers of himself. To break through and accomplish major
change, he has to unveil the "central nucleus—that whorl of
the self which possesses absolute wisdom and self-knowledge." These words are from Irvin Yalom, a senior psychiatrist and professor at the Stanford University medical school.
At first, only the therapist realizes that a core of wisdom and
self-knowledge exists. The patient himself, under the influence of his mental distress, is alienated from this part of his
psyche. Therefore the therapist's role (I am speaking here of
classic "couch therapy") is to give the patient the courage and
freedom to bring his deepest self to light.

In almost every case, the first step is to convince him that
the deeper self is real. The patient must be shown and then
made to experience that part of his mind which transcends
crises, which registers life with crystal clarity even when the
conscious mind is reeling in bewilderment and panic. It is not
an easy exploration. Ever since Freud, depth psychology has
proceeded on the notion that the knower is buried under layer
upon layer of painful experiences. It cannot be confronted
directly; therefore it must be tricked out. The patient is thus
presented with dreams, slips of the tongue, and free associa-
tions that betray what is actually happening under all the layers of disguise.

Once I was discussing the current high divorce rate with
another internist and happened to ask if his parents were divorced. "No," he said. "Believe it or not, they are still married
after forty-five years. They're almost museum pieces in this

day and age. I should have them put under grass." Before I could react, he caught himself. "My God, I meant 'under glass,' of course." Eighty years ago, he could have dismissed his Freudian slip lightly; now he has to wonder at the disguised wish that popped out between the cracks of his psyche.

One of the great cultural differences between East and West is that the quest for the knower, which we undertake as a cure for disorders like neurosis or depression, is a normal goal of life in the East. In India, finding the knower is considered life's great adventure. Although a highly personal adventure, the way is marked by a tradition of knowledge— amounting to a science, really—called Yoga, from the Sanskrit word for "union."

The union a yogi seeks is not with anything outside himself; nor is it a union with God, ecstasy, or the supernatural, although each of these may be manifested at one time or another. The yogi's union is more ultimate, rooted in his craving to find the speck of himself that experiences reality directly, without filters or masks.

The legacy of yogic knowledge in India is ancient and extensive, and very bewildering to outsiders. If they bother to define it, most Westerners assume that Yoga means practicing various physical exercises that, if taken to extremes, twist the body into grotesque postures. This discipline is properly called Hatha Yoga and is just one of Yoga's eight "limbs," or divisions (and by no means the most important).

Since the search for the knower is not an exclusively Indian project, neither is Yoga. Its aim is to systematically uncover the silent witness inside us, a possibility open to anyone at any time. Here it appears in thirteenth-century China, distilled into four lines by the poet Wu-Men:

> *One instant is eternity,*
> *eternity is the now.*
> *When you see through this one instant,*
> *you see through the one who sees.*

The great Sufi poet Rumi beckons us to freedom with just two tantalizing lines:

> *Out beyond ideas of right-doing and wrong-doing,*
>   *there is a field.*
> *I'll meet you there.*

If we want a more literal idea of what Yoga amounts to, we must turn to the whole problem called identification, for this is what will be solved when union has been achieved. All of us move through life by identifying with one thing after another. *My* house, *my* career, *my* wife are all forms of identification that give us comfort and security—but not permanently. The mind has to keep shifting its focus of identification because conditions change: my house gets too small to live in, my career slumps, my wife grows bored. If I can shift smoothly with these changes, it is possible to remain relatively secure, but there is always the risk that the bottom will drop out because I have attached myself to something totally insecure. In Lou's case, he identified with his disease, not because he consciously chose to, but because identifying with one's body comes naturally. When the body falls sick, its pain might not have to be a problem, but it turns into one automatically if the idea of "my" body is strong enough.

Because identification is built into the mind, one cannot abolish it. Rather, the yogi solves the problem of identification by turning it on its head. Instead of identifying with things, a person who practices Yoga—primarily through meditation—begins to identify more and more with the silent witness inside. The process is like following a gossamer thread until you reach the spider that spun it. My thread may be very different from yours, because I have spun the web of inner reality according to my unique experiences. I may believe in a certain master, school, method, or book. Or I may not even have heard of Yoga as such. But the central issues remain much the same. Do I have a thread to follow? Will it lead back to its source before it breaks?

Once the goal is reached, Yoga is said to liberate the seeker from the limitations of ordinary life. The separation between body and mind is healed, allowing the person to enter into a higher state of functioning, both physically and mentally. I have already mentioned the ability of some swamis to stop their respiration and heartbeat at will. True yogis, however, would not stoop to consider any such feats as a primary part of their development. They are too intent on establishing, once and for all, the truth about mind, matter, and spirit. In that sense, they are scientists in their own realm, keenly observant and completely grounded in their inner experience.

My spiritual grandfather could not get enough of yogis, whom he revered in the traditional manner as living saints. I vividly remember his account of one. He came back from a pilgrimage to the Himalayas breathless with excitement. "I have seen the most amazing sight!" he exclaimed to my mother. Then he noticed me perking up my ears in the corner —I must have been about eight—and his face clouded. "It might frighten him," he said anxiously.

"No, it won't," I protested, not quite sure.

"No, no," he demurred, shaking his head. It was a long time before I found out the story. My grandfather had visited a distant cave on the Ganges where a yogi lived, passing most of his day in meditation. The yogi greeted my grandfather and his companions cheerfully. As they talked, my grandfather could not help but notice numerous double scars covering the yogi's exposed arms and legs.

"What are those?" he asked one of his companions in a low voice. The other man shrugged his shoulders, then all at once both of them realized that these were the results of snake bites. That area in the lower parts of the mountains was infested with cobras. The two visitors looked around nervously, and in a moment they spotted a large cobra lazily moving in the grass.

"Baba," my grandfather exclaimed to the saint, "you are living with snakes all around you."

"Snakes?" the yogi said. "I've never seen one here."

"But you are covered with bites," my grandfather protested.

The yogi gazed at him with penetrating sweetness. "Perhaps you see snakes here, but I see only God, and believe me, sir, He does not bite."

At eight years old, I marveled at this story and believed it, but it did not take. For me, the concept of Yoga became meaningful only in adulthood, when it was paired with the concept of Maya. Yoga is the process that makes Maya less convincing, so that eventually one is free to choose a wider reality than the one automatically presented by the senses. The senses present a cobra, but the saint sees only God—and reality shifts. What would have killed another man cannot touch him because he has already died; he is dead to the old, sense-dominated reality.

A subtle aspect of identification is being overcome here. Generally we cannot help identifying with the world. When the image of a rose falls on the retina, it automatically makes an impression on the visual center in the brain. No choice is consciously made, because the nervous system has taken in-stant possession of the image. Until the attention wanders to another object, one's awareness is imprinted with a rose. This is therefore a kind of union, or Yoga, but a false one, because it is so weighted in favor of the object. Seeing the rose, I forget myself.

Most people have no idea that looking at things can be a kind of bondage. A rose is a rose, fire is fire, water is water—all these natural facts arrange themselves into a unity that seems preordained, thanks to the automatic process of identi-fication. But to the yogi, the bondage of the senses is a serious handicap, because it commits us to things "out there" and to our memories, which are totally filled with things from the past. If I break my leg and feel intense pain, my response seems unchallengeable when in fact it is merely a repetition of an old way of responding that I learned years ago. Can this old lesson be unlearned?

Anyone can distract himself from a mild headache by talking to a friend or becoming absorbed in a book. The rea-son these distractions work is that we have more choice over identification than we realize. Even though the senses stick to the world like glue, we are still free to pull them away to new objects of fascination. There is no reason why this element of choice has to be foiled by pain.

The Christian martyrs whom the Romans fed to the lions in the first and second centuries A.D. often welcomed their fate, seeing it as an opportunity to prove their faith. In *The Gnostic Gospels,* Elaine Pagels cites letters in which con-demned Christians begged their friends not to intercede and save them from death. Motivated by their zeal to literally imitate the events of Christ's life, the martyrs competed in the arena to show as much patience as they could, singing hymns and looking upward with expressions of angelic joy as the beasts attacked them—we have this from reliable accounts by amazed Roman onlookers. As much as anything else, Christianity conquered the pagan world by first awing the pagan mind, proving beyond dispute that human will dictates to matter and not vice versa.

Modern theories of pain concentrate on the complex neural pathways of the pain signal and the various chemical triggers that accompany the sensation of pain. Yet believing in Christ is not a chemical event; it is a choice made in the mind. That is why the yogi's vocabulary, which deals in such abstract terms as identification, is actually truer to life than the scientist's concrete terms. To get at the switch that turns pain off and on, one has to step over the line that separates visible molecules from invisible beliefs. In this abstract field people decide whether or not something will hurt them. They attach their sense of "me" to some events and detach it from others.

There is a notable medical case, described by Stephen Locke and Douglas Colligan in *The Healer Within,* concerning a foundry worker whose legs fell into a vat of molten aluminum. Taken unconscious to the hospital, he was hypnotized the instant he woke up by a psychiatrist attached to the burn unit. The suggestion was planted in the burned man's mind that he had fallen into cool water instead of 700°F. molten metal. This suggestion took root and worked so well that it not only canceled out the pain, but the patient recovered quickly and with minimal scarring. This is the practical result of a purely mental detachment.

A man who has solved the problem of identification may still feel pain as a signal from his brain, but he will not convert it into *my* pain, and that minuscule but all-important difference cuts the cord of suffering. He no longer makes the mistake of thinking that perception is flooding in to create his awareness; rather, awareness is going out to create his perceptions. By returning our minds to the depths of awareness where we are free to make our own experience, Yoga opens up the possibility for uprooting all suffering at its source.

Can the Mind Free Itself?

Breaking down the mind's illusion sounds desirable as an ideal, but what does it amount to in practice? Many people try to substitute "positive thinking" for the disturbing thoughts they want to eliminate. On the surface this tactic may lead to some signs of improvement. The mind can be forced into identifying only with pleasant or uplifting things. But in time the feared thoughts will surface again (Freud called this "the return of the repressed"), and until then there is the exhausting effort of trying to maintain constant self-control.

Some time ago I was consulted regularly by a woman who was fixated on positive thinking. She had been successfully treated for breast cancer two years before but remained extremely worried about a recurrence. Her anxiety was obvious to everyone around her, but it was the last thing she herself wanted to confront. If I even entertained the notion of saying, "You're scared, aren't you?" her fixed smile and upbeat manner made me feel gratuitously cruel. I also felt increasingly nervous just being around her. She seemed like a taut wire on the verge of snapping.

Finally, after not so subtly hinting that she might be creating a false mood, I asked her point-blank to stop being so relentlessly positive. "You mean it's all right for me to have negative thoughts if I want to?" she asked with touching incredulity.

"Yes, when they are natural and unavoidable," I said.

Suddenly she burst out laughing. "Thank goodness," she exclaimed, "I needed permission from someone. I have read so much about the damage you can do to your body with negative thoughts that I spent the whole year after my operation dreading the least sign of one. Then it occurred to me that dread *is* a negative thought. You don't know how confused that made me feel."

I considered this quite an impressive insight on her part. Many people, in their well-intended efforts to accent the positive, do not escape their problems but only increase them. They want to put an end to suffering but mistakenly choose the tactic of denying their true feelings, on the grounds that the feelings are "too negative" to express. I went deeper into this whole issue with my patient. "Paying attention to one's fear and pain is a great source of guilt in most people," I pointed out, "because it seems like self-pity, a trait we think of as wrong. But denying pity to yourself, when you would give it willingly to others, is also wrong. We all have hidden pain inside, and trying to suppress it is not a virtue. It's only an impossibility.

"You may consider it very important to maintain a good attitude, but in itself an attitude is not very reliable. After all, who's keeping whose spirits up? Everything inside you is just you, even though you might split it up into a brave you that is trying to suppress or defeat a fearful you. If one part is addressing the other, saying, 'All right now, don't give in, don't turn hopeless,' isn't that really just a kind of game?"

She admitted that this was probably true, but it was not very reassuring. "I always feared that if I didn't keep up this game, as you call it, my negative thoughts would swallow me up."

"Does opposing your negative thoughts lessen their power?" I rejoined. "Doesn't it just delay the day when they will come out in one way or another? Think about it. You probably put in a lot of time not thinking negatively. It must require constant vigilance and effort on your part. Yet as soon as the pressure is off, don't these denied feelings rebound with doubled intensity? In your position, I couldn't lay my head on the pillow at night without armies of negative thoughts assaulting me."

She agreed that going to sleep had become a torture. "Negative thoughts come on their own, even in the face of our strongest opposition," I said. "It's just something we all have to accept. If we keep playing this game of opposing thoughts that are not acceptable to us, we will always lose. The serious question is, Can I give the whole game up? Very few people consider that alternative."

After a second's reflection, the woman commented, "No matter what you say, I don't think the game will be so easy to quit."

She is right, of course. Our conditioning to keep going in the same direction is very powerful. The ancient Indian sages,

or rishis, noticed this and concluded that the mind cannot
free itself through any mental activity, whether of struggle,
vigilance, or repression. Thinking your way out of thought is
like trying to get out of quicksand by pulling yourself up by
the hair. At bottom, any thought, however positive, is still in
the realm of thought. Yoga opens another way, and its secret
is just this: there is more to the mind than thinking. Indeed,
thinking is another mask of Maya, less solid than things we
see and touch but just as untrustworthy.

In an ancient Indian text called the *Shiva Sutras,* one
hundred and twelve ways are given for a person to escape
Maya by the only means possible—transcending it to experience the deeper reality of the silent witness. Here are a few of
the techniques, delivered directly by the god Shiva, the traditional teacher of yogis:

> When vividly aware through some particular
> sense, *keep in the awareness.*
> When on a bed or a seat, let yourself become
> *weightless,* beyond mind.
> *See as if for the first time* a beauteous person or
> an ordinary object.
> At the edge of a deep well, look steadily into its
> depths until—*the wondrousness.*
> Simply by looking into the blue sky beyond
> clouds, *the eternity.*

Although they stress *seeing* the world in a different way,
all of these techniques are actually based upon a shift in
awareness, for as we have discussed, awareness is the source
of seeing. Seeing a beautiful person "as if for the first time"
might happen by chance, out of the corner of your eye, but
never as a constant state, not in everyday awareness. I cannot
see a certain small, shy, devout Indian woman without seeing
my mother, nor can she see me without seeing her son. We are
used to each other, accustomed to looking through so many
layers of ourselves.

My father looks at her and sees a different person, in fact,
several different people superimposed one on another: the
sheltered girl with downcast eyes who was at first a stranger,

then an object of timid courtship, next the new bride and mother, and ever since the intimate adviser and companion whose words and thoughts have intertwined into his almost like a second self. Each layered image contributes something of its own value when he sees her. The shaping force that has made them almost one is no less powerful because it has worked so slowly and invisibly. A shared reality flows in, over, and between them both.

Their intimacy gives my father and mother a privileged relationship, but at a price. Until the masks are lowered, he will never see my mother *except* as his wife. Her beauty will remain at a certain distance. In a happy relationship, this price is worth paying, many times over. In the absence of true intimacy, the price becomes too high. A father may say to his son, "I only criticize you because I love you," and in his own eyes that may be true. But the son has to untwist love from criticism as best he can. This is why so many people, after they've grown up, feel a core of suspicion toward being loved.

From childhood onward, we all learned to cope with a complicated situation where the most basic feelings and perceptions were blended with one another much of the time. Life would be simpler if we could see directly into the crystal-clear ideals, the wondrousness and beauty, that the yogi declares to be at the heart of life, meaning our own hearts. But Shiva's teaching barely penetrates the shell of modern skepticism. A skeptic often harbors an idealist within who has suffered the pain of disillusionment one too many times. If idealists are born to be disillusioned, why not be disillusioned to begin with? Again and again, Freud stressed the importance of "the reality principle" as an index of psychological health. The reality principle is the recognition that you are not the world's creator. Your ego stops at a certain boundary, beyond which you have no influence.

A baby is thus considered primitive because he feels that he *is* at the center of the world, indulging the fantasy that everything is himself. As a child grows up, he is supposed to shed this infantile illusion of boundlessness. "Me" and "not me" congeal into their separate spaces, and hopefully it is not long before "me" learns how to cooperate with "not me." Parents are generally quite anxious to promote this cooperative attitude, even when their child is obviously too young to adopt it. They ignore the child's discomfort out of fear that he is being selfish. It is hard for them to see that their own hidden anxiety is being reflected here—they are afraid themselves to be fully self-accepting. Their own parents signaled that being self-centered was wrong, and this value judgment is being passed along now by seeing most forms of satisfaction as "selfish."

The raw selfishness of a newborn baby is not a model for future behavior, needless to say, but it needs to be tempered naturally into more selfless behavior. If the growing-up process sacrifices a child's very sense of being, then something has been lost that is too precious to lose. Being carries with it a subtle feeling of uniqueness, and out of that feeling comes a sense of union with the world, of being bathed in beauty and love. This is reality, too, but of a higher order.

Many young children report experiences that fit remarkably well with the supreme goals of spirituality. One woman writes of a vivid childhood memory: "At age four I was lying in the grass making pictures with the clouds. At a certain point I realized that they had stopped moving. Everything around me was very still, and I felt merged into the sky. I was everything and everything was me. I don't know how long this lasted, and I've never felt that way since. But it's possible."

Her experience closely mirrors the meditation in the *Shiva Sutras* that goes, "Look into the blue sky beyond clouds" in order to sense *eternity*. Many children recall moments just before they fell asleep at night when they had the sensation of lightness or floating—again, this echoes the meditation whose instruction is to be *weightless* while lying in bed. A spiritual exercise that seems so difficult to an adult, "seeing a beauteous person as if for the first time" is completely effortless for a four-month-old. He greets the sight of his mother, the most beauteous person in his universe, with adoration and delight, day after day. As long as she is in the room, his eyes remain fixed on her, unable to see anything else. To be, for a newborn, is to be in the center of a magical world.

Some children can remember the magic suffusing into much later stages of development. At five and six, the poet William Wordsworth saw the mountains, lakes, and meadows around him "apparelled in celestial light," and had to cling to a tree to remind himself that material things were not visions. Without this effort, he tells us, he would have been swept away into an ideal world of pure light and divine feeling. Seeing through Maya, then, may be much more natural than we suppose. Who knows how many of us have played in fields of light only to lose the memory of it? What is certain is that our current ideal of a sound psychological upbringing is rooted in the real, not the ideal. Through many repeated lessons a child is taught that the rough bark of a tree is more real than divine feelings; as soon as he is old enough to go to the playground he finds out that sidewalks skin knees and fists hurt when they hit your face.

In meditation, a yogi erases this rough sense of reality and points himself back toward the light, the ideal, the divine. Yoga aims for perfection, which means living from one's creative core twenty-four hours a day, without disguise or evasion, free of any form of unreality. The successful yogi does not simply contact the all-knowing nucleus, he *becomes* it. As beautiful as that sounds, the adult mind instinctively holds aloof. Our experiences of pain and disillusion are extremely convincing, whereas the premises of Yoga seem far removed. "Anything can be accepted as true today," a friend of mine likes to say, "as long as it isn't the Truth." He has understood the reality principle all too well.

The Flash of Insight

Fortunately, higher reality has a way of breaking out unexpectedly. There are moments when the all-knowing nucleus of the self defeats the mind's narrow prejudices. We call these flashes insight, and they give us a good sense, at least in passing, of what it must be like to be enlightened. As the Vedas put it, the enlightened mind is like the sun, compared to which all other minds are like candles. But a candle has value, because once it is lit, the darkness cannot be total. In the flash of insight, a corner of the self is revealed for what is really there.

One silently exclaims "Aha!" and a bit of the truth is brought out from under wraps.

Insight is not always deep or lasting—psychiatrists spend huge amounts of time shoring up new insights and making sure that the patient does not lose hold of old ones and regress. Nor does the body always follow the mind's lead into a healthier state. Even so, the moment of insight often manages to shift the entire self, and that is the key to its power.

A social worker in his early forties tells this story: "I was walking down the hall at work, and I was casually sharing some opinions with a friend. I told him that I felt he was taking his cases too personally and might be applying a lot of unnecessary guilt to them. Suddenly he turned on me and snapped, 'You're imposing your own emotions on me, and I resent it.' Then his voice softened a little and he said, more reasonably, 'It's just something you should work on. I've noticed that you have a habit of imposing your own hostile feelings on other people.'

"I didn't know what to say. I figured he would apologize for attacking me. Instead, he simply walked away. When I got to my office, I sat down at my desk, but it was impossible to work, I was feeling so angry.

"I simmered for a few minutes like a child on the verge of throwing a tantrum. I felt outraged and extremely sorry for myself. Why would a friend betray me like this? To discharge my anger, I started talking out loud to him, imagining that he was in the room. 'You don't seem to care how much you're imposing *your* hostile feelings on me! You have really hurt me, and I have to tell you that your accusation is totally and completely unfounded.' This ploy made me feel better for a few seconds, but some rational part of me knew that I wasn't merely the victim of a pointlessly cruel remark."

At this point a surprising process of emotional release began. "All at once, I began to split into layers. It was the most extraordinary thing. To describe it completely would take a long time, so many images began to flash by in my mind. I saw my self-pity as a defense against a huge amount of anger, which was out of all proportion to what my friend had said—I wanted to kill him! Then I saw my father as he looked years ago. He was asking me to do chores around the house, something I hated as a boy. Clearly the same overblown resentment was at work.

"That stage lasted no more than a split second. Images were still whizzing by in my mind; it was like watching myself from the viewpoint of a pebble falling down a well."

In rapid succession, he saw that his anger at his father was connected to feeling that he could never win his father's love. Then he saw that he had never been able to take criticism from his brothers or male friends, either. Images of them flashed by, stirring up a whirl of emotions and memories.

"By now only half a minute had passed, but the pebble was still plummeting, faster and faster. Instead of feeling giddy and disoriented, my mind was actually quite clear. I was appreciating every new angle and seeing it truthfully. Strangely, whenever my feelings started to run away with me, a detached, calm, inquisitive voice in my head kept repeating, 'Well, is it true? Do I impose my feelings on others?' Wherever this voice was coming from, it wasn't going to be dismissed with half-truths."

During this entire process, this man had lost consciousness of things around him. He was concentrating with intense focus, as most of us cannot, on the dynamics of moving out repressed feelings. In a few more seconds, the sensation of being a rock plummeting down a well ended.

"The thing is, I didn't feel myself hit bottom. I passed through all these layers, expecting to wind up God knows where. Instead, all that happened was that I came to again and noticed that I was sitting at my desk. I took a deep breath —apparently I had been holding it the whole time—and went back to work, feeling calmer though still wounded. It was only an hour later that the insight came. I was sitting at lunch with a few co-workers, people whom I know inside out and who frankly have ceased to interest me for years. Suddenly, they seemed appealing, even fascinating.

"They looked at me with affection in their eyes, they laughed when I said something funny, and I laughed with them. It was the most peculiar thing, until I realized, with a flash of recognition, what had happened: I wasn't imposing my feelings on them anymore. It hadn't occurred to me that these people had nothing new to offer because I wasn't giving them a chance. As soon as I backed off, they opened up, like shy flowers. The change in my awareness had released something new in them. To see them open up like that was very intimate, and at the same time it came as a great relief."

Craig's Story

At the flash of insight, psychiatry and Yoga are one—the revelation of the knower is the goal of both disciplines. However, psychiatry is content with a flash: insight is basically a tool, not a permanent state. Patients come to therapy for various reasons—to relieve unhappiness, to sort out unwarranted guilt or anxiety, to correct self-defeating behavior, and so on —but they do not come to wake up from the dream of Maya. If anything, that would be seen as a confused, disabling fantasy, far removed from the sensible, rational end product of successful therapy.

Psychiatry is an imperfect healer because it is wounded itself. Its reality does not include a core of magic; in fact, many therapists do their utmost to stamp out any signs of magic in the patient's mind. Only the most exceptional people manage to rise above the reality principle; they alone can begin to appreciate how simple the state of total insight might actually be.

Here I am thinking of one patient whose experience of transcending his physical boundaries seemed to make the difference between life and death. "For the last year I have been aware of a battle raging inside my body, but in my heart, I am like the happiest, most carefree of children. I have found the part of me that cannot be touched by my cancer. I am so much more than it, so far beyond it. Sometimes I feel totally in command of my illness, at other times I simply pay no attention to it. In either case, illness cannot mar my sense of being alive and whole, though surrounded by chaos and destruction."

Craig Reed had been diagnosed with terminal cancer when he wrote these words in a letter; he showed it to me after he had recovered. Craig Reed is a meditation teacher in his thirties from upstate New York. Three years ago he visited his family doctor with a severe sore throat, only to discover that he had contracted a fast-spreading form of lymphatic cancer called lymphoma. He had probably had the disease for six months before noticing any symptoms, which meant that the cancer had metastasized throughout his body. Two days later Craig checked into a large teaching hospital in Boston where he was assigned to a leading specialist in lymphatic cancers.

"Our only choice," his oncologist told him, "is to try to kill this thing with everything we've got. It will be very rough, I warn you, but absolutely necessary."

When Craig asked how rough it would be, the oncologist smiled grimly and said, "First we run a truck over you, then we back it up to make sure we didn't miss." In private, he wondered if Craig would live long enough to complete the first round of treatments. But from the very outset, Craig was a highly atypical case. His first treatment went unusually smoothly. The fever he entered the hospital with resolved and the balloonlike swelling in his face subsided. His psychological readiness to face the trials that lay ahead began to grow.

At this point Craig wrote the letter from which I quoted. It mentions that he practiced meditation every day and had been doing so for seventeen years. He had developed a remarkable ability to stop identifying with his disease. Though centered in his mind, this attitude of nonattachment also had a profound effect on his body.

Two months into his treatment, his temperature began to rise alarmingly; Craig was rushed to the hospital, where it was determined his immune system was severely compromised. His white cell count had been cut to the bone—it stood at 200, whereas a healthy person's is between 4,000 and 11,000. Chemotherapy is known to cause these crises, which put patients in grave jeopardy from any passing infection, no matter how minor. Discouraged, Craig's oncologist left his bedside wondering how many weeks they would have to wait before the white count crept back up. Three days later, a second blood test was taken. It showed that Craig's count had bounced back to 4,000, from near-fatal to near-normal. The doctor associated with the case had rarely if ever observed or read about such an occurrence.

Despite the odds, Craig was rebounding rapidly, and the cancer was in retreat. He was released from the hospital after four months, having chosen not to undergo a bone-marrow transplant, despite his doctor's insistence.

In Craig's mind, there was no doubt that being able to distance himself from his disease was crucial. "The emotional ups and downs are endless, the ordeal has dragged me through every imaginable emotion, but something in me is not involved. I still laugh and cry, celebrate and grieve, but I remain apart at the same time. I have discovered how to free my life from hysteria, and when the hysteria went, I was healed." It has been nearly three years since Craig left the hospital. He leads a completely normal life and remains free of disease.

It is very heartening to see that patients can pick up the thread to freedom. And what about Lou? He now stands at a halfway stage, no longer a prisoner of his fear but not quite believing that he has escaped.

As things turned out, Lou went in for his surgery, which was supposed to remove the tumor on his pancreas while leaving the majority of the organ intact. But his surgeons discovered that the tumor was much larger than they suspected. Lou was judged inoperable for either a partial or a total removal, and the incision was immediately closed.

When he came out of the anesthesia, he shocked his oncologist by taking the news in high spirits. "I never wanted surgery in the first place," he told me in his hospital room, "and by a circuitous route I got what I wanted."

We both mused on this. I didn't realize at the time that something critical had happened—Lou's sense of being under a dark enchantment was broken. He flew back to Europe and a fate I could not predict. Six months later I was delighted to see him in my office again, looking well and without any discernible weight loss. He had a normal appetite and no digestive difficulties. Lou did not seem as happy with this situation as I was, however. "Do I look all right?" he asked nervously.

"You look wonderful," I enthused.

"That's what everyone tells me, but inside I don't know how I feel." It became apparent that Lou's uncertainty still cast a shadow, and yet if he only knew it, he had smashed through huge barriers.

I remember how we parted that day. We had been talking for quite a while. I paused and glanced outside. It was April, a rare spring day in New England when the sky was a perfect, crystalline blue. The crocuses were up, yellow and violet jewels splashed across the lawn, and the trees were bursting in their first glory of golden green.

I saw that Lou was looking outside, too, but dully. All at once, I knew the utter loneliness his sickness had brought. "Look," I said, "why don't you go outside for a little while. It's a beautiful day, isn't it?" He nodded sadly, still alone inside his impenetrable gray space.

I had to break through, if only for a moment. "Think of the beautiful days you used to love," I said, surprising myself with emotion. "Where are they now? They must still be here, inside you. You breathed the air, and it became part of your blood. You looked at the sky, and the sight became engraved on the neurons of your brain. You felt the sunshine, and its warmth was absorbed by your skin.

"It's all there now, not just in your memory, but turned into you. So don't long for the good old days, Lou—*you are them*. Outside this window is another day that wants to turn into you. You aren't outside life. Like all the rest of us, you're blended into it, creating it as you are being created. This day cannot last without you to keep it alive. Will you give it a chance?"

When I was through, Lou said very little, but he embraced me warmly when we parted. We had come to an understanding. As I stood by the door, I caught one last glimpse of him from the back. He was just stepping outside, and from the eager way he looked around, I sensed his happiness at being welcomed by the warm spring light.

7

~~~~~~~~~~~~~~~

The Importance of Feeling Special

The instant he started to fall, Ray was probably dead. Twelve thousand volts of electricity had violently hurled him off the roof where he was working, helping a neighbor to install a new television antenna. What should have been a harmless ground wire turned out to be a live high-tension cable. When Ray picked it up, he had no protection against the massive surge of current, which almost certainly stopped his heart on the spot.

The horrified neighbor rounded the corner and found Ray's body in a heap on the ground. His right arm was shattered where the current had entered; the charred right knee of his work pants marked where it had exited. When the neighbor gingerly touched Ray's chest, however, he felt a beating heart. We will never really know why.

Perhaps—given just the right angle and velocity—hitting the ground restarted his heart. When defibrillator paddles are not available for shocking the heart back to life, thumping the chest is a standard procedure in emergency resuscitation. Yet, even in the hands of a doctor, it is a crude, risky method. You can just as easily damage the heart as save it, and in the process crack a rib or puncture a lung. Falling from a roof would increase these risks considerably. But how else could Ray Shepard's heart have started again? It was an intriguing circumstance for the doctors on the trauma team to speculate about later. When he heard about it, however, Ray began to call this moment, out of all the remarkable ones to come, "the gift."

Medical services are modest in the rangeland of eastern Washington where Ray runs his horse ranch. Now barely conscious again, he had to endure an hour-long ambulance ride without painkillers. A helicopter airlifted him to the nearest burn center, in Seattle, and intensive surgery began. Over the course of sixteen hours, the trauma surgeons removed his right arm at the elbow and carefully preserved the tissue that could be salvaged at the other two sites hurt worst in the accident, his right knee and left wrist.

His sister picks up the story in a letter written six months later:

"Ray was remarkably clear-headed and calm from the moment he entered the hospital. He did not sink into depression during his extended period of treatment, and despite the intense pain of his burns, he insisted on a minimum of medication. He underwent five surgeries over the next six weeks. It took that many procedures to remove all the dead and damaged tissue and to begin the massive work of reconstruction. A very delicate flap graft was required to cover an exposed tendon on his left wrist. The right knee was so devastated that it wound up being reduced to arteries, bone, and nerves, all exposed to the air."

Healing is a highly individual process, and in complex cases like Ray's, a "normal" recovery is almost a self-contradiction. Most of us cannot imagine what we would do if our nerves and bones were opened naked to the air. Certainly we would feel a great deal of discomfort, and the physical sensation of pain would begin a complex series of psychological reactions to produce what is called suffering. Most people believe that pain and suffering are more or less identical. This was not true for Ray, who experienced immense pain but never converted it into suffering. He had an explanation for this:

"I felt that a decision had been made in the split second while I was falling, pulling me back from certain death—it didn't have to happen that way, but it did. It was a gift. My mind went back to that moment many times, and I found that the memory triggered a different awareness in me. I can only compare it to meditation: I was in a place pain couldn't reach. I had a sense of floating and of great calmness.

"Sometimes the nurse would be packing my knee wound, which was very uncomfortable physically. I would see her doing it, and the signal of pain registered, but instead of stinging my mind, so to speak, it made me feel intense—what?—not exactly pleasure but a sensation hard to name, intensely sweet, very intimate. It was pain turning to tingling joy. Every time that happened, I would wonder at it and be very glad."

Once he slipped into this privileged state of awareness, Ray could divorce himself from his pain for hours at a time. Significantly, he had practiced meditation since he was eighteen, virtually all of his adult life, and was familiar with settled states of awareness. He soon showed that he was doing much more than evading pain. His sister writes, "When I first saw the surgical wound around Ray's right knee, I was frightened at how much muscle they had been forced to remove. Despite the grafts, there was nothing visible but tendon, and when we returned to Seattle, several specialists advised that muscle tissue be brought around from the back of his leg for a new graft.

"That meant major surgery, and Ray's doctor decided to postpone it. Keeping the tendon exposed raised the chance of infection, but he wanted to wait and see for another month. In that time, Ray healed himself amazingly. We dressed his knee twice a day and showered it with loving attention. (Ray would say afterwards that he could lie back and literally feel this attention being soaked up by his body.) Ray meditated a great deal and was up and around, tending the new colts and enjoying his life to the full.

"When his doctors saw him four weeks later, they were in a state of disbelief. New muscle had started to come up around the tendon spontaneously, appearing in every gap, and new skin was rapidly advancing to cover it."

Muscle regeneration is a highly uncertain process, and there is no guarantee that it will occur at all if the damage is this extensive. One would certainly not predict the rapid granulation of new tissue that appeared in Ray's destroyed knee. With undisguised wonder, one of his doctors exclaimed, "I don't know why, but you're a great healer, Ray." No further surgery was required.

Much has been written about what makes certain people heal better and faster than others. Ray embodied many of the most desirable qualities. He had the courage to get up out of his hospital bed and walk on his leg within days after his accident. When his arm had to be amputated, he immediately learned to tie his shoes with one hand. He unhesitatingly and hungrily accepted love when it was offered by his family and friends. These are rare qualities of heart and mind.

Although every doctor has seen such patients, "great healers" have proved to be too rare and too individual to study as a class. Therefore, we do not really know their secret. I believe that what makes such people extraordinary is not anything they do: it is something they *are*.

We all are. That is, we all have the certainty that we exist. A clever debater can make you doubt almost anything you ever believed in, but not this. "I am" lies at the core of every person, a rock-solid certainty he has no reason to doubt.

Unless you are caught in a tortured dilemma like Hamlet, to be or not to be is *not* the question. Existence comes as inevitably as being born. Strangely, some people take more advantage of this state than others. They do not do more or feel more or think more. Somehow, like light passing through a crystal-clear lens, life comes through them clearer, brighter, and sharper than through people who exist dully.

This fact has not been lost on psychiatry, though it is seen from the opposite end. Very few people come to therapy exhibiting clarity. They come feeling extremely needy and dependent, or feeling so much anxiety that they can barely face up to the ordinary challenges of existence. Sometimes they are so depressed that nothing in their lives, however vivid and moving, registers as more than a gray smudge. In all these cases, something has gone wrong, not just in thinking and feeling, but in being. They have lost the gift for living.

The Feeling of Specialness

Where does the gift come from? In Ray's case, it seems to express itself first and foremost as a bedrock sense of security: "I was sure from the first that I was going to recover. There's no explaining why—it was like a secret I shared with God. I called it a gift because there are no real words to describe it. I was given a chance to remake myself. I didn't know how to do that, only that it was going to happen and nothing could stand in its way."

By now almost everyone has read accounts of the brief near-death experiences that occur to thousands of people every year. The details change from story to story, but a common theme is the sudden descent of a complete sense of security. People who come back to life after their hearts stop beating frequently report that as they "went into the light" or hovered above their bodies looking down on themselves, they felt completely protected. Often this feeling lingers when they reluctantly take up the burden of their bodies once more. They now find it difficult to worry about the things one is supposed to worry about, especially dying. It may be that this is how we are meant to feel even without the near-death experience.

To be may not be a choice, but the way you feel about it certainly is. Some people grow up nurturing a secret feeling that they are somehow special. They feel guarded by providence, although they may not reveal such a reckless belief to others. Dr. Irvin Yalom writes about one such woman who believed in her specialness for years, only to come out of it quite traumatically: she was deeply shaken one day when she became the victim of a purse-snatcher in a restaurant parking lot.

Yalom writes, "Most of all, the robbery illuminated her ordinariness, her 'I never thought it could happen to me' reflecting the loss of belief in her personal specialness." He is not referring to any special talents or gifts that this woman possessed. It is highly rational for people to prize that kind of specialness. But we also have an irrational sense of specialness, Yalom asserts, which serves as "one of our chief methods of denying death." However, far from deeming it a valuable trait, psychiatrists tend to regard this way of feeling special as undesirable, and when the woman came to Yalom for treatment, his chief focus was to bring her to terms with her ordinariness. This meant that he had to strip away her sense of feeling protected against death.

Here we are confronted with the ambiguous role of the psyche's need for self-protection. To feel safe from death is not something we can easily do without; on the other hand, if the fear of death is being forcibly suppressed in the depths of our subconscious, it could be spreading underground terror that we ignore at our peril. As Yalom goes on to say, "The part of our mind whose task it is to mollify death terror generates the irrational belief that we are invulnerable—that unpleasant things like aging and death may be the lot of others but not our lot, that we exist beyond law, beyond human and biological destiny."

I grant that it is a worthwhile goal to dispel delusions and even more worthwhile to rid the mind of hidden fear, but beyond the goal of mental health lies the goal of freedom. Where is freedom to begin if not in "that sense of specialness, of being charmed, of being the exception, of being eternally protected" that psychiatry wants to stamp out? All of these feelings are ones that Yalom labels as self-deceptions. However, to think that they are illusions may itself be a greater illusion—or so the yogis declare.

The starting point for Yoga is just this sense of being special or charmed or protected. Without it, the only sane course in life would be to come to terms with the solid, sensible world before our eyes, complete with its burden of pain, aging, and death. At best one would put up an "ironical struggle," in a famous phrase by Montaigne, fighting the enemy who is destined to win from the first moment of combat.

Many people, perhaps all, would leap at the chance to feel special again, but their conditioning flatly closes off that possibility. Lawrence LeShan is a highly regarded psychologist who more than thirty years ago pioneered the startling theory that cancer has a personal component. He argued that becoming a cancer patient is the end product of neurotic mechanisms that go back to childhood. LeShan was also among the first to use psychotherapy as a means to revive the cancer patient's buried instincts, particularly the instinct to heal.

LeShan found that he had to begin by turning the methods of conventional therapy on their head. If a breast cancer patient goes to a conventional therapist, he would focus primarily on her symptoms. Confronted with her psychological pain, he would try to identify the precise source of that pain and reduce it. LeShan, on the other hand, attempts to make cancer a turning point, with the aim, not of reducing symptoms, but of pushing the patient to new heights. He focuses on the patient's uniqueness and individuality: a breast cancer patient coming to him would be told that she has "a special song to sing in life," a source of joy that belongs only to her.

On the first day of therapy, when LeShan looks at his patients and announces this goal, he very often gets a blast of hostility and rejection in return. The following are some typical responses, taken from his book *Cancer as a Turning Point:*

> "If I found my own music, it would be so discordant that I wouldn't like it, and no one else could stand it either. My own 'natural' way of being is ugly and repellent. I learned a long time ago not to express it if I wanted to have *any* relationships with others or to be able to live with myself."

> "If I found my own song and tried to sing it, I would find that there is no place in the world for anyone like me."

> "My own song would have such contradictions built into it that it would be impossible."

In their acute distress, these patients feel the therapist's helping gesture as a huge threat. They reject his "impossible" goals and hold on desperately to the "unselfish" values they were taught as children. These values include being modest and polite, never losing one's temper, deferring to the wishes of others, and so forth. In our society, every good child has learned them. Yet from the mouths of LeShan's patients, these values sound dreadful, as if someone's soul has been stifled.

Most of us accept the same values, however, and to some extent we, too, do not feel that the world wants to hear our music—our most personal expressions of feeling and desire— just because it is ours. A profound lack of self-acceptance is being revealed in this attitude. But since we are healthy enough to stay out of therapy or a cancer ward, we have no occasion to defend our vulnerability quite so nakedly as these women.

Whenever people actually find their own song to sing, their deep-seated sense of self-doubt begins to be released, leaving a space for creativity to fill. The song turns out to be beautiful; people find that they can sing it without being punished and even earn a living being themselves. "In addition," LeShan notes, "in every case the song was socially positive and acceptable. *I have never seen an exception to this.*" Beneath the fear of being unique, each of us has a powerful craving for as much uniqueness and specialness as possible.

In essence, LeShan is simply asking his patients to be themselves. Why is that prospect at first so horrifying? Deep down, as much as we might deny it, all of us have been hurt by having our childhood wishes trampled on, but we accepted it "for our own good." A child needs and demands to be respected as a unique person, but being small and helplessly attached to his parent's approval, he will sacrifice his own feelings to win the reward of their love. For most of us, our parents fed us their own concept of "being good," and we conformed to that even if it rankled our still-selfish childish egos. As the noted Swiss psychoanalyst Alice Miller points out, we were all taught to be good before we *wanted* to be good.

This may sound like a fine distinction, but in later life it makes all the difference between freedom and slavery. As an adult, I may be firmly habituated to being good. Whenever I give to others, I feel superior for being able to give and sorry for anyone who cannot. Yet the acid test is how I feel when I am doing the giving. Am I joyful about it or merely self-righteous? Do I expect something in return, such as gratitude, deference, and respect? Or do I let the other person feel what he feels, whether it is anything or nothing? Giving can be a mark of genuine freedom, the willingness to do with less so that someone else may have more. But a person who has learned to put on a mask of giving is in total slavery. To what? To the memory of what he must do to make his parents happy.

Beginning with our desire to please our mothers, we have learned to read like perfect scholars the faintest hints of acceptance and rejection in other people. As we subtly mold ourselves to this outside pattern, it becomes second nature, a kind of false self. A gap is created between true and false emotions, between what I should feel and what I actually feel. The process is subtle but treacherous. If it goes on long enough, one forgets what it is like simply to be, to let happiness and sadness come when they will, to give or keep as the moment dictates. For the false self does not really feel; it calculates.

A life lived truly is the joining of heart and mind. As feelings come, the mind approves and delights in them. It is not difficult to test if someone is leading such a life, because he will readily tell you that the best time he has ever spent is the present. This is a sure sign that the mind is not running ahead of the heart in anticipation or lagging behind in nostalgia. The Chinese poet Wu-Men counsels:

> *Ten thousand flowers in spring,*
> *the moon in autumn,*
> *A cool breeze in summer,*
> *snow in winter—*
> *If your mind is not clouded by unnecessary things,*
> *this is the best season of your life.*

If the balance between heart and mind is disturbed, especially if the subtle feeling level has been destroyed, there begins a process we call rationalization. Why am I not happy at this very moment?

"I'm too busy now. I'll be happy when I'm successful."

"Today's not a good day; I'll be happy tomorrow."

"I can't be happy with you, you're not up to my standards."

"Others need me so much that I have to be responsible."

"Life is less risky if you are good and measure up to the norm."

"I'll be happy when I get what I want."

In each phrase one hears the victory of the head over the heart. Being happy is no longer immediate; it has become a distant or near prospect, an idea rather than a feeling. In meditation the yogi tries to clear a path for feeling, removing "unnecessary things" from his mind so that he can actually experience the bedrock of inner satisfaction that all the ancient scriptures declare to be our birthright. Whenever a person succeeds in joining head and heart, that is Yoga. The reward of this union is immense: every moment will become the best in the person's life.

A yogi balances the qualities of intellect and feeling, but I often think of him as a protester on behalf of the heart. Surrounded by people (even in India) who pursue achievement without gaining fulfillment, he chooses fulfillment first. He will not let the mind rob him of the subtle feelings of joy that come as freely as leaves blown by the wind and are as easily swept away.

The Mystery of Elaine

I sat on the edge of the emergency stretcher looking down at Elaine in bafflement. It was midnight, and we had just had her rushed from our clinic to the hospital with uncontrollable vomiting and severe abdominal bleeding. The crisis had erupted with little warning.

When Elaine became my patient two weeks earlier, her complaint had been menorrhagia, or excessive menstrual bleeding. This condition, which caused acute pain during her periods and lasted for as long as fifteen days a month, had persisted for more than a decade. There was also a secondary complaint, which, combined with the first, made her mysterious in my eyes. Although she had never given birth, Elaine spontaneously secreted milk from her breasts, a condition called galactorrhea.

Medically speaking, these two symptoms are contradictions of each other. A particular pituitary hormone, prolactin, could have caused her milk secretions, but another major effect of prolactin is to stop the period. To compound matters, Elaine's tests failed to reveal any abnormalities in her hormone levels. I had been pondering various explanations for her condition when she suddenly suffered this midnight attack.

The young Indian doctor who was on call at our clinic that night had sounded panicky when he phoned me, reporting that Elaine had vomited twenty times in less than three hours. He noticed a droop in her left eyelid and a slight facial tic, which made him fear some kind of brain incident. He guessed that a tiny tumor, probably in the pituitary, was beginning to hemorrhage, and he therefore had had no choice but to get her into an ambulance as fast as possible.

Now Elaine was no longer in pain and lay on the stretcher sedated. Her symptoms had receded as unexpectedly as they had begun, and a CAT scan, much to my relief, disclosed no sign of a brain tumor. Incredibly, her entire sheaf of test results still indicated that she was perfectly healthy. Nothing made any sense.

As Elaine slept, I looked down at her worn, drawn face. It occurred to me that this was the most relaxed I had ever seen her. In her first office visit she had presented herself as a secure, successful businesswoman. She owned her own public relations firm, with twenty employees under her (they were all men, she took pains to inform me). Whatever lay beneath this confident persona, I wasn't going to find it that night. I scheduled an office appointment on her chart and in the meantime called her family doctor in Houston to see if he could clue me in. He was not encouraging.

"Elaine?" he said. "There's nothing wrong with her, not that I have ever been able to find. She has had about sixty of these attacks in the past ten years"—Elaine had neglected to tell me that when she came up to Boston—"and I recently told her that there was nothing more I could do."

I asked him for his best guess at an accurate diagnosis. "Hysteria," he shot back. "No doubt in my mind. You'll never be able to shake her of this thing, but good luck trying." With obvious satisfaction he abruptly ended the conversation.

The next morning I asked Elaine about the previous attacks. Looking embarrassed, she admitted that these had occurred off and on for fifteen years, dating from when she first got married. Did she have a happy marriage? She turned red and looked away. "I was raised a strict Catholic, and I feel I have a duty to remain in this marriage. Happy? My husband treats me very well, and I respect him as a good man." It turned out that because of a preexisting organic condition, her husband had never been able to have intimate relations with her. She described their current relationship as caring and close but platonic.

"Do you know what your doctor in Houston thinks is wrong with you?" I asked.

She answered angrily, "He thinks I'm hysterical, of course. I'm sure he told you that."

"Do you know what is meant by the term hysteria?" I asked. She admitted that she had only a vague idea. "I'm not a psychiatrist," I said, "but in layman's terms, an hysteric is someone who is the victim of self-deception. He presents all the signs of a physical illness and is completely convinced by them, yet no one else can find a 'real' cause for his symptoms. On the other hand, deceiving yourself can also be considered a real cause in its own way."

Whereas the word "hysteric" had deeply offended her, I noticed that Elaine looked interested in the line of explanation we were now pursuing. "People find numerous reasons for deceiving themselves," I continued. "You've already mentioned that your marriage lacks certain types of normal fulfillment, such as having sexual relations with your husband and becoming a mother. Your doctor has concluded that your symptoms are basically born out of frustration. I don't know how frankly you can talk to your husband, but I'm sure you've made all these connections on your own already."

She said nothing, which I took to be assent. She was extremely startled, however, by my next words. "You're not an hysteric, Elaine. I think there's a flaw in your doctor's reasoning. The fact is that you are quite conscious of what is missing in your life, which is not true of a deeply deceived person. I would feel more comfortable if we dropped the psychological jargon and looked at your problem much more directly."

"What do you mean?" she asked nervously.

"Let's start with a very basic thing," I replied. "How do you feel at this moment?"

"Right now?"

"Yes. What word would describe Elaine right now?"

"Empty," she said without hesitation. "But I have lived with that for a long, long time."

"Why?" I asked.

She looked at me hard. "Do you think I have a choice? That's just the way I feel."

"Does feeling that way make you happy?" I asked.

"You may not believe this," she said, "but I think I'm basically as happy as the next person."

"Really?" I asked. "You just said you feel empty much of the time. A lot of people feel that way, or are afraid that they feel that way, but a lot of people don't."

"How do you feel?" she asked.

"Can't you tell?"

"Well, no. How could I?"

"I'm giving it off."

"You are?"

"Sure," I said. "In my tone of voice, the look in my eyes, and in many other subtle ways, I give off feelings, just as you and all other people do. We are having a conversation in feelings, though it may be taking place below the verbal level. Right now I feel interested in you. I am worried about why we can't explain what is happening to you, and at the same time I must admit that I am excited by exploring your emotions. It's an intimate moment."

Elaine didn't comment. "Can't you sense those feelings?" I urged. "Don't you have much the same ones?" She nodded her head reluctantly.

"Like an underground stream, the life of feeling keeps running on," I said, "even when the mind denies it. You aren't empty, but you have an *idea* that you are. This is the split that is causing so much confusion. We know that you have a full range of feelings, both powerful and subtle, because your body is expressing them as symptoms. However, these feelings have not registered clearly in your mind. Perhaps there is too much frustration for you to easily cope with, or on the other hand too much happiness. Have you ever considered that?"

She looked completely disbelieving. "Too much happiness? Are you joking?"

"The feelings we are told not to have as children become lost on us as adults. The child inside you could be roaring with laughter or wild with ecstasy, but if you have learned that roaring and going wild are not permitted, you won't experience those feelings directly—you will find a substitute feeling that is more acceptable, like being proud of your work."

"But I *am* proud of my work."

"It's very right and good that you are," I said, "but by opening up that one channel so wide, you may be cutting off others, equally valid but more difficult for you to experience."

A guarded look came over her face. We were on the edge of a psychological precipice, but I had no intention of pushing her over. Elaine's intimate life had to be healed at a pace that was comfortable to her. What I wanted her to see at the moment was something much more general. Sometime in the past she had made a fatal choice common to many people. She had decided to control her unhappiness instead of expressing it and letting it go. Humans seem to be unique in facing this choice. If a cat stalks a sparrow in the grass, pounces, and misses, its whole body reacts with frustration. The cat paces, twitches its tail, licks itself, and then falls asleep. These various reflexes manage to clear the slate of the cat's nervous system, and the next time it stalks a bird, there will be no shadow of the earlier failure.

The human nervous system, although equipped with similar automatic reflexes, is far more elaborate, and it gives us much more complex reactions in the face of frustration. If a cat thought like a person, it might resort to denial ("I was just practicing"), blame ("Someone's been scaring the game around here"), self-recrimination ("I knew I should have

sharpened my claws this morning"), or guilt ("Why can't I
stay away from those sparrows?"). As things stand, human life
is inconceivable without these reactions. They are part of our
nature, however much we suffer from them. In a psychologically healthy person, guilt, shame, self-recrimination, and
blame serve as symptoms of unease. When the unease is corrected—when we face our guilt, confess our shame, or confront the person we have blamed—a feeling of ease returns.

An illness is a localized form of unease (as the term "disease" implies), and it is not surprising to find that for many
people, a much broader unease underlies it. What I try to do
with patients is to reveal this very general unease, just enough
so that they are not entirely caught up in the narrow boundaries of their symptoms. In Elaine's case, there were intimate
details of her life involved in her illness; I am sure a knowing
psychiatrist could probe into her fundamental feelings of guilt
and shame. (To begin with, why did she remain devoted to a
man who had failed to tell her of his sexual incapacity before
their marriage? Did she deny her anger because she felt too
guilty to demand sexual satisfaction as her rightful reward?)

It would be foolhardy and cruel to explore a patient's defenses simply to expose them. These boundaries exist for good
reason: the person is trying to salvage shreds of happiness by
isolating himself from areas of distress. This is what I meant
by saying that we choose to control our unhappiness instead
of letting it go. If, like a cat, we could wipe clean the slate of
our memory, then living with guilt, shame, disappointment,
and self-recrimination might not be inevitable. As nature
made us, however, we turn our distress into ourselves, just as
we turn food into ourselves. What can we do but try to devise
the best defenses we can? If anything, a compassionate doctor
would try to reinforce them, limiting his treatment to the local problem while mercifully ignoring the general one. Unless, that is, he understands how to reveal a deeper mercy.

I have no illusion that my words are enough to change a
person's deep unease. Each of us is a walking universe. Our
inner space spans huge distances, with unreachable horizons
in all directions. We contain black holes of lost memory and
white holes of erupting joy. A mysterious center of gravity
keeps all our mental processes in delicate balance. To change

this vast, intricate, ever-evolving system, you must know how to overturn worlds. The only person who can do that is the god who presides over this inner cosmos, and when I presume to break into a patient's mind, it is to implant the idea that he is that god. By thinking, feeling, and acting, he is altering the universe that is himself. If a person can gain that insight, even in a brief glimpse, anything in his life can change.

Here I am thinking of a woman in Canada whom I have never met but who wrote me a fascinating letter. At the age of twenty-four she married a man she had loved for six years. Because the couple had very little money, they waited four more years before trying to have a child. The woman was unable to conceive, however, and it was eventually discovered that her husband was completely sterile due to a testicular disorder.

The woman was bitterly disappointed, but she remained caring and considerate toward her husband, whose psychological state became very fragile. A few months later she woke up in bed one night and found a lump in her abdomen that was hard to the touch. By morning it had swollen so large that her belly was distended. She rushed to a doctor, who informed her that she was at least five months pregnant. The woman carefully explained why this was impossible. For some inexplicable reason, the doctor then advised her that the problem might be a bladder infection, and she was sent home with a two-week prescription for antibiotics.

When the swelling refused to subside, she returned to the clinic, and a second doctor made a careful physical examination. He, too, confirmed that she was pregnant. The woman had no choice but to assume that a miracle had occurred. She started wearing loose dresses and spent her time in maternity shops. But then the swelling became tender, and she experienced vaginal bleeding. She returned to the clinic, where she was met with harsh skepticism. Her doctor assumed that she had been having an extramarital affair and was now trying to induce a miscarriage. Various tests were performed, and at last the mystery was solved: she was suffering from a massive ovarian tumor. The woman immediately entered the hospital, where one ovary was removed and the other repaired.

The letter ends: "My surgeon insisted that such a large

growth must have taken at least five years to reach that size. I am the only one who believes that it appeared overnight. Although I was bitterly disappointed to be deprived of a child for the rest of my life, I have gained something, too. I realized that nothing—or everything—is as real as what I make it. If getting sick is in my power, so is getting well. To this day, more than ten years later, I have not allowed myself to catch so much as a cold."

I find myself moved by this story, not just because of its poignancy, but because a veil has parted. Whenever reality shows itself, even in the midst of crisis, there is the hint of joy, and if we could see further, there would be no limit to it. That was in my mind when I was talking to Elaine. "Look at that tree out there," I said to her, and pointed to a huge old copper beech outside the window. "Tell me what you see."

"I see a large tree with purple leaves and gnarled bark," she began.

"It's very beautiful, isn't it?" I interrupted.

"Yes," she agreed.

"Now can you look further and see more?" We both paused and she continued to look. "Do you have a sense of its gloriousness? Do you see the living light being tossed off by each leaf? Doesn't that old tree seem to possess the air around it like a monarch?"

Elaine laughed. "Sure, I can sort of see all that."

"But you notice that we had to work at it a little," I said. "The first tree you saw was not so glorious. If that tree had looked truly glorious to you, you would have stared at it from the moment you walked in. Gloriousness is pretty hard to ignore. Now tell me, what do you see when you look at Elaine?"

She gave a startled jerk of her head.

"Are you glorious?" I asked. She looked embarrassed, and in a gentler voice I said, "It might take a little work to see yourself as glorious, and right now it's not your first reaction, just as it wasn't to that copper beech. All the same, the gloriousness could be there. It really could."

For the first time, her face softened and she looked genuinely touched. "Feeling the glory of life means feeling it in yourself and about yourself," I said. "You can look at beautiful trees and listen to beautiful music, but these substitutes, however gratifying, are still substitutes. The fact that you can appreciate them means that your own inner beauty wants to come out. It is seeking its own kind.

"What is that tree's glory but your own, seen in nature's mirror? If you wanted to, you could turn the mirror around and see yourself directly. The glory in you is not painful to see. It is the opposite of pain. Shall we try to bring it out?" With obvious pleasure, Elaine shyly agreed.

The Polished Mirror

Turning the mirror inward is a metaphor for the actual process I wanted Elaine to discover, meditation. Medically speaking, meditation has proved particularly helpful in cases like hers where the patient's physical and mental states have become severely disjointed. I advised her to seek instruction in Transcendental Meditation, or TM, the technique that I practice myself and have recommended for a decade.

In my eyes, TM's primary advantage is that it is natural—it allows the mind to discover its own subtlest layers without force, as they are discovered in moments of calm quietness in normal life. To unveil the most delicate feeling level of the mind, a meditation technique has to be as effortless as possible; otherwise, one is just forcing the mind into a preconceived mold. (The opposite of a natural meditation would be one where intense concentration is used.)

In English, the classic description of a natural state of meditation is provided in the poems of William Wordsworth. As an adult, Wordsworth could no longer see the celestial light that made his childhood so glorious, but his mind was acutely attuned to itself—he had turned the mirror inward. In a contemplative passage from his great poem "Tintern Abbey," he describes with marvelous precision

> . . . *that serene and blessed mood,*
> *In which the affections gently lead us on—*
> *Until the breath of this corporeal frame*
> *And even the motion of our human blood*

Almost suspended, we are laid asleep
In body, and become a living soul;
While with an eye made quiet by the power
Of harmony, and the deep power of joy,
We see into the life of things.

Reading these lines, I always get a sense of reassurance from one particularly telling touch: the use of "us" and "our." Wordsworth is making clear that all of us share his inner experience. We may lack his gift for expressing it so beautifully, but that does not matter. We all exist on the basis of one common being, immersed in "harmony and the deep power of joy."

These experiences sound beautiful, but until thirty years ago, no one had understood that they are crucial for human development. It was widely thought in the East and in the West alike that yogis and swamis were hermits who wanted no part of the vanity of the world. The most magical thing about them—that they renounced the world in order to regain it anew—was entirely missed. It has taken hundreds of research studies into the physiology of meditation to reverse this mistake. These studies were begun in the early Sixties, in both American and European universities, at the suggestion of Maharishi Mahesh Yogi, the founder of Transcendental Meditation.

Stepping from the Himalayas, where meditation is so tangible and alive that it has soaked into the very stones and forests, Maharishi faced a wall of skepticism in the West. Here even the very educated held that meditation was a vague, highly suspect mixture of mysticism, psychological illusion, and religious faith. Maharishi proposed quite the opposite: meditation was an objective, repeatable phenomenon that could be validated by the means of science. It was actually a universal experience, although it happened to be cultivated in the East and largely neglected in the West.

During the Sixties and Seventies, doctors and physiologists tested thousands of college-age meditators. After monitoring heartbeat, blood pressure, respiration rate, oxygen consumption, brain waves, and all the other bodily signs that change during meditation, Western researchers soon agreed that they were seeing something real in their own terms, a new phenomenon that was not just a variant of ordinary sleep or hypnotic trance.

Measurements of TM subjects as they enter into deep meditation indicate that they are recreating the state Wordsworth so carefully described. There is a gradual suspension of respiration and decreased heart rate (a stilling of "the breath of this corporeal frame" and "the motion of our human blood"), the body approaches the lower metabolic rate associated with sleep, and yet the mind remains alert, even heightened in its clarity (the "eye made quiet by the power of harmony"). And the mind feels secure, at peace, and protected (united with the "deep power of joy").

No two people meditate exactly alike, since the byways of every mind are different. But if taught a natural, correct technique, everyone, I believe, would experience inner glory. The human nervous system is innately capable of seeing directly into "the life of things," as Wordsworth tells us, so long as the brain is not clouded by disease or toxic substances. In time, meditation makes the nervous system extremely sensitive, so that it registers every subtle impression vividly and without prejudice; then the world itself changes.

The change might prove to be much more far-reaching than anyone supposes. To modern ears, the seers of the ancient Vedic scriptures sound almost otherworldly because they took it for granted that human life is essentially perfect. A typical verse from the Veda says of humanity that we exist in bliss, or pure joy: "Of bliss these beings are born, in bliss they are sustained, and to bliss they go and merge again."

Like all Indians who have any awareness of their inherited tradition, Maharishi was raised hearing these expressions about *ananda,* or bliss. Yet he could not reconcile the idea of pure joy with what he saw around him: "There is such a gap between what life is declared to be and what life is found to be. I was naturally and deeply moved between two realities: life being lived on such a completely wretched level and life described on the most exalted level. There was no connection between the two.

"And yet there was no reason why there should be a gap, because it's so simple for the individual to be on the level of universality and immortality. It's so simple. This was the natural feeling that was deep in my mind—something should be done so that people don't suffer, because there is no reason to suffer."

The true yogi stands apart from ordinary experience by seeing that suffering is a completely false state. As we really are, we are creatures of bliss, but this reality is totally dependent upon experiencing it. All bliss vanishes when the mind takes on suffering; all suffering vanishes when the mind takes on bliss. The reason this must be so is that our inner mirror, unlike one made of glass, actually *becomes* the image it reflects.

What the yogi proposes is that each of us should locate the level of pure joy that is behind the mirror. It cannot be expressed in words, because language is another image in the mind's mirror. Once the experience of bliss is achieved, it may spill over into words, as it did for Wordsworth. The crucial point is that bliss is not our goal but our starting point. Unless it is present, one has no foundation for climbing to any of the higher spiritual states.

The deeper nature of the world is barely guessed at in our present situation. I was reminded of this fact by a breast cancer patient of mine, a longtime meditator who recently sent me her latest progress report. It begins,

> January to August have been completely pain-free months. I continue to rise above all the old routines that remind me of being a cancer patient. During this whole period I have enjoyed increased energy and activity. Finally I felt I had the time to enjoy myself, doing what I wanted to do, eating what I wanted to eat, and leading a normal life.

At the height of this happy period, the freest she had experienced in seven years, this woman noticed the return of chest pain and a feeling of pressure in her lungs. A recurrence was strongly suspected, and her oncologist resumed the course of chemotherapy. However, her discomfort continued to increase, to the point that she had difficulty walking or even sitting up in bed. Then something new happened:

Despite the discomfort, my husband and I decided to camp out in the woods one night—we live in Alaska now. It was a starry night, absolutely clear. Around midnight the aurora borealis unfurled across the sky. We woke up the next morning and did our usual meditation sitting cross-legged on the mossy forest floor.

When I opened my eyes, the trees all around me had changed from their ordinary flat brown and green to pinpoints of sparkling golden light, then gradually back again. In awe I watched this transformation repeat itself, as the forest pulsated with energy, turning to light and back again, in and out. Everything around me was intensely alive, and I felt so intimately connected to it, as I had never felt before.

Her whole body was suffused with the gentle, living quality of the scene she looked at: "It was not an experience of joy but of sublime peace." Without warning, she had fallen into a special state in which the rough reality we all accept had turned into a flow of pure light and divine feelings:

I have said that I felt peace rather than joy. The joy came later, intensely, when we walked back through the forest, caressed by the soft air, listening to the birds and watching the antics of the squirrels. There were signs of wildlife everywhere—we saw bear tracks and many ptarmigan. At one point a large red fox walked across our path without showing any sign of alarm.

On her return home, she noticed how tired the two-hour walk had made her, but at the same time she felt something very gratifying. There was no longer any chest pain or pressure in her lungs; her breathing was completely clear for the first time in a month. The next night she sat up in bed talking to her husband, and a new phrase slipped out in passing, "I had breast cancer." Always before, she automatically said, "I *have* breast cancer." She was surprised but greatly relieved at this change:

> After I said it, I realized how spontaneously the words had come out. Most importantly, they felt like the truth. The words were strong and clear, spoken without hesitation. At the same time, a new feeling began to rise in me, a deep sense of gratitude for all the gifts I had received in such simple ways.

I have little to add, except for one caution: the sense of fulfillment that surfaces when the inner mirror is polished must be spontaneous to be true. The dull mirage of the world "out there" does not change to glory all at once; the personality is not instantly lifted to sainthood; the body does not lose all its imperfections. (This woman was not miraculously healed; she continues to undergo regular treatment for her cancer and calmly accepts whatever outcome the future holds.)

The whole process of renewal happens in one's consciousness, at a level deeper than thought. It does no good to try to be newer, better, more insightful, and so forth. Rather, the nervous system undertakes the metamorphosis deep inside itself, using its own recuperative powers. As the Upanishads declare, the yogi "dies and lives again" with each meditation, which is another way of saying that he cleans the mirror and holds it up to reflect a different light.

The light will surely come through, even under conditions that seem to be overwhelmed by darkness. One of my friends is a TM teacher who has taught extensively in prisons, and because he speaks fluent Spanish, he has helped start meditation programs for prisoners in Central America. On one trip he found himself walking into the courtyard of an old governor's palace from the days of the conquistadors. A moldering ruin now, it was built like a medieval fortress, with several thick stone walls nested inside each other.

"The gloom and oppression of that place were terrible, even compared to other places like it," he remembers. "I got inside the third wall and then the fourth, and when the guards let me through the last gate, do you know what I saw?

"Very high up near the roof was a single small barred window. Sticking out of it was a man's arm. His hand was open, and he was reaching, as hard as he could, for the sky. The arm didn't move the whole time I passed through the yard. More than words ever could, it told me the dread of being in there."

He found horrendous conditions inside. The cells were huge open rooms, each holding a hundred men, whose rope hammocks were stacked in layers up to the ceiling. The cramped room set aside for my friend's lectures had wide cracks between the plank flooring. When he looked down he could see the prisoners milling in the cells below.

"We taught large groups of these men, who seemed very eager to learn to meditate. They had good experiences, too, because of the huge contrast between their present condition and the quietness we were giving them inside. I gathered together the first thirty who had learned and asked them to volunteer what they were getting out of it. There was a general stir, but no one really wanted to volunteer. Then Juan Gonzalez raised his hand, and everybody laughed raucously.

"You see, Juan Gonzalez had the lowest status in the entire prison. He was an old peasant who seemed to be mentally retarded. He shuffled along with his head bent down and rarely spoke. All he did was take care of the prison chapel, a tiny, bare room with nothing in it except a few wooden benches and a rough-hewn cross on the wall. All the decorations and altar pieces had been removed long ago, or stolen.

" 'Don't mind them,' I said to Juan Gonzalez. 'Stand up and tell me what you feel in your meditation.' He slowly stood up and climbed onto his chair—I will never forget it—then he spread out his arms as wide as possible, tilted back his head, and said, *'Mas amor, señor, mas amor.'* "

"Do you know what that means?" my friend asked me.

"I do," I said, seeing Juan Gonzalez in my mind's eye and wondering at our kinship although he was so far away. "It means, 'More love, sir, more love.' "

8

~~~~~~~~~~~~~~~~

The True Self

When my old friend Liam woke up one morning, got out of bed, and had a heart attack, he didn't bother to tell me. I only found out a week later when another doctor casually asked, "How's our man Liam enjoying his bypass?"

"What?" I stammered, dumbfounded.

He stopped being so lighthearted. "You didn't know? He was admitted for a triple bypass last week. Don't worry, I understand it was a minor infarction"—meaning that only a small portion of the heart muscle had suffered permanent damage. "If you ask me, he was lucky to find out the way he did. He could have walked around with three vessels blocked and dropped dead tomorrow."

I was relieved that Liam was safe but at the same time hurt that he had left me out. Our friendship went back more than fifteen years. We had both just immigrated to this country—he from Ireland, I from India—burning to make a career for ourselves in Boston medicine. We shared the exhausting grind young residents are put through, seeing more of each other at the veteran's hospital than we saw of our families at home.

Liam was a star even back then. When the rest of us were slumped in the residents' lounge at four A.M., too tired to lift our fifth cup of coffee, he would be retelling the day's clinical findings with undiminished enthusiasm. His brilliant mind never rested, it seemed, and his store of medical knowledge was bottomless. All he could think of was internal medicine, and his way with duller, less committed colleagues was merciless. He had all the senior residents cowed, and more than one department head gave him a wide berth.

The flip side of this diamondlike hardness of mind was Liam's soft way with patients. If a sleepy intern took thirty seconds too long to come up with a proper diagnosis, Liam would be jumping down his throat, but a burned-out alcoholic could ramble on for half an hour and still hold his undivided attention. In return for his ability to truly listen, Liam won his patients' adoration. One ominous detail stands out in my recollection, however—Liam was already a heavy chain-smoker, working his way from two to three packs a day.

When I started writing books, Liam had already made his way into mainstream medicine, operating a flourishing oncology practice in Atlanta. Whenever he called, he took care never to refer to my involvement in alternative medicine. One night, however, he announced that his four partners, all senior oncologists, had passed around one of my books. Their reaction was violent. "They're outraged, Deepak," he said. "They don't believe in these spontaneous cures. They think your patients will have recurrences sooner or later, and they say that you are undermining the legitimate practice of medicine. You've blown them out!"

After Liam had reported their reaction in great detail, I hung up feeling depressed. It wasn't the hostile skepticism of four strangers that upset me—I suspected that Liam was speaking his own mind indirectly through them.

Now it was two months later, and Liam had had a premature heart attack at the age of thirty-eight. I reached him at home. "Sorry to be so mysterious, Deepak. It wasn't a big deal," Liam started off, sounding weak and gloomy. He was reluctant to share any details of his attack. Yes, the infarcted area was minimal, localized to the posterior of the left ventricle. The bypass had gone very well; he was steadily recuperating, and there were no complications.

In the midst of this rather impersonal exchange, Liam

suddenly blurted out, "I know exactly why this thing happened, you know. It's not the smoking, not really. For two
years I've been growing disenchanted with oncology. I don't
feel like doing my job anymore, and the prospect of seeing
another cancer patient fills me with revulsion. But what are
my options? I feel trapped."

I was caught off guard, but Liam rushed on without taking a breath. "Cancer shakes people up, Deepak. Some of my
patients are stiff with fear. 'I just don't want chemotherapy,'
they insist. You and I know that chemo is effective a lot of the
time. When it isn't, I don't feel like pushing it, but if I don't
push it, of course I don't get paid. A doctor can't make a living
just talking to patients, not nowadays. You have to run the
procedures that insurance companies reimburse you for. My
conscience hurts me, but I push chemo anyway.

"I mean, look, all I'm trained to do is give chemo. If I
don't, the patient's relatives start screaming, lawyers get involved. It becomes very complicated very quickly. You get
swallowed up in a system that you didn't invent. And everybody is very skeptical, every step of the way."

I began to sense a Liam very different from the one I had
known—guiltier and more vulnerable, but potentially far
more self-aware. At the moment, however, this budding self-
awareness came out sounding very confused. "I'm caught in a
terrible dilemma," he said as his outpouring was winding
down. "I don't want to go back to work. As far as I'm concerned, work gave me this heart attack. But my cardiologist
says my vessels are open. I passed the treadmill stress test, I
can walk three miles without chest pain. So I'm cured—the
fact that I hate my job and can't stand to go back doesn't
count."

The immediate need was to calm the panic I kept hearing
in Liam's voice. "Look, you're not really trapped," I began.
"You could make a new start tomorrow if you wanted to."

"Deepak, everybody treats cancer this way."

"You wouldn't be the first oncologist to change fields," I
replied. I reminded Liam that he was selling his brilliant
clinical abilities far too short. "I can think of half a dozen
internists who would give their eyeteeth to have you for a
partner," I said, mentioning a mutual friend of ours who had

abandoned the city for a rural practice in Maine. "He'd love to have you join him. You would be doing the small town up there a service, and taking the pressure off yourself can only help your heart."

"You're right, you're right," Liam kept saying in response to my encouragements. He thanked me profusely, promising to pursue the lead, and we hung up.

This incident preyed on my mind for the rest of the day and for days afterward. What did I think about Liam now? My reaction was not simple. When someone feels psychologically trapped, his body can often speak louder than words. Liam was basically apologizing for being so heartless as to have "pushed chemo" on frightened, resistant patients. Perhaps he had to have a heart attack to prove that he still had a heart. I felt very sorry for him if it had come to that. I berated myself too for not having more insight when he first called venting his partners' complaints. Was he trying unconsciously to ask for help? It certainly looked that way in retrospect.

And what would happen now? People who find themselves caught at the crossroads of a life-threatening disease also face many deep, painful choices in their psyches and must make them with no guarantee that they will choose right. It is much easier to settle for the bypass. Patch up your heart, pay the bills, and hope the pain stays away. This is the common tactic, but it is a perilous one. Being a doctor, Liam knew that his fresh new graft was not a cure. It was basically a stopgap, and in five years or so he would probably have to go in for another patch up, with possibly a third one five years after that. Would his bypassed emotions be any more merciful?

After Liam did not call for a month, I heard—again at secondhand—that he had returned to his oncology practice. I also got a call from our mutual friend in Maine.

"By the way, have you heard from Liam recently?" I asked in the middle of our conversation.

"Liam? No," he said. "Don't tell me he was thinking of coming up here."

"I don't know," I said, feeling more disappointed than I had any right to be. "Why should he?"

The Song of Truth

No one knows why people make sudden breakthroughs into self-awareness, but when they do, the effect is often short-lived. The moment of liberation may be earthshaking, but it passes quickly, leaving no deep or lasting transformation in its wake. There is no great mystery to this. The forces that uphold our familiar world have returned with renewed tenacity. Inertia, fear, the pull of old habits—they all warn us to remain where we are. Who knows what the unknown might bring?

Could a completely new self even survive in this rough world? As children we all learned not to be too sensitive, too open, too vulnerable. We saw the obvious advantages of being as tough as possible, of getting what you want from other people. In this way there arose a very troubling conflict—the clash between love and power—that found lodgings deep inside each of us.

Liam found himself confronting this conflict head on. Instead of his having power over his patients because he could make life-or-death decisions for them, their pain was starting to have power over him. He was being put in a very awkward position: one part of him keenly wanted to retain control over others, while another just as keenly wanted to feel compassion for them. Compassion is a form of love; it takes others as they are, without judgment or a sense of superiority. It is therefore not the easiest feeling for the ego to adjust to. On the other hand, compassion is true, and that is its great attraction.

By "true," I mean that compassion is found at the core of human nature, underneath the covering layers of selfishness. In our time, psychology has dwelt on selfishness as a fundamental drive in the human character, but in the yogi's eyes, this is a profound misjudgment. To him, compassion and its root feeling, love, are primary in humankind. Whenever they appear, even in a flash, it is our true self appearing, like the sun breaking through clouds. To the yogi, love and nonlove are not striving for dominance. Love is eternal; nonlove is temporary, a twist of the psyche that the small, limited, fearful self falls prey to.

I am not sure this position can be proved, but one can certainly witness that love is welcomed with relief and joy whenever it is sincerely given. This joy is the self's natural response when it sees its truthful reflection. The same cannot be said for nonlove: to achieve enormous power is rarely a joyful event.

In *Love and Will,* Rollo May portrays a young patient who fell victim to the unloving influence that power generally wields. This boy, whose father was treasurer of a large European corporation, entered psychotherapy with May during his early years at college. When therapy was about to begin, the father called up to discuss "maximizing the effectiveness of my son's treatment," exactly as if he were conducting a corporate board meeting. He had a controlling interest in his son, although he would have called it paternal love. When the boy fell ill at school, his father flew out immediately to take charge of the situation, but at the same time he became furious when his son held hands with his girlfriend on the front lawn of their resort house.

May points out that the father was superb at taking care *of* people but had never learned to care *for* them, could give them his money but not his heart, could direct them but never listen to them: "The strong 'will power' which the father thought solved all *his* problems, actually served at the same time to block his sensitivity, to cut off his capacity to hear other persons, even, or perhaps especially, his own son."

This man exercised power over others casually, even unthinkingly. At dinner one night he proudly told how he was negotiating to buy a small business owned by one of his son's friends, but when the negotiations went too slowly, he irritably canceled the deal, showing no remorse about driving someone into bankruptcy with the snap of his fingers. It is no wonder that his son had great difficulty finishing school and spent years of anguish before he could accomplish anything worthwhile on his own.

One of the reasons that the yogi can endure our false world with so much patience is that he believes in the eventual triumph of truth. Despite the endless display of selfishness in every society, he is able to witness the possible emergence of love in everyone. Like gravity to a physicist, love is the primordial energy in the yogi's universe, which no lesser force can abolish or successfully oppose, not in the final unfoldment of time.

But it is not necessary for the millennium to creep on before the truth triumphs. The yogi is living proof that inner unfoldment can be hastened; the pure joy of love can be achieved in one lifetime. So our only choice is how long to delay the moment when we transform ourselves. The bound, ego-driven self has much to offer—comfort, security, continuity, power—but the truth sings its own song, and for some mysterious reason, we are tuned to hear it.

I remember a tender, beckoning line from Rumi, the great Sufi poet: "Come out of the circle of time and into the circle of love." This is the change that must happen. Right now, everything we know about ourselves as individuals has been built up over time; therefore time is also our psychological enemy, reinforcing the boundaries that keep love out. One must go beyond time to experience the real value of oneself, which is what a breakthrough accomplishes.

It is not a bad sign when a breakthrough makes one feel vulnerable and undefended, as Liam so acutely felt. These are actually desirable emotions, because they announce the possibility of a new life. They are not safe emotions, however. To be new is to feel terribly exposed, like a fragile hatchling. A spiritual teacher was once giving a talk on going beyond the confinement of time, seeking the timeless in every moment, when a member of the audience anxiously interrupted, "But if I go beyond time, won't I miss my morning train?" One's first reaction to the unknown is often like that: a worried anticipation that the familiar world, with its trains that run on time, will be pulled out from under.

However, the poet Alfred Lord Tennyson affirmed that for him the feeling of being totally free of boundaries was "not a confused state but the clearest of the clear, the surest of the sure, utterly beyond words—where death was an almost laughable impossibility." This certainty was a tribute to the clarity of his experiences. In keeping with many others who have transcended the waking state, Tennyson concluded that those rare instances when individuality "seemed to dissolve and melt away into boundless being" had shown him "the only true self."

If Tennyson was right, then each of us is living outside his true self. We are not clear and sure; we are trapped in time and the pain it brings; we are mortally afraid of death. One might surmise that the intensity of "the only true self" must be reserved for saints and poets. But ordinary experience, the kind all of us have, is much more profound than we give it credit for.

To begin with, we spend a large part of every day in the supremely creative act of constructing our self. If this self has flaws, it is not because we are incompetent builders; rather, the problem is that our past mistakes have turned into us. Since adulthood, the process of making a self has been left in our own hands, but its roots go back to earliest childhood, when we had no choice but to imbibe our parent's version of selfhood. Without knowing it, we started to be shaped.

In an ideal childhood, we would have been nurtured, in Alice Miller's words, "by the presence of a person who was completely aware of us, who took us seriously, who admired and followed us." Awareness is the prime prerequisite here; it is much more important than the words and actions in themselves that a parent directs toward a child. The words "Mommy loves you" or "You're a good boy" mean very little outside the look and tone of voice that accompany them. A loving gaze turns the words into nourishment; a troubled, hesitant, or angry gaze can turn the same words to poison.

Life has proceeded, of course, on a less than ideal basis for generation after generation. Alice Miller describes a Greek man, a restaurant owner in his thirties, who told her very proudly one day that he never drank alcohol and had his father to thank for it. When he was fifteen and came home one night extremely drunk, his father beat him so severely that he could not move for a week. From that time on he could not stand to taste so much as a drop of liquor. This man was on the verge of getting married when Miller talked to him, and she asked if he intended to beat his own children. "Of course," he replied, "beatings are necessary in bringing up a child properly: they are the best way to make him respect you. I

would never smoke in my father's presence, for example—
and that is the sign of my respect for him."

This man was oblivious to what he was actually propos-
ing, that it is good to break a child's spirit. Without a qualm,
he felt it necessary for a child to live in fear of severe punishment. After all, for him the word "respect" basically meant
"terror." This sort of untruth gets passed on because one generation fails to solve the problem of the false self and then has
no choice but to pass the problem on. Broken spirits do not
see anything wrong in breaking the spirits of their children.

The ideal parent would serve as a sensitive extension of
the child's psyche. As father and mother mirrored the child's
feelings, he would see the reflection coming back to him, and
conforming to it, he would be shaped by both his own psyche
and theirs. A cry of rage would meet, for example, with an
understanding look that said, "I know why you are angry,"
and in that unspoken compassion, anger would run its course
and dissolve. It is our checked feelings, the ones that our parents labeled "bad" in their eyes, that cause so much hidden
conflict later. Without this sensitive, loving interaction, which
must begin from birth, we walk through the rest of our lives
wounded, unable to accept ourselves but never fully knowing
why.

Having missed the ideal upbringing, one can still repair
the lack of a totally aware parent by becoming totally aware
oneself. The ancient Indian texts often compare Yoga to becoming your own parent. The image of "dying to your father
and mother," which is frequently found in the Upanishads,
does not mean running away or turning your back on them.
Rather, it means taking on their role yourself, developing inside your own heart the give-and-take of awareness that fash-
ions a complete person out of the raw material of existence.

The Art of Not Doing

The morning sun sends bright shafts of light onto the Ori-
ental carpet in my bedroom, but I do not see them. I am sitting in an armchair, my eyes closed, meditating. Thoughts run

through my head; I hear the sparrows squabbling outside my window and the clicking digital clock in the room; I scratch my ear or shuffle in my seat as the spirit moves me. The picture of meditation that many Westerners have in their mind's eye is not this. It is of an austere, disciplined setting, with saffron-robed monks sitting row upon row at stiff attention. The room is dark, silent, and unbearably cold. The watchful eye of an old abbot is fixed on the novice monks; he is ready to strike them with a bamboo stick if they nod their heads or slump their shoulders.

This aura of renunciation tends to overawe most people. As much as they might respect the inner fortitude being displayed, Westerners are very reluctant to endure the same rigors themselves. Yet the outer picture is deceiving; the inner experience of meditation can be had without any kind of forced discipline. The outer trappings—how one sits, breathes, dresses, and so forth—are really irrelevant.

When I sit down to meditate, my inner experience can best be described by what I am not doing: I am not focusing my mind or contemplating any idea. I am not in a spiritual or introspective mood. I do not count, time, or control my breaths. No effort is being made to cause certain thoughts to come or go. There is no particular feeling I try to either induce or avoid. I do not pay attention to my body in a special way or attempt to relax any part of it. If I start to fall asleep, I do not resist the impulse.

What am I doing, then? The best answer is that I am just *not* doing; I am engaged in getting the normal activity of the mind to turn into silence, but without coercing it to do so. I am getting past the inner noise of thoughts and feelings in order to reveal what the silent witness inside me is really like. This is how the mind naturally opens to itself and heals.

"Not doing" sounds like doing nothing at all, but there is a subtle difference. The thinking, feeling mind is in constant motion. If it has the thought "Slow down, be silent," that is a movement, too, and will not make the mind stop. No thought can make it stop. One might try just sitting, waiting for the mind to stop of its own accord. There are meditations of this sort in the vast tradition of Indian and Zen practice, but most novices who try this method find it extremely exhausting and unproductive. A mind left to its own devices tends to run here and there like a drunken monkey, as the Indian scriptures say. To watch one's mind reel around for an hour can be intensely disturbing. Moreover, there is no reason why the mind should reach silence during the vigil.

One can try gathering the mind to a point, which is called concentration. This form of discipline is often compared to trying to make a candle flame hold still in the wind. Concentration is not like active thinking, but it still falls under the category of motion, since the mind has to be brought back to its focus every time it wanders. Enormous strain is involved, and the results may be very small compared to the effort required.

The deeper you go into it, the more difficult "not doing" seems to be. How can any form of mental activity ever make the mind be still? The ancient rishis mastered this extremely exacting art after they observed that the mind has various layers. In this observation, they agreed wholeheartedly with Freud. However, they were not interested in the *meaning* of each layer (whether it stores away childhood fears, repressed anger, or submerged sexual desires). They simply observed that the mind's deeper layers are not in as much motion as the superficial ones.

This insight made them realize that meditation must be a vertical process—a dive into the mind's depths—not a struggle on the surface. Somehow the meditator's attention has to penetrate the chaotic surface activity of the mind, pass through all the layers of subtle thought, and at last arrive at silence. Instead of subduing a drunken monkey, the appropriate metaphor is much more subtle: Meditation is like creeping through a herd of sleeping elephants without waking them up.

In order to dive through every layer of the mind, one needs a vehicle that can carry one beyond the thinking process. In Transcendental Meditation the vehicle is called a *mantra*, a specific mental sound derived from Sanskrit but with no verbal meaning. A mantra is chosen solely for its ability to gradually bring a person's attention to quieter and quieter levels of the mind.

Since everyone's mind has innumerable layers, the choice of a mantra and the precise instructions for using it are extremely delicate. If chosen, taught, and used correctly, a mantra is as nearly effortless as mental activity can be. It begins like a normal thought but fades to fainter and fainter degrees of sound without getting lost, until it disappears entirely, leaving the mind in complete silence.

Many forms of meditation use some kind of sound or visual image as their vehicle. That might make it seem that one technique is as good as another. However, there are any number of important issues to consider when evaluating a form of meditation—above all: Did my mind actually find the silence I was seeking? Was I psychologically comfortable during and after the meditation? Did my old self begin to change as the result of having meditated? Is there more truth in my self?

Every person has to decide these crucial issues for himself. Patrick, a friend of mine, is a ten-year meditator who began TM to rescue himself from a disastrous personal and financial fall. "In the late Seventies I was just barely emerging from the rockiest period in my life. For several years I had invested heavily in the real estate market, accumulating rental properties quickly on a very speculative basis. It was an exhilarating venture at first, and I found myself in a powerful financial position, at least on paper, with assets in the multimillions.

"You never know the exact point when things start sliding beyond repair. The ups and downs of the market seemed to be no worse than before, but I couldn't keep my grip somehow. My real estate holdings began to crumble, and no matter what I did, the collapse accelerated. I had started drinking heavily, and my wife was very distraught when I stopped relating to her and the children. It wasn't deliberate on my part; I had become swept up in a financial nightmare, and all I could think of was how to save myself."

Spiraling deeper into his troubles, Patrick learned to meditate. He learned almost on a whim, but from the outset the impact was dramatic. "The first time I meditated came as a revelation, if for no other reason than the comfort I felt in letting go of my huge internal struggle. The moments of actually transcending—that is, reaching the silent level of the mind—were very brief at first. Several times I asked, 'Is this all there is?' There was not much clear transcending in my meditations, only the coming and going of periods of silence. However, I couldn't deny that when I opened my eyes, I felt changed."

A single meditation can change people because it has allowed them to release part of the false self for good. Without our realizing it, holding on to old feelings, habits, and lifelong conditioning takes effort. The isolated ego defends itself by remaining constantly on the alert. Is this situation a threat? Is that person going to do what I want? The constant need to protect oneself psychologically may be too subtle to notice, but it occupies an enormous part of everyone's unconscious life.

As we saw, meditation does not deal in meaning. The old conditioning is released without talking about it, feeling it, or having much conscious experience of letting it go. Instead, the mind is shown how to cross over from activity to silence, and this process accomplishes the desired result. The stresses lie in the gap between the active and silent mind; touching this gap with one's awareness is enough to release them. Since it takes mental activity to keep the false self going, ending the activity loosens the false self's grip. It is not that a person tries to detach himself from his fears; they detach themselves from him.

"Meditating made me feel that I was putting the pieces together again, but I was not out of the woods yet," Patrick recalls. "The damage done to my personal life ran very deep. One day I came home to find that my wife had locked me out of the house. No one answered the phone when I called, and I felt angry and hurt. Miserably I walked over to the park and sat down to meditate. It didn't seem to do any good. I felt restless and upset the whole time.

"But when I opened my eyes, a remarkable thing happened. My mind was suddenly very quiet. I tried to think a thought, and one came, but it immediately settled back into the silence, like a drop merging into a still pool. I began to notice that the light around me looked brighter than usual, and when I heard some children playing nearby, their voices struck me as being the most joyful sound I had ever heard.

"It is hard to recapture how free I felt just at that moment.

It was like having all these dead layers fall off to expose some sensitive, living part of myself. I walked around a little, and everything had taken on the same vibrant quality. My intense feelings of aloneness and shame were now completely gone. I was totally different from the suffering person who had sat down on a park bench half an hour before."

I believe Patrick *had* hit upon the breakthrough that meditation causes: the self expands beyond the confines of the ego, at first gradually, but with greater and greater intensity, until it is in complete union with everything. "I and the world are one," an ancient Upanishad declares. The transformation of the small, isolated self into something universal may come only in glimpses, but this is the true self. It is only a matter of time before one lives its truth permanently.

At the height of his experience, which lasted for half an hour, Patrick was approached by a panhandler. "Up to this point I was completely lost in myself. I saw this derelict walking towards me—it makes me ashamed to use that word. He did not look like a derelict to me then; he was beyond that kind of value judgment. He was as alive and vibrant as everything else.

"When he was about three feet away, I looked right into his eyes. For some reason, they were changed. They looked shining and soft. I asked him what he wanted, and he hesitated, confused. Then he said, 'I don't want nothing. I just hope you're happy, man.' It sounded funny coming out of him, and I could see his surprised reaction to his own words. It was as if he had been drawn into my experience. In an amazingly joyous voice, I said, 'Yes, I'm happy, very, very happy.' I mean, I wanted to embrace this dilapidated, filthy guy.

"He was walking away by now. I turned and started to go off in the other direction, but when we were about twenty feet apart, I looked over my shoulder. He was staring at me with disbelief. When he caught my gaze he turned away for good. I wonder what he saw in my eyes at that moment? Probably disbelief, too, but I hope he saw more. For a few seconds back there, I deeply loved him."

Unconditional Love

This strange encounter between Patrick and the derelict brings us to the issue of unconditional love, which has become a catch phrase in popular psychology. The objection I have felt about unconditional love is that it runs completely against the grain of normal love, which is based upon relationship. The love that exists between husband and wife is not the same as that between mother and child. The difference is based upon the type of relationship the two people have. Where there is no relationship, it is hard to see how love can flow.

In this case, though, Patrick had no relationship whatsoever with the derelict. They were total strangers who had every reason to feel suspicious and hostile toward each other. However idealistically one may want to feel, a shambling, smelly man in raggedy clothes is an object of love to practically nobody; usually he is an object of revulsion whom we assiduously avoid in order not to be exposed to feelings of fear and contempt.

But it is at the point where all relationship ceases that the opportunity for unconditional love actually arises. When you have no relationship to another person, you are automatically thrown back upon yourself. The feelings that come out have no basis in what you need or want from others—they simply come out. If I get bumped in the street and feel angry, the emotion arises spontaneously. I may feel guilty about it the next moment, but in that split second it was the only choice my self could make. My level of awareness did not offer me a better response. In Patrick's case, his level of awareness had leaped far beyond its normal limits; this expansion dictated the response that spontaneously poured from him. I imagine his meditation on the park bench was not the sole cause of this sudden change; in India they speak of the "Yoga of desperation," a breakthrough into higher consciousness resulting from a predicament so terrible that the psyche can find no other way out.

Whatever the precise mechanism, Patrick found himself in a state transcending normal perception. Like a flyer breaking through a dense cloud layer to find blue sky and brilliant sun above, he discovered that to look at anything was to see it in the light of love. He could not help himself, just as I could not help my anger on being bumped in the street.

The rishis speak of unconditional love, in fact, as a transcendental quality that becomes infused into the mind during meditation. When the mind goes beyond normal waking awareness, the transcending process brings one in contact with unconditional love in its silent, unmanifest state. "Unmanifest" means that this love is not directed at anything; it simply vibrates within the nature of the silent witness, like a radio signal silently waiting for a radio to pick it up. At the end of meditation, the person returns to the waking state bringing some of this transcendental quality into his everyday consciousness. A new vibration has been added that alters, however subtly, the person's former awareness.

This explanation is a twist on the usual understanding of unconditional love. By definition, you can love someone unconditionally only if your love does not alter no matter what the other person does. This aspect of "no matter what" implies a superhuman effort of will. One cannot help but imagine a plaster saint who returns rudeness, anger, jealousy, inconsideration, and every other sort of unloving behavior with sweetness and light. For all its apparent goodness, this situation smacks of self-denial and even masochism.

The rishis' version of unconditional love contains no effort at all. A person who feels love "no matter what" is simply following his nature. In truth, this is all that can be asked of anyone. Acting according to your own level of awareness is inescapable. In order to smile at the stranger who bumps into me on the street, I need to feel like smiling; otherwise, my behavior will be calculated. As we saw before, calculation is the primary strategy of the false self. It has to calculate when to smile because it is too afraid to show the emotions actually being felt. Tact and diplomacy, which most of us applaud as "nice behavior," can also be seen as the subtle skill of lying.

All of us are radiating our awareness out into the world and bringing its reflection back to us. If your awareness contains violence and dread, you will meet those qualities "out there." On the other hand, if your awareness contains unconditional love, the world, even the eyes of a derelict, will mirror that love. The curative value of this kind of awareness is enormous, as I would like to illustrate with a moving story told by R. D. Laing.

At the age of fourteen, a Scottish boy named Phillip came home from school one day and found his mother on her bed in a pool of blood. A long-term tuberculosis patient, she had died from a sudden hemorrhage in her lungs. Instead of consoling the boy and helping him to overcome his shock and grief, Phillip's father berated him, telling him again and again that he had killed his mother by putting her through the exhaustion of pregnancy, birth, and raising him. This went on for two months. Then Phillip came home from school to find that his father had committed suicide.

Six months later, Laing came across the boy in a Glasgow mental ward, in a bizarre state of psychological and physical deterioration. As Laing vividly recalls, "He smelled awful. He was incontinent of urine and feces, given to staggering and walking peculiarly. He gesticulated in strange ways without speaking, seemed almost completely self-absorbed, and could not care less about his surroundings and the people in them."

Although he was in the midst of doctors and nurses whose job was to care for him, Phillip had pushed the limits of compassion. He was too strange and disgusting for anyone to be around for more than a few minutes, much less to help. He had developed a stutter, along with a peculiar collection of tics: blinks, darts of the eye, and twitches in his cheeks, tongue, hands, and fingers. Worst of all was his total I-could-not-care-less attitude, which had alienated the other patients and turned the whole staff against him.

Two months in the hospital made little change in Phillip's condition. "There was no question of the diagnosis," Laing recounts. "He was an acute (probably becoming chronic) catatonic schizophrenic. When he had anything to say, it was clear that he was hallucinated, very paranoid, and very deluded." Laing felt drawn to this shattered creature. Phillip had no remaining relatives or family friends to take him in. That he would be put away for the rest of his life was a foregone conclusion.

Instead, Laing took Phillip home with him, to his wife

and three children under the age of four. He made this extraordinary decision because, when talking to Phillip alone in his office, outside the setting of a psychiatric ward, he noticed that the boy became calmer. Phillip started to talk intelligibly, and although his talk was about "crazy" things—his feeling that the ward was a gigantic sphere with himself as a pin in the center, his visitations by interstellar beings, his hallucination that a black man's voice was speaking gibberish to him in the night—he did not seem completely gone. His tics and twitches also subsided in Laing's office. For an hour at least he controlled his bodily functions, and most telling of all, a shadow of gratitude passed over his rigid features when Laing offered to help him.

Laing had the insight that perhaps the doctors and nurses were *keeping* Phillip crazy simply by the way they felt about him. "Phillip generated in *everyone* who came near him mixed feelings of revulsion, at the sight of him and the *smell* of him, and feeling sorry for him, just because he was so repulsive, as well as at his evident misery. The result was that hardly anyone could resist trying to appear to him to be kind and loving, but fleeing out of sight and smell of him as quickly as possible —not because they could not stand him, but for some other necessity."

Phillip was being kept crazy because the attempt to love and care for him was tinged with hypocrisy and he knew it. As soon as Laing took the unheard-of step of bringing a catatonic schizophrenic into his home, Phillip improved with astonishing speed. His incontinence ended the moment he entered the house. Within a couple of weeks he had stopped staggering, although he still shook. He began to talk falteringly but coherently. Three months later he was well enough to be moved into a foster home. The threat of a lifetime spent locked up in a mental ward had been removed.

Laing did not use psychotherapy on Phillip while he was under his roof. The boy was treated honestly, without emotional hypocrisy, which meant that what was good or bad about him was reacted to as such. Fifteen years later, he returned to the house to report his progress. As Laing puts it with a shade of dry wit, "He was married, had two children, had a steady job, and was taking evening classes in psychology."

It is hard to deny that Phillip's sanity depended to a huge extent on projections from the minds of others. The superficial "love" and "caring" in the mental ward kept him imprisoned in a false self because these feelings were equally false. Behind them lurked the real message: "love" was just a means to keep him under control—it was a power ploy.

Fortunately, in Laing the boy found someone who looked upon him in the light of love. To me, that is the most touching part of the story. Laing does not raise the issue of love. He puts his motives on a simple human basis: "I felt very sorry for his plight and very much wanted to help him, if possible." Yet in Laing's presence, a rapport was established that was an honest reflection of one awareness with another. The intensity of life, so clear, sane, and loving, radiated from Laing and touched the boy. That seems to be the most natural part of what happened between the two, and what should happen between all of us. One true self speaks to another, using the language of the heart, and in that bond a person is healed.

Safe to Love

If the rishis are right, the end of the false self spells the end of fear, and the desperate need for power that fearful people cannot help. Power is a form of self-protection, and when fear is gone, there is no need for protection. The true self *is* love, and being able to love all the time is the most one could want. The clash between love and power then has no meaning. As Tagore so decisively wrote, "Love is not a mere impulse; it must contain truth, which is law." I deeply believe that, because I have met people who suddenly found themselves living under this law.

"I was driving down the highway looking for the exit onto the turnpike when I noticed an unusual sensation in my chest. It began as a warm or tingling feeling, which I recognized from meditating. Generally the feeling is pleasant but temporary. Now it began to intensify, and instead of physical warmth, wave after wave of emotion started to sweep over me."

Chris's eyes shone as he talked on: "It was love, but much purer and more concentrated love than I had ever felt. I have read in various scriptures about the heart opening like a flower—one never thinks such things are going to happen in real life, on a six-lane road. But this was it: my heart was unfolding like a flower, almost drowning me in the exquisite sensation of love. Strangely, I could still keep my attention on the road, but I decided to pull off. I walked into a hamburger stand and just stood there looking down at the salad bar, having the most wonderful experience of my life."

I see my friend Chris every once in a while, usually at the Boston TM center. He has worked as a bank manager and a community organizer; he is a hardheaded sort, not the man you would pick to have his heart unfold like a flower. But that is wrong of me. His voice sounds kind in an unforced way, and he has a very accepting manner with people; it is easy to believe that he has experienced his heart very deeply.

Seventeen years ago, when Chris began meditating, he had a conventional, though deep-felt regard for relationships. "I was just testing the water as a community organizer then, trying to bring together people who would normally take no notice of each other. All around me I saw so much hatred that had no real basis—people simply had never crossed color barriers or social lines to meet each other.

"I helped organize a large food cooperative in a poor neighborhood; anyone could join, regardless of class or income. We would purchase food and sell it at cost, but each member had to put in some time, usually about an hour a week, to go to the wholesale market at Faneuil Hall or sweep the floor at the co-op or something. The idea was that if people helped out, they could not avoid seeing the results of their actions. The store wouldn't open if they didn't buy the food. It would open late if they didn't sweep the floor. Prices would go up if the cash register was shortchanged.

"I had never been more hopeful than the day the co-op opened, but a month later I was practically in despair. People didn't seem to care—they shirked their work, they didn't sweep the floor, they stole money from the cash register, and they found it very easy to live with the consequences of their actions. This experience convinced me that institutions cannot bring about a fundamental change in human nature. And yet it seemed unbearable not to do something."

As he became more disillusioned with the social crusade, Chris's commitment to meditating deepened. "I desperately wanted to foster cooperation and love among other people, but it was never possible to make intimate enough contact with them, not in the long run. There were always barriers and personal hangups; disappointment was inevitable, whatever my ideals said.

"Seeing no way out of this painful dilemma, I let it continue. I decided to work on myself, since after all I was a crucial part of every relationship I wanted to improve. Gradually a profound change came about. I felt less anxiety about situations and warmer feelings towards people who had been stereotyped in my eyes as 'bad' or 'uncaring.' As a result, people began to emerge from their stereotypes. For a long time I found it hard to believe that I was the focus of this change. But how could I account for the love that people directed at me, whether I knew them or not?"

At this point Chris was far along into the change of awareness produced by unconditional love. In conventional psychology, a person is told that altering his own attitudes is the best way to improve the behavior of others. Chris now found that he could walk into a bank and soon everyone in it would be smiling. When he presided over community meetings, where the clash of opinions was usually very tense, the atmosphere seemed to be softer, as if troubled waters were mysteriously stilled.

"I could not come to terms with this inexplicable phenomenon," Chris recalls, "until I radically changed my sense of myself. My world view had always been centered on individual ego and effort. The effect you might have on the world depended on doing something, or at least thinking. I wasn't doing anything, other than existing. So I had to conclude that what I *am* was having this effect."

I asked him to fit in his experience on the highway, when he felt waves of love engulfing him. "That experience, I think, brought a certain part of the whole process to a climax. After believing for so long that I could not expect or receive love without relating to another person, suddenly it was all happening inside me. I was shocked at first, because it meant that in some way the failings of other people, their selfishness and hatred, was somehow centered in me as well. And yet these experiences were undeniable: as I changed, everything around me changed.

"In time, I quit wrestling with this thing intellectually. I became used to it. No longer did I find myself depending on other people for my basic sense of loving or being loved. By connecting with myself I started connecting with others better than I ever had before.

"When it came, the experience of my unfolding heart was overwhelming, but only for about forty-five minutes. The most fortunate thing is that the breakthrough lasted. It has been two years now, and I am still that loving person inside. I don't mean that I always exude kindness no matter what other people do to me. I can get angry and criticize others when I think they're wrong, but there is no destructiveness in it."

I was thinking of how hard we try to protect ourselves from being hurt emotionally, not realizing the intensity of life we have walled out in the process. It is necessary to defend the heart when it is too weak and frightened to love, yet at some point all that changed for Chris. It became possible for him to let love flow when and where it wanted. He was able to welcome others, without defenses, without fear, into the expanded space of his own being. Something he said particularly sticks with me: "I used to try so hard to love, and now it's the one thing I can't prevent, no matter how hard I try." He smiled, and I felt the tender affection of someone who has not torn down the walls of pain but flown over them.

Part Three

Unconditional Life

9

⚞⚞⚞⚞⚞⚞⚞⚞⚞⚞⚞

"Why Aren't I Real Anymore?"

The day after I first met Karin, I was driving home when I felt a sudden urge to hear her voice again. I found the tape of our interview and slipped it into the machine. There it was, the soft, melodious soprano of a woman who kept reminding me, hauntingly, of a child. I don't mean that she sounded childish. She spoke like an adult, talking about serious adult problems, yet blended into that I could hear a precocious eight-year-old who was very puzzled by the grown-up world.

"Why am I punished for telling a lie when Mommy lies about her age? Why do I have to clean my plate when Daddy leaves his Brussels sprouts?" All children go through some stage like this. By challenging the ready-made values handed down by adults, they begin to formulate their own values, which is a necessary step toward gaining a real identity. Karin, however, continues to issue challenges right and left.

I once went to a clinic where they treat obsessive-compulsive disorder. I didn't think I was obsessive-compulsive, but it had me worried. The first thing the doctor did was to hand me a test. "I'm sorry, but I don't want to fill this out," I said.

"Why not?" he asked.

"Well, the first question wants to know if I read things more than once. I didn't read very much in school, and now I sometimes do reread books to make sure that I am getting everything out of them. But if I say yes to your question, you will interpret it as an obsessive-compulsive trait, like hand washing."

He still wanted me to take the test. "I'm not a test score," I protested. "I'm a human being. I need to be dealt with for what's going on with *me*."

He said, "That's a sign right there of obsessiveness."

"Has it ever occurred to you," I said, "that because you run a clinic for obsessive-compulsive disorder, you may be obsessed with making a diagnosis of obsessiveness?"

"No," he said, "that has never occurred to me."

I laughed out loud listening to the tape, just as I had when Karin first told me about this run-in. Like many children, she has a sixth sense for when she is being manipulated.

Okay, so I went to another doctor, a well-known psychologist. It took me a while to get hold of him, and when I finally did, he said, "I think you didn't want to meet me, anyway."

"What makes you think that?" I asked.

"Because you got my answering machine three times."

"Oh really?" I said, "but what about the fact that you got *my* answering machine three times?"

Karin sounds rather feisty set down on the page. In person she is actually much less that way. She talks excitably about herself and likes to dramatize her story. Underneath the drama, however, one senses that she is a gentle person—I find it easy to believe her when she says that she has never deliberately hurt anyone. She has soft, pleasing features and lively eyes. Still unmarried at thirty-five, she successfully runs a small catering business with two women friends in suburban Boston.

By her own count, Karin has been to ten different doctors in the past two years, none of whom has helped her. To begin with, her basic complaint is extremely difficult to pin down. She says that she doesn't feel real anymore. In everyday situations such as talking on the phone, walking down the street, or eating in a restaurant, she has persistent doubts about her existence: "Someone will call my name, and I'll go through one of my experiences: 'Did I answer that? Is this really me?' Sometimes I'll be talking and think, 'How come I can talk? How can I breathe?' It's as if my mind is going, 'Does not compute, does not compute,' and I start to cry."

Physically, Karin no longer feels comfortable in her own body, a sensation that psychologists call derealization: "It's as if someone else is in my body, doing everything with me, or for me." Her feeling of being unreal becomes quite profound at times, and yet she continues to function normally. Other people have a hard time believing that there is actually anything wrong with her. "When I'm miserable, my brother will say, 'Look, I have the same thoughts you do, but I don't have the same responses. I don't want to ruin my life over the question, *Why am I here?* or *Who am I?*'"

Her brother is right in spotting that Karin is wrapped up in a great deal of intellectual confusion. She is constantly assaulted by questions that seem crazy to her: Can one be real and unreal at the same time? Is thinking that you are unreal the same as being unreal? When her head begins to whirl with these existential riddles, she becomes as bewildered as Alice down the rabbit-hole.

I asked Karin if she felt real talking to me. She said that she did and she didn't: "I am sitting here having a conversation with you, but a part of me says I'm not. It's impossible. How can I be saying such a thing to myself? My mind doesn't comprehend it. I *know* I'm talking to you, but another part *knows* I'm not. I can't figure that out."

As a yogi would see it, there must be some element of witnessing involved here—that is, Karin is having an experience and at the same time watching herself have it. That does not have to be an unreal way to relate to things. Quite the contrary—it could be seen as the *most* real way, once the silent witness is acknowledged as the core of the self. In ancient India, witnessing would have been calmly accepted and welcomed as a gateway to higher spiritual experiences.

Karin was not totally surprised when I brought this up to her, but it did not make her any happier. "People have told me that my awareness has risen too high, that it has become my enemy," she said, "but I don't know how to turn it off." Turning her awareness off is all she wants to do at this point. Time and again she has intuited things that I would consider profound truths, only to reject them as "sick." Here is one example:

"I have this experience of talking to someone and feeling that I'm on automatic. It's like a reserve mechanism kicking in. I want to shut it off. I want to be able to walk into a room and not think, 'Oh, look at that. I converted myself into matter.' The top layer of my mind is now above automatic, but that doesn't seem like a gift to me, it's just neurotic. How do I get rid of this high awareness or sensitivity, whatever you want to call it?"

I told her that other people have spent years on the spiritual path trying to achieve the very state of nonattachment that she has fallen into. To a spiritual person, the feeling of being "on automatic" implies that God or the higher Self has taken over from the small, isolated self. Many saints, both Christian and Eastern, have reported that they lived in such a blessed state. They considered it a kind of second birth, freeing them from the bondage of the flesh and the ties of the past. After this rebirth, a person has nothing to fear from the snares of Maya and can go forth to explore what lies beyond.

Yet the everyday world seems to have no relationship to the boundless one, and to stand on the threshold of the higher Self, where Karin finds herself, can generate deep fear. No one can feel her experiences with her. There is no objective standard for weighing them, and their scientific validity remains marginal (the renowned English physicist Sir Arthur Eddington once remarked that any attempt to scientifically measure a subjective experience was like trying to find the square root of a sonnet).

In this light, the words that have come to us from the ancient spiritual traditions are all the more valuable, since they can serve as lifelines to the present. In India the *Bhagavad-Gita* is taken as the quintessence of the collected wisdom on the nature of reality. There, Lord Krishna tells the warrior Arjuna that every person shelters a "dweller in the body" who is wholly unlike the isolated, vulnerable ego:

> *Weapons cannot cleave him,*
> *Fire cannot burn him,*
> *Water cannot wet him,*
> *Wind cannot dry him away . . .*
> *He is eternal and all-pervading,*
> *Subtle, immovable, and ever the same.*

Although this invulnerable dweller may seem to be a religious concept—what most devout people call the soul—Lord Krishna asserts that it is the same self that gives everyone his sense of "I am." In Sanskrit several different words are needed to describe the full range of the self, from the most local to the completely universal. Each of us has an individual spirit that undergoes unique experiences in life—this is called the *jiva* in Sanskrit; it comes closest to being the soul.

If you remove all personal boundaries, the jiva expands into the *Atman,* pure spirit without individual experiences. Emerson and the other Transcendentalists called this the Over-soul. (I will follow the simple convention of calling it the Self with a capital "s.") When jiva and Atman fuse, merging the individual and the cosmic self without losing the qualities of either, one arrives at *Brahman,* or totality. A person who has realized Brahman retains his individuality but experiences himself as universal, "under the aspect of eternity," as the church fathers phrased it. Brahman is also used to describe reality as a whole, taking in both the objective and subjective fields of existence, the manifest and the unmanifest. Beyond the all-inclusive Brahman, there is nothing.

The jiva, then, is like a single wave on the ocean; Atman is the water that all waves partake of equally; Brahman is the ocean itself. If you ask which of these three is you, the answer is "all of them." To say that one aspect of the self is different from the others may be useful on an everyday basis, but it is not the final truth. The self I call "me" seems to respect the boundary of my skin, but at the same time I naturally feel my kinship to other selves. When a child suffers in Afghanistan, I feel the pain. My sensation may not be as intense as when I cause pain to my own body, but that simply says that I do not share a particular set of nerves with the child.

The ancient sages knew that each person is grounded in a concrete reality that gives him his bearings in time and space. Nevertheless, they maintained that all selves are woven into the same fabric of life. Karin could easily be stumbling into this state of greatly expanded self. However, she wants no part of it. She has frequently stated to me in crisp tones that she did not have a religious upbringing and finds no spiritual significance in what is happening to her. Clearly there is a knowledge gap here. No tradition validates her experience for her; no elders or guides exist to educate her further. She has been cast adrift.

On the Outside Looking In

It is not easy to live with an original experience, and Karin would much rather return to the mundane experiences that all of us put on like ready-to-wear clothes. "I want to watch TV on Saturday night, drink a glass of wine, and not think about anything," she complains. "I want to be upset when my car gets dented and not feel detached about it. I want to go back to feeling like I'm a part of life. Is that even a possibility anymore?"

At moments like this, one realizes how much in limbo Karin is. Since no convincing version of her present reality exists, she remains committed to the unreal. Yet she is not as detached as she appears. I sense that she is trying to connect with others all the time but in hidden ways. I might have missed this except for a telling incident. At one point during our first talk, I wanted her to know how impressed I was with her level of insight, and I started out by saying, "For a brilliant person like you—"

She cut me off with a strange look. "Why did you say that?" she demanded.

"What?"

"That I'm brilliant. What makes you say that out of the blue?"

"Well," I explained, "it is obvious that you have more self-awareness than ninety-nine percent of the people I deal with."

"How can you tell that after one meeting?" she asked suspiciously. I said I just could, and she let the matter drop. Half an hour later, she interrupted herself and asked, this time rather timidly, "Do you really think I'm brilliant?" I repeated that I did. Again, the matter was quickly dropped. When we met a few days later, the first words out of her mouth were "I've been thinking about why you called me brilliant."

Then I couldn't help but notice that my compliment held a special charm for her. It was a token, not just of my respect, but of my affection. By calling her brilliant, I had said, "I feel close to you." Replaying the tapes, I find that Karin also managed to call *me* brilliant several times that day—apparently quite unconsciously—and whenever she did, one heard a shy, embarrassed intimacy in her voice.

Why was this little game of emotional hide-and-seek so important to her? I think it's because she finds it much easier to intellectualize about feeling unreal than to openly express the much more wrenching feeling of being lost. Before their emotions get covered over with a thick coat of denial, many children feel lost, set apart. Karin reminds me of a wide-eyed child one might find on the fringes of a social gathering—a wedding reception, cocktail party, or Thanksgiving reunion—peering at the adults like a fascinated spectator at the zoo.

What the child wonders at is quite ordinary and yet very disturbing: the casual deception of daily life. Behind the words "I love him" or "I love her" lie guarded feelings and secret betrayals. People who put on a show of generosity turn out to be secretly the most selfish. Jealousy lurks under a smile. Children do not know how to live this way, and Karin still doesn't have the knack for it. From her perspective, other people are living securely inside a shared reality, while she is outside looking in—"I live in another dimension," she mourns. This persistent feeling of isolation makes things very fearful for her. She has no security. The rest of us are at home; she is the eternal stranger.

Many sensitive people feel this way. Wisdom and poetry can arise from the situation as easily as anguish. But given how lonely such people generally are, I can see why anguish is the most common response. It is by relating to other people, after all, that most of us manage to feel real in the first place.

Three years ago, Karin asserts, she felt completely normal and connected—she is particularly adamant on that point. She was thirty-one and had just decided to break up with a man whom she had been seeing steadily for several years. "From the very beginning of our relationship," she said, "I knew that Rodney was not 'the one,' but we cared for each other and really enjoyed each other's company." What made her finally break off with this man was her decision to seek someone whom she really might want to marry. This reason satisfied her, and the breakup occurred without rancor.

But Karin immediately started having doubts about what she had done. She glossed over that part with me: "When Rodney and I broke up, I felt a sudden sense of loss. I wondered if I had done the wrong thing, if I should get back with him, you know, blah, blah, blah. Then I went on with my life." Within a month after the breakup, she met another man, a customer at her catering business.

She fell deeply in love with him and continues to say that their relationship, which was brief but intense, was the closest she ever came to marrying anyone. From the very outset, however, she knew that his parents, who were Orthodox Jews, strongly disapproved of her because she was Catholic. "At first it was okay, because I was confident and elated, and I didn't allow them to become involved in my life. But after a certain amount of treatment that I considered worse than torture. . . ."

Karin stopped speaking at that point. I gathered that there was a tempestuous breakup and she had a "collapse" or "nervous breakdown." Whether in fact she suffered an actual psychosis is not clear. She did develop a morbid fear of having AIDS. "Whenever I gave blood I would shake like crazy. Three times they needed my blood that year, and I was terrified that I would be infected." Several times she called the local AIDS hotline in a panic, always to be reassured that she had no real reason to be afraid (a fact confirmed by all her blood tests).

It was in the midst of this difficult period that she first began to feel unreal. She says that the sensation was quite new and unexpected when it first arrived. Never in her life had she ever had the feeling of "being out of my body" or "having my awareness up here" (holding her hand above her head). When I told her that many people have similar feelings without being disturbed, she curtly responded, "What does that matter if I still feel miserable?"

I tend to believe Karin when she says that she began to feel unreal all of a sudden. On the other hand, I cannot buy her story that her life was so perfect before "something happened." She has an unshakable nostalgia for the past; it is the flip side of her refusal to open herself to the present. She says that her only wish is to return to the way she was three years ago, before the unfortunate love affair. That period has become fixed in her mind as a rapturous ideal:

"I felt centered and relaxed then. I was confident, and I had a purpose. I felt integrated: I had a relationship, I had money, I had peace of mind. I felt good about what I did and was able to feel humble about it. I felt I was on a nice road to growth. I felt like a part of the universe, like I really wanted to be here. People looked up to me, and I was able to make them feel good."

Karin has split time into then and now, the good and the bad, with no gray in between. It is no wonder that her situation ties her in knots, because it cannot be resolved as she has set it up. On one hand she has this need to make sure that the split in her life continues (in order to preserve the myth of the perfect past she left behind), while on the other she longs to feel real again, which would mean jumping back into the flow of things. For the time being, clinging to her black-and-white view of the world feels like the only safe course.

Don't Tell Me I'm Not Crazy

Karin is surely real; she has just had the misfortune to find herself moving from one level of reality to another, like an infant who one day realizes that crawling, which he has thoroughly mastered, is starting to give way to the uncertain prospect of learning to walk. Babies make this transition instinctively, and their parents guide them over the rough spots with encouraging attention. But when an adult psyche begins to test the possibility of a completely new perspective, the transition period is fraught with difficulty.

There are no guidelines for "normal" experiences of a higher Self. The image we have of saints suddenly pierced by a shaft of divine light is far too simple; even the greatest spiritual attainments take place within the limits of daily mental life, with its doubts, fears, hopes, and denials. What people need is the same encouraging attention that parents give to a wobbly toddler. Sadly, our society is bereft in this area, and each of us has to row alone to the foreign shore that is beckoning us across the waters.

But what is even more disturbing is that the growing pains of self-awareness might get mistaken for the goal. Karin was making this mistake, and her self-doubt echoes a culture that feels profoundly suspicious of spiritual experiences. I am not just referring to the accusations of insanity that surround anyone who breaks out of the normal ways of thinking, seeing, and behaving—that problem exists in all cultures, unfortunately. The deeper worry is that our society is so fearful of the Self that we equate it with death and dissolution. When Freud was confronted with the fact that every psyche has a hidden longing for unboundedness, he coined the phrase "death wish" or "Nirvana instinct"—the two were more or less the same in his eyes.

Nirvana is not death, however. It is a Sanskrit word for Being, the primary state of the Self. By and large, psychiatry still ignores this clarification, and the fear persists that total self-awareness is a kind of annihilation. Irvin Yalom describes the moment when he had brought one of his neurotic patients, after much struggle, to the stage where he began to open up to self-awareness:

It is the time when one stands before the abyss and decides how to face the pitiless existential facts of life: death, isolation, groundlessness, and meaninglessness. Of course, there are no solutions. One has a choice only of certain stances: to be "resolute," or "engaged," or courageously defiant, or stoically accepting, or to relinquish rationality and, in awe and mystery, place one's trust in the providence of the Divine.

To think that this is the long sought-for *goal* of therapy! It would be kinder to believe that the patient had not yet begun. In fairness, I should explain that Yalom is an "existential" therapist, meaning that his cornerstone belief is unbelief: life has no intrinsic meaning or purpose other than the one created (through an arbitrarily chosen "stance") by each person.

Many, perhaps most, psychiatrists might agree that life's dilemmas have no solution, only they would not preface their opinion with the words "of course." Outside the therapist's office, lay people echo the same pessimistic world view, if not in so many words, then in their endless search for pleasure and escape from pain. Karin grew up with no better version of reality, so she resists her "high awareness," turns her back on insight, and longs to watch TV with a beer on Saturday night—anything but to see what she actually sees and feel what she actually feels.

When I tried to put her experiences in a good light, Karin turned on me. "This standing outside myself all the time isn't natural. People tell me that I'm functioning well, so what's the problem? I know I'm still functioning well, but I'm afraid. I have times when I look at a calendar and think, 'How can there be dates? What is time?' The experience is too much. Am I insane? Luckily, someone told me that you can't go crazy after a certain age. . . ."

I responded with the strongest assurances I had yet given her, "You're not crazy. At all. You're having experiences that you can't handle. They're coming too fast. But they're all right. What's happening to you isn't completely healthy, because it causes you panic, anxiety, and so on. Yet there is an element of witnessing here. Do you know what I'm saying?"

"Um. If you remember that obsessive-compulsive doctor," Karin rejoined, "he saw everyone as obsessive-compulsive except himself. When I'm with you, I like talking to you, and I can see that you're used to conversing with minds far above mine, but you're trained to look for this witnessing. Maybe you see my symptoms as opening up a new avenue, but I see them as neurotic."

I immediately backed off, waiting for things to happen naturally and at their own pace. But I couldn't help feeling sad that Karin is so conditioned to see herself as "sick" rather than normal or even gifted. She tosses around a good deal of unflattering psychological jargon to describe herself. At one point I was going to say, "I think you're really on to something." As soon as I said the words "I think you're," she jumped in with "an acute schizophrenic?" Finding a satisfactory label is very important to her.

At various times in our first talk, which lasted less than an hour, she also referred to herself as obsessive, neurotic, depressed, anxious, insecure, hyper, and crazy. Actually, her deep worry that she might be insane is one of the surest signs that she is not. She describes her symptoms with clarity and insight. She does not hallucinate or have delusional thoughts. I could even get her to admit, grudgingly, that she sometimes feels pleasantly detached from her symptoms and can see through them. This admission came out when we talked about the ten doctors she had seen before me. "Ten specialists each gave you ten different diagnoses, and each one happened to be the diagnosis that he specializes in," I said. "So what does that tell you?"

"That that is how they view it," she replied evasively.

"But what does that tell you about what you have?" I insisted.

"Well, it might tell me that they have seen these symptoms before," she said. "Maybe my need to go to ten different doctors *is* obsessive. I could have all ten of those things or none of them."

"Which is it, do you think?"

"Probably a combination, if that makes any sense. Obviously I have anxiety, I have depression—I have what they term 'derealization.' On the other hand, sitting here now, I question whether I have any of that."

If Karin had not made this last comment, I would concede that the chances of turning her interpretation around would be remote—we are lucky that she is not totally sold out to the idea of being sick. She is intelligent enough to pick out the weak points in even the best doctors. "I told one therapist that when I was two I had a pet ghost," she said. "It was my imaginary friend. This psychiatrist said, 'Well, no doubt that was your longing for a penis.' Now, at two years old, who cares if it was or it wasn't? I felt normal three years ago, and I feel terrible now."

"Did you really have a pet ghost?" I asked.

"Yes, I did—I wouldn't make up a thing like that. Many children have imaginary friends, don't they? And if they don't, I still can't see how that affects me," Karin said.

"What happened to your friend?" I asked.

"I don't know," she answered wistfully. "As I grew older, he just . . . I don't remember. He is no longer with me."

As much as I appreciate her knack for seeing through self-important doctors (including me, I'm sure), Karin isn't happy scoring points against them. She wants to be accepted, like everybody else. These two sides of her personality have created a major conflict in her life. "You can see how hard it is for me to tell if I am right in wanting to be dealt with for myself," she said. "Am I a bright person who is just over-analyzing other people's motives? Or am I so self-righteous that I won't listen to anybody else?"

Relating to the Self

The more I think about Karin, the less peculiar her situation seems and the more she appears to be only a slight exaggeration of many other people I know. The common theme in all her experiences is a drastic loss of confidence in her relationships, a leaking away of trust and security, which leaves a vacuum of distrust and loneliness. Everywhere one looks, relationships are in a similar crisis. Preserving a stable marriage and a loving family life has turned into a heroic enterprise, doomed to failure more often than not. If Karin really is as I see her, not "sick" but just acutely self-aware, perhaps her sensitive awareness is leading her to a solution.

Relationships are based on two opposite values: feeling close to someone else and yet feeling apart. Feeling close enables us to have rapport, to share our feelings and to exchange words and ideas. Feeling apart enables us to retain our own egos, so that "me" does not bleed into "not me." As long as a person has a healthy sense of how to share himself but not share too much, the machinery of relationship runs smoothly enough. The crux of Karin's problem is that she has tumbled headlong into feeling separate without the balance of feeling close:

"I have started to walk around without being able to fathom my existence. My mother isn't my mother anymore. I look at my brother and it isn't, 'Hi, Rich,' but, 'Who is this person?' I know he is my brother, but how can he be? Looking in the mirror at my body I say, 'How can that be me?' I just feel that the world is over *there*, and I am looking in on it."

Far from being delusional, Karin's feelings of intense self-absorption could be hitting upon a deep truth. All of us retain a part of ourselves that stays aloof from others, no matter how intimate the relationship. As people who define ourselves by how we relate, we have mothers, brothers, houses, jobs, and so forth. The scene around us changes, and we change with it. As witnesses who stand back and observe the scene, however, we are as fixed as stars, and our changeless nature is utterly still, calm, and wise.

In one of the oldest Indian scriptures, called the "great forest teaching" (*Brihadaranyaka Upanishad*), which dates back at least a thousand years before Christ, we are told the deeper emotional basis for the kind of feelings Karin is having:

> Truly, it is not for the sake of the husband that the husband is dear, but for the sake of the Self.
> And it is not for the sake of the wife that the wife is dear, but for the sake of the Self.

And it is not for the sake of the sons that the sons are dear, but for the sake of the Self.

Yajnavalkya, one of the greatest of the ancient sages, is speaking, trying to convey to his wife what is most real and lasting in life. He is raising the Self above any relationship one might have with husband, wife, or children, but this is not to degrade those relationships. Rather, the sage is stating a psychological fact, that each of us is more intimately connected to ourselves than to anyone around us. Relationships begin "in here," with our ability to love ourselves, to know ourselves, to be ourselves. As Yajnavalkya tells his wife, "Indeed, my beloved, it is the Self that should be seen, the Self that should be heard, the Self that should be reflected upon, and the Self that should be known."

The reason these words have survived for more than three thousand years is that in every generation, the Self wakes up and demands to be known. When it does, other relationships begin to pale by comparison, at least at the outset, because the intimacy of one's own being is quite overwhelming. The world becomes a wraparound mirror, reflecting oneself on all sides. Let us begin to examine how that might feel.

Sitting in my chair meditating, I feel like myself, a person isolated in time and space. I have thoughts, each of which takes a tiny amount of time, but every once in a while my mantra fades away and I experience silence. Sometimes this silence grows deep, and I am left in it for moments at a stretch. When that happens, I do not feel like my finite self anymore. I have entered into the Self. How does this feel, exactly? Think of a man exploring a long, dark hallway with a flashlight. All he sees is the next object that falls within his beam; the rest remains in darkness. This is like the waking-state mind, which knows its contents one thought at a time. Now suppose that all at once the whole corridor lights up, revealing every object in it.

The Self is like that, a total awakening to all that exists in awareness, but unlike the lighted hallway, there are no physical restrictions—no objects or walls. Awareness simply sees itself in pure form. To give another analogy, imagine a genius resting on a couch. He could be thinking any number of brilliant thoughts, but he is not having one right now. He remains a genius nevertheless, because his ability lies in his *potential* for being brilliant. Similarly, the Self is a state of potentiality, of untold possibilities that unfold one at a time in the manifest world.

Entering the domain of the Self can be a surprisingly modest experience, and many beginning meditators miss the significance of their inner quietness. I had one patient who had suffered from anxiety attacks since childhood and found it difficult to accept that he was meditating correctly. In an encouraging tone I asked, "Do you notice any periods of silence in your meditations?"

"Never," he shot back. "At least not that I know of. Wouldn't I know it? I'm looking for it all the time."

I told him that noticing the silence might or might not happen at first. "But intellectually," I said, "you realize that the mind can be silent?"

"Not mine," he said.

"Why not?"

"It's too quick."

"But even a quick mind has gaps between thoughts," I pointed out. "Each gap is like a tiny window onto silence, and through that window one actually contacts the source of the mind. As we're talking here now, there are gaps between our words, aren't there? When you meditate, you take a vertical dive into that gap."

"Sure, I can see that," he rejoined, "but I don't think I experience it in meditation." I asked him what he did experience. He said, "The only thing that makes meditation different from just sitting in a chair is that when I open my eyes after twenty minutes, I often feel that only two or three minutes have passed—I am intrigued by that."

I said, "But you see, this is the very best clue that you have gone beyond thought. When you don't have thoughts, there is silence. Silence does not occupy time, and in order to contact the Self, one has to go into the field of the timeless. Your mind might not be able to register this experience at first, because it is so accustomed to thinking. You may feel that time has simply flown by, or that it was lost somewhere. But the 'lost' time was actually spent immersed in the Self."

It was helpful for this man to gain a better intellectual grasp of what was happening to him, but the timeless Self is not a concept one has to believe in or even comprehend. It is only necessary to travel back and forth from thinking to silence, over and over, until the full experience of silence registers. When the yogis escaped the field of time, they did not intend to remain away forever. They knew that as long as they possessed a body, its organs had to function according to natural laws; as long as they used their brains to think, their minds had to accept the same sensations, memories, and desires as the mind of any other person.

All this was absolutely necessary. What was not necessary, however, was the tangle of pain and sorrow that is caused when one is a prisoner of events. For the duration that he could experience pure silence, the yogi's nervous system was free to untwist the old knots of stress and thus heal the wounds of time.

Once a person is convinced that his meditation experiences are real, he begins the process of ripening the self into the Self. That is, he begins to experience what it means to abolish all the divisions that keep people apart. Ordinary life does not provide much experience of this state. We are conditioned never to forget that "me" and "not me" are different, with one notable exception: falling in love. To fall head over heals in love is to share your self with another. The ego's barriers fall for a time, and the lover and his beloved agree that they have merged into one identity. For as long as the enchantment lasts, one feels the other's emotions, breathes the other's breath. There is an invincible sense of union that makes being alone too painful to endure.

In our culture, we tend to dismiss this union as a passing psychological illusion and probably unhealthy if prolonged much beyond the first flush of courtship. ("Love addiction" has even entered the lexicon of abnormal psychology recently.) The yogis, however, would say that there is no reason why a person cannot have two perspectives on himself, one local (the self) and the other universal (the Self). A yogi adopts both perspectives at once. He has stabilized his awareness of the Self without losing the self. An intense feeling of love accompanies this new state, but unlike falling in love, the yogi's merging does not depend upon another person, even a beloved. He merges with everything, including it all in his Self. Once he can see everything as part of his identity, there is no isolated "me" to defend. Love is all that remains.

A person living in the Self feels intimately connected to others, not because he is skillful at the usual give-and-take of a good relationship, but because he gives everything of himself. He holds nothing back, and therefore he flows effortlessly beyond the boundaries of his isolated self. Could this be our natural state?

At the turn of the century, the great photographer Alfred Stieglitz was growing up in a well-to-do German family in New York City. During one viciously cold winter, a wandering organ-grinder showed up at the back door. As soon as he heard the organ-grinder's tune, Alfred jumped up from the dinner table and ran outside to give him a penny. The next evening the organ-grinder reappeared, and the little boy ran out again to give him a penny.

This ritual repeated itself day after day, through snow and sleet. The family became quite impressed, and one evening Alfred's mother told him how wonderful it was that he would brave the cold to give money to a beggar. Alfred looked up in surprise and said, "But Mama, I am doing it all for myself." When I first read this anecdote, it gave me a thrill of recognition, for I could see that the most intensely selfish motive can also be the most selfless.

In another instance, the renowned Jewish philosopher Martin Buber went through a shift in perception from the small to the larger self when he chanced to spot a shiny rock by the side of the road:

> On a gloomy morning I walked upon the highway, saw a piece of mica lying, lifted it up, and looked at it for a long time; the day was no longer gloomy, so much light was caught in the stone. And suddenly, as I raised my eyes from it, I realized that while I looked, I had not been conscious of "object" and "subject"; in my looking the mica and "I" had been one; in my looking I had tasted unity. I looked at it again, the unity did not remain.

This is not a mystical moment; it is just true experience, stripped of the veils that make us think we are *not* one with the rocks, trees, mountains, and stars. For a brief moment, Buber had replaced relationship with unity, catching on the wing a vision of the world that could be captured permanently. That rarely happens, because the nervous system of ordinary people is too active, too conditioned by years of non-silence.

If a moment of unity lasts long enough, the perceiver has time to appreciate what it would be like to remain in a state where "me" and "not me" peacefully coexist within the same mind. In his journal, the English essayist Mark Rutherford writes about one spring morning when he was walking in the woods and chanced upon a huge old oak. The tree was just leafing out, bursting forth as a billowing cloud of greenish-yellow buds. Caught by the splendor of so much new life, Rutherford suddenly felt that "something happened which was nothing less than a transformation of myself and the world."

The oak was "no longer a tree away from me and apart from me. The enclosing barriers of consciousness were removed. . . . The distinction of self and not-self was an illusion. I could feel the rising sap; in me also sprang the up-rushing from its roots, and the joy of its outbreak, from the extremity of each twig right up to the summit, was my own." Fused with the being of the tree, he thought the words *Thou in me and I in thee.* The key to his experience lay in the unity that this sentence conveyed. "I cannot explain; it will be easy to prove me absurd, but nothing can shake me. *Thou in me and I in thee.* Death! what is death? There is no death: in thee it is impossible, absurd."

Countless people have had similar experiences. They have fused with nature for a moment and realized the Self. Isn't it possible, then, to go further and think of a state where a person fuses with nature permanently? That is the yogi's challenge to our everyday conception of being. To be human, the yogis say, is to experience the one silence underlying everything. Indeed, life *is* silence, and in the fellowship of silence all life is oneself.

Going into Silence

At the end of our first talk, I decided to ask Karin to maintain strict silence, speaking to no one for the next three days, after which we would meet and talk again. She was staying as a patient at the clinic outside Boston where I see patients, so her daily needs would be taken care of. At the same time, this period of silence would be a good opportunity to deepen her experience of meditation, which she had just learned the previous month.

Karin was very reluctant to try my experiment. "Do I have to be totally silent?" she asked nervously.

"Yes," I said. "When you need anything, you can write a note and pass it to one of the staff."

She only looked more nervous. Karin is used to keeping up a constant shield of words, partly to relieve her anxiety, partly to cover it up. I could see how the prospect of being quiet seemed like having her oxygen tent taken away. "Please, just have a little faith," I implored. "You might be surprised at what happens."

She wavered. "Can I at least call my brother to wish him a happy birthday?" she asked. I nodded. "And then not a word to anyone?" she said.

"Not a word," I replied.

Asking a patient to go into silence is a very unusual step— I hasten to add that spending days in silence is not a requirement for successful meditation—but I couldn't think of any other way to keep Karin from constantly verbalizing every tiny thing that happens to her. Using words as an escape route, she runs away from me, from anyone else who has tried to help her, and ultimately from herself. Also, it seems to me that she has a basic misperception about her problem. She believes that she is outside reality trying desperately to get back in. I often feel, on the contrary, that she spends just as much of her energy making sure that she *stays* on the outside.

Why does she do that? Participating in the everyday world brings with it a mixture of pleasure and pain, but Karin prefers to float above the world like a balloon barely tethered to earth. This distant vantage point doesn't provide much pleasure, but it certainly helps to isolate her from any more pain. Karin knows that her escape plans haven't succeeded. She is still tied to the ground, by her memories, by her distress, and above all by her longing to rejoin the rest of us. I didn't expect a few days of silence to mark a major breakthrough, but at least I could be there if she happened to come to earth and meet herself again. It would be a highly charged moment, I knew.

When the three days were up, I felt that some kind of change had taken place. Karin looked rested and less anxious; she did not return obsessively to the same litany of complaints. She looked at me inquisitively, and after admitting that she felt a little more cheerful, she asked, "What was I supposed to get out of that?"

"What do you think you got out of it?" I asked in return.

"Well, I still feel like a lit-up Christmas tree," she laughed ruefully, "and I still want to pull the plug so the lights will go off." She stopped.

"Anything else?" I urged.

"I don't know," she mumbled evasively. "I walked around a lot. There was one thing."

"Yes?"

"There's a big maple in your woods that was cracked by lightning and has a hole in the middle, about shoulder high. I happened to pass by when I noticed something moving inside the hole. Walking closer, I saw a bird's nest with a single blue egg in it; an adult bird was standing beside it, not moving. I was surprised that she didn't fly away, but when I looked closer, I realized what was happening. The egg was hatching, right at that moment. Tiny cracks appeared, and then the brown point of a bill.

"I stood very still, holding my breath. For a second I wondered if I should help, but I have heard that touching a hatchling will make the mother reject it. So I just watched and very slowly moved my hand until it was only a foot from the nest. Still the bird did not fly away. The chick must have gotten exhausted, because as soon as one large patch of shell fell off, it didn't move for several minutes. I decided to go back." Neither of us said anything.

"Do you know why the mother bird didn't fly away?" I asked. "It's because you were truly quiet. You were carrying around your inner silence and projecting it. You may not notice yourself doing it, because you may think that a silent mind shouldn't be able to think. You can think and be silent at the same time. They are two different levels of yourself. The thinking mind goes on, yet the silence remains."

What Karin had experienced was a small window of quietness. I told her that the world seen through that window is very different from the one we are used to. Far from radiating silence, most of us radiate hysteria, reflecting the mental turmoil inside. When that inner turmoil subsides, it leaves a space for change to begin. "Your mind is quiet by nature," I said, "but you have to settle down to realize this. Everything sorts itself out correctly and spontaneously once you become quiet. In the light of calm, steady self-awareness, a feeling of wholeness will wake up inside you. This wholeness is not a thought of any kind; it is simply your own mind, empty of thought but full of *you*. You do not have to do anything to reach this state; the process is effortless. You do not even have to consciously let go. A quiet mind is all you need."

This, the second time I talked with Karin, was also the last. Her week-long stay at the clinic had only a couple more days to go. We had been alone in each other's company for less than two hours, yet I felt close to her. She has staked so much on being true to herself. Just before we said good-bye, she seemed ready for the first time to talk about her future—I mean the possibility that she actually has one and is not going to waste her life protesting the present or mourning the past. "I came here to find out if there was a way to go back to what I've lost, even though my mind already told me there wasn't. I have to go on," she said.

"Wouldn't it be too sad to exist on a memory?" I asked. "That is what the past is." Softly she agreed.

I went out of town the next day, but the nurses told me afterward that Karin seemed much more cheerful and outgoing before she left. She noticed for the first time how sick some of the other patients were and spent several hours walking and talking with two older women who had advanced cancer. I really feel now that Karin is not lost but in transition.

She is about to arrive at a new and much higher conception of who she is.

"You keep asking who you really are," I said at our last meeting. "If you want to know intellectually, then you are pure awareness, the changeless background against which all thoughts occur. This pure awareness is a continuum. It is not broken up by time or space—it just is, ever and always.

"When you witness yourself, what you are experiencing is your real nature. This is the key to freedom. Freedom is the experiential knowledge of one's own nature. You already have elements of this. Many times you definitely seem to be witnessing your body and your environment. You've said that to me, over and over. You even stand aside from your own thoughts.

"Right now, the experience is not creating joy, but why shouldn't it? You are exploring your own corner of immortality as separate from all things mortal. Can't that be exciting?"

"I can accept that as a concept, but I don't feel it yet," she said.

I respect Karin's honesty on this point. We do not live in an age of faith, and many people have problems with any view of life that includes as chancy a word as immortality. "Life? I already know what life is," the isolated self declares. "It is thinking, feeling, breathing. It ends when they end. I don't need to go beyond." But I am not asking Karin for faith, only the willingness to explore inside and wait for the facts to emerge. More than one person has lain half-awake in a rowboat, drifting under a cloudless summer sky, and felt something immense, quiet, and endless. In a certain relaxed state, this something seems to be everywhere, both inside and out. It does not smile at you or frown; it just is.

It takes repeated dips into silence, in and out every day, for a person to accept that this immense, motionless, eternal state of being is himself. Then the door is open for an experience that truly does transform oneself and the world. The person realizes that everything he has been doing in isolation —thinking, feeling, breathing—was taking him on a hidden path. The self has always wanted to connect; it exists so that it may marry the Self.

10

❧❧❧❧❧❧❧❧❧❧

Paradise Remembered

Stan will tell you that the flute saved his life, but there is more to it than that—the flute *is* his life. A day does not go by that he is not either playing the flute or teaching others how to play it. He fulfills dozens of concert dates every year as a flute soloist. He owns a shop downtown where he repairs, tests, demonstrates, and even builds flutes from scratch. On the way home at night, he hangs onto the subway strap reminiscing about all the bright silver instruments he has caressed and polished that day.

One can only imagine, therefore, the horror of what has recently happened. Stan woke up one morning five months ago, suspecting nothing unusual, only to find that the sound of the flute was no longer pleasant to his ears. The sinuous melodies, scales, runs, and trills of his own flute playing had become ugly, sounding as grating as fingernails scraping across a blackboard. Overnight, without reason, the greatest pleasure in his life had turned to pain.

"Where is this harsh sound coming from?" I asked him. "From any one instrument?"

"No, it doesn't matter what instrument I pick up," he replied gloomily. "It's still my energy being transmitted through it. I have always gotten a certain tonal quality that my peers

198

hear as gorgeous but that I now hear as annoyingly shrill. It's become so annoying that I can't stand to play anymore."

Stan's haggard, drawn face looked up at me. "And this all happened out of the blue?" I asked.

"Completely."

"Without any warning? Think back," I urged.

"All I can tell you is that everything seemed to be going all right in my life when a psychiatrist told me that I shouldn't keep on taking a certain antidepressant. I had relied on it for a period last year after I broke up with my old girlfriend. When my psychiatrist told me to go off it cold turkey, I said, 'Is that really okay?' He said, 'Sure.' The next morning I woke up with my ears zooming and ringing, as if someone was playing the flute inside my head."

Stan's psychiatrist has carefully explained to him that the sudden change in his hearing could not be blamed on discontinuing his medication, but Stan is not reassured. He has consulted various specialists, all of whom are baffled by the peculiar mixture of the physical and the psychological in his symptoms. "Whenever I swallow," Stan told me, "I get the sensation that my ears are filling up with fluid. It's like there are trees in my body with branches, and as I swallow, they crackle and fill with fluid. I went to four ear specialists. Two said there wasn't any fluid, two said there was. Only one thought he could treat it, but the medicine he gave me didn't work. My hearing tests come back normal or above normal, just like before, but I know I'm not right anymore."

"Since so much of your life is tied up with your sense of hearing," I pointed out, "do you think some kind of emotional problem could have become localized through this symptom in your ears?"

"I don't know," he replied. "A few months ago I began to think, 'Maybe it's not physical at all. Maybe there's something I need to work through.' People said to me, 'Go talk to someone,' so for months it's been talk, talk, talk, but the psychologists aren't telling me anything I don't already know. Let's assume that my problems are neurotic. Well, Merry Christmas, we have an answer, but I still feel like I'm doomed."

Stan's audiences apparently hear nothing wrong with his playing. To them, his music sounds the same as before, and his peers still praise him specifically for his sensitive, expressive tone. The fact that he now hates his own playing has therefore become a deep, dark secret.

"Perhaps it's temporary. No one has complained to you yet," I pointed out.

"No, but they might," Stan said anxiously. "I keep dreading that someone will catch on and begin to hear my sound the way I do. It's bound to happen, isn't it?"

"I don't know," I said, feeling as puzzled as he was.

As things stand, Stan finds it harder and harder to uphold his integrity, both as a person and a musician. Palming off his dissonant sound on others is a constant source of guilt. More than that, he has depended on the flute for his happiness ever since he was a boy growing up in Brooklyn and his teachers discovered his musical talent. I can imagine the small, defenseless thirteen-year-old he must have been.

Today, at thirty-five, Stan is still small. He wears fragile wire-rimmed glasses and has a full lower lip that curls outward just so, making a perfect perch for the edge of a flute. He speaks in a nervous whirlwind of words, barely touching ground before rushing off to something new. I can't help but think that he was lucky to find the flute when he did. A boy like Stan could easily have been trampled on the streets of Brooklyn.

Without the pleasure of his flute, he is growing more moody and isolated every week. "I'm playing a concert on Sunday with an orchestra that is mostly doctors and lawyers. There's a cello player who's very wonderful. She's cute, and I think she kind of eyed me. I would like to get together with her. We could have a lot of fun, both of us musicians. I am as good a player as she is, if not better. But I'm afraid to pick up my flute and play duets with her, so I can't ask her out."

For a man who sees dating a woman as basically "playing a duet," not being able to perform has proved catastrophic. One could glibly point to the sexual overtones in what Stan is saying. He is like a sharpshooter without his pistol, a policeman without his nightstick, but I don't think the sexual overtones are nearly as important as the drastic loss of purpose that he has suffered.

"It has never mattered if anyone else liked my playing, so

long as I enjoyed it. You can impress people for ten minutes and get a quick high, but those endorphins or whatever they are up here"—Stan pointed to his head—"they're just morphine. I want to feel it for myself. I want fulfillment; otherwise my playing has no meaning."

He sighed wearily. "Maybe it's like meeting a woman for the first time. You're so elated, but then you learn that she's just a person. The magic gradually wears off, and your perception shifts. Maybe the flute is just a flute to me now. I've already had my love affair with it, and now I'm hearing it the way it really is—who knows?

"Every day I start to play, hoping it will sound beautiful again, but then I'll hear that shrillness. I try to talk myself out of it by saying, 'Stan, your sound couldn't have changed. Your ears are just plugged up.' But my symptoms tell me something else. I rationalize to myself, 'Look, people are walking around with multiple sclerosis and things that are much worse,' but it doesn't help. I just don't want to live this way." Stan stopped, and his face looked more morose and baffled than ever. Hurled out of paradise like a fallen angel, he cannot get over the shock of where he has landed.

Now and Forever

The difference between Stan and a fallen angel is that paradise is handed to the angels while humans have to create their own. Not that anyone has ever succeeded. Stan was privileged just to create a corner of intense happiness through his music. As every true artist must, he lived from the creative core of himself, until the sinister day when the flow of creativity was interrupted. A gap appeared between the maker and the thing made, and even though the thing made was still beautiful, it was not *his* beauty that others admired. In that gap, that emptiness, all his earlier happiness was lost.

This problem is not unique to Stan, or to artists as a class. No matter how gratifying one aspect of life becomes, its satisfaction is limited. It wears itself out unless one finds a way to remain connected to the source of renewal. Renewal is one of life's primary urges, like love and freedom, but even more important, since all of life needs renewing to keep ahead of the tireless process of destruction. There is never pure destruction in nature but creation and destruction together, so closely spliced that they cannot be separated. We are constantly dying and being born at the physical level. Each minute, millions of our cells divide, sacrificing their old existence in a death that gives birth to two new cells. The impulse of creation pushes life ahead even while the past is gobbling up life from behind.

We all have a deep psychological drive to keep pace with this process. Alice Miller puts it with beautiful conciseness: "There are needs that can and should be satisfied in the present. . . . Among these is every human being's central need to express himself—to show himself to the world as he really is —in word, in gesture, in behavior, in every genuine utterance from the baby's cry to the artist's creation."

The key to this inspiring affirmation is that life needs to be satisfying *in the present.* It is not that easy to define "the present," however. From one perspective the present is the thinnest possible slice of time, the fleeting instant that allows the future to flip-flop into the past. From the opposite perspective, the present is eternal, because it is ever-renewing, like a river that is never the same twice. "The present is the only thing that has no end," Schrödinger once declared.

To create paradise could mean nothing more or less than living in the present, enjoying the happiness that is both now and forever—but who can manage that? The boundaries that the human mind lives within are invariably fashioned from the past. It is yesterday's hurt that I am defending against today, last year's glory I want to relive, a bygone love I want to find again. The boundary-maker who wields such enormous power over us is the intellect, the part of the mind that judges and categorizes our experiences.

We have already seen that the mind creates boundaries for its own self-protection. Because it can push dangerous feelings out of sight, shoving our childhood fears and primal aggression back down into the underworld of the unconscious, the intellect plays a crucial role in making us feel safe. Anytime we find ourselves in a psychologically threatening situation, the mind faces a decision. "Will this person hurt me? Is it dangerous to feel this emotion? Dare I say what I really think?" Whatever answer the mind comes up with becomes the provisional reality we act upon, and the shifting, jumbled heap that these provisional realities amount to is Reality itself.

Since life never ceases bringing us a new wave of challenge every day, the intellectual decisions we make spin on forever. The number of questions that arise over the tiniest experience is awe inspiring. Is it desirable or undesirable? To be repeated or not to be repeated? Right or wrong, good or bad, nice or nasty? Once each decision is made, it gets filed away in memory, to serve as a reference point for future experience. Let us say that my first time horseback riding made me feel better / was good / nice / worth repeating. The next time I think of going riding, these judgments will color my decision. They do not force me to get back up on a horse, but I cannot totally discard them either.

Two years ago I gave a lecture in Germany. A woman came up afterward to say that she worked for a large municipal aquarium and had often observed an interesting phenomenon there. Whenever the thick glass partitions in the main tank were pulled out to be cleaned, the fish would swim right up to the spot where the glass used to be, and just before crossing it, they would turn back, warded off by a barrier that didn't really exist.

My imagination was quite caught by this observation. Our own uncrossable boundaries are nothing more than wrinkles in our mind that another wrinkle labels as too ugly, fearful, loathsome, or terrifying to confront. If I see an old enemy who insulted me ten years ago, I will find it almost impossible to overlook my former injury. The old judgments crop up in my mind automatically, erecting a wall, and the person who could be my friend is shut out, rejected in advance. In turn, when he senses my coldness, his defenses are raised, until we both find ourselves hiding behind barricades that serve no purpose, that lack all reality. The moment soon passes, and yet there has been no relationship at all, only the stale repetition of outworn memories. And the most frustrating part is that my tormentor today is myself left over from yesterday.

The rishis pondered this problem posed by the intellect, which is like a bread knife, constantly cutting the flow of life into neat slices of experience, each one labeled and judged. They saw that this slicing up of reality, although necessary to the thinking process, was basically false. Life is a river, not a dripping faucet. The rishis therefore contended that any experience which depends upon slices of time and space is not an experience at all. It is a fiction, a shadow, a notion of life that has no actual life in it. By endlessly interpreting the world in bits and pieces, we are losing it at every instant, allowing it to slip through our fingers like sand. To have reality that is whole and thus truly real, one must rise above the intellect, discarding its neat slices of experience. Like day-old bread, they only go stale anyway.

"I Am the Field"

In place of a world sliced up into bits and pieces, the rishis offer us a continuum—a flowing river—that begins inside our awareness, expands to create all the things and events "out there," and then returns to its source, dissolving back into awareness again. Ultimately, the rishis' perception can only be tested by rising to their state of consciousness. But let us suppose that they might be right. Then it should be possible, if only for an instant, for us to see what they saw. A teacher I know from Oregon, now in his early forties, apparently had just such a glimpse as he was meditating. The experience began in familiar territory:

When I started to meditate one morning, I felt as if a powerful magnet was pulling me down into myself. For some minutes I continued to sink deeper and deeper, using no effort on my part, until all sense of outside stimuli faded away. I sat with my breathing stilled, but my mind was alert in the unbroken silence. I knew that I had transcended to the point where my individual self had dropped out completely, taking with it all sense of time, space, direction, or any kind of thought.

At this juncture, a person usually continues to experience the transcendent silence or else begins to rise toward the surface of the mind, carried by a sudden thought or feeling. However, this time something new happened.

Out of the absolutely uniform field of silence, a faint point of awareness arose. It was the most delicate feeling of "I-ness," just a wisp of personal consciousness, and with it came the sensation of "turning"— that is the only way I can describe it. This turning must have acted as a spark, because suddenly I was surrounded by an enormous expanse of light. There was nothing existing but light, and I intuitively knew it to be intelligence, or consciousness, taking on visible form.

Even though I was sitting with my eyes closed, I could see that everything outside myself was also made of the same brilliant white light. My body, the tables and chairs, the walls and windows, the building and all that lay beyond it—everything was molded from this intelligent light, which pulsated with life. After a moment or two the light gradually faded. I was left alone, sitting in silence again, but now it was different, as if I had swallowed the world and for the first time felt full.

Extraordinary as this experience is, it strikes me as even more remarkable that my friend found it *normal.* He said that the "turning" which sparked his vision could also be called a "self-reflection." In other words, he felt that behind the alluring surface of his vision, he was actually catching sight of himself. After a lifetime of being distracted by things "out there," he finally saw the seer. Yet we can't fully comprehend his experience until we get closer to what this inner "turning" of awareness is and how it can carry us out of ourselves into the field where light and mind, nothing and everything, mingle as one.

It is extremely intriguing that the word "field," which modern physicists use to describe the most fundamental forces in nature, was a divine word in ancient India. When Lord Krishna reveals his infinite greatness to the warrior Arjuna in the *Bhagavad-Gita,* he says, "Know me as the field and as the knower of the field." The Sanskrit word, *kshetra,* can mean a battlefield (Arjuna and Krishna happen to be talking in the middle of a battlefield, just before two mighty armies clash), but the deeper meaning of *kshetra* comes very close to what a physicist means when he says "quantum field" or "electromagnetic field." These fields are infinite and all-pervasive; without them, reality could not exist. Lord Krishna was making the same point about himself.

Before there can be a photon of light, there must be the field of light; before an individual electron, the field of electricity; before an isolated bar magnet, the earth's magnetic field. The field of light that my friend saw as the source of everything around him was not a physical field, however, but a field of awareness. He was perceiving his consciousness *as* light, but this is not so different from ordinary perception as it might seem. When we see light, our brains are actually selecting totally abstract qualities from out of the field and interpreting them *as* light. In fact, everything we see, touch, hear, taste, or smell has been selected from the infinite reservoir of vibrating energy in the field.

Think of a rose leaf and a rose thorn. Both are nourished by the same sunlight, being constantly bombarded by the sun's entire light spectrum. Photosynthesis is basically the same in each, and if you delve into their cellular structure, you would see mostly the same molecules at work, and their DNA is identical.

The difference between a leaf and a thorn is a matter of selection. The thorn takes sunlight and turns it into something hard, sharp, and pointed. The leaf takes sunlight and turns it into something soft, rounded, and translucent. By itself, sunlight has none of these qualities. Could you claim that light is hard or soft, sharp or rounded? Somehow the various qualities get pulled out of the field even though they do not appear to be "in" it—they exist as possibilities that the field can manifest.

Like the rose, I practice selection, fashioning my life as my relationship to the field alters. In one state of awareness—deep sleep—I have no interaction with light at all. In dreaming state, I produce images of light in my head. In waking state, the light appears to be "out there." In actuality, the light was always a potential of the field, waiting to be activated by my mind.

The field, it must be understood, is not a thing—it is an abstraction that we shape into things. To help prove this to ourselves, we can turn to those people who lack the complete creative abilities the rest of us take for granted. In *Pilgrim at Tinker Creek,* Annie Dillard writes eloquently about an entire class of people, those born blind, who do not live in a world that contains space, size, distance, or many other qualities we accept as given. Several decades ago, when eye surgeons first learned to remove cataracts safely, they could restore sight overnight to people who had been blind from birth. Suddenly released into the light, the newly sighted did not feel freed. They were plunged into a mystery that was at times overwhelming. "The vast majority of patients, of both sexes and all ages, had . . . no idea of space whatsoever," Dillard writes, drawing from the notes left by surgeons. "Form, distance, and size were so many meaningless syllables. One patient 'had no idea of depth, confusing it with roundness.'

"Of another postoperative patient the doctor writes, 'I have found in her no notion of size, for example, not even within the narrow limits she might have encompassed with the aid of touch. Thus when I asked her to show me how big her mother was, she did not stretch out her hands, but set her two index fingers a few inches apart.' "

One patient was used to telling the difference between a cube and a sphere by touching both to his tongue. After the operation, he looked at the same objects and could not tell them apart by sight. A second patient said that lemonade was "square" because it gave his tongue a pricking sensation, the same way a square object gave his hands a pricking sensation.

The newly sighted faced a baffling world because they lacked the visual creativity we all take for granted. Vision was plopped into their laps formlessly, which is how it really exists before the mind turns it into something formed. Some patients did not realize that a house is bigger than one of the rooms inside it. A building one mile away looked as close as a nearby one, only taking a lot more steps to get to. A dog that walked behind a chair was no longer in the room. Shapes were seen as flat patches of color, and when some patients walked past a tree, they were amazed to turn around and see that it was now behind them.

"For the newly sighted," Dillard comments, "vision is pure sensation unencumbered by meaning." Adding the meaning proved too much for some of them. They reverted to closing their eyes when they were alone, feeling objects with their hands and tongues, or climbing the stairs with eyes shut to avoid the dizzying prospect of going straight up a wall. Poignantly, the glut of visual images caused almost every person to lose the serenity that is so striking in those born blind. It was particularly disturbing for them to discover that they had been *watched* all their lives, since this was a personal intrusion totally alien to the blind.

In the end, some adjusted better than others. It was startling but also wonderful for them to find that everyone in the world had a different face; it was awesome to realize the vastness of the heavens and the earth itself. But space mostly remained elusive. One girl was shown some paintings and photos. "Why do they put those dark marks all over them?" she asked. "Those aren't dark marks," her mother explained, "they are shadows. That is one of the ways the eye knows that things have shape. If it were not for shadows, many things would look flat." "Well, that's how things do look," the girl replied. "Everything looks flat with dark patches."

Just because we are so used to the usual construct of the world, that does not mean it must already exist. Other people may not accept our code for reality if they do not accept our code for seeing. The eye refuses to see what the mind does not know.

I am reminded of stories told about Turks who ran in panic from the theater when they saw their first movie, thinking that the image of a locomotive was leaping out of the wall; of forest pygmies in Africa who were led onto a plain for the first time and thought that distant water buffalos were actually two inches high; of Eskimos who were confronted with photographs of themselves and saw no faces at all, only a jumble of gray and black blotches. These are not "primitive" responses but responses from another code, another world. Yet every person accepts some code. The human race is bound in cords of sight, with only the rishis to tell us that we are free to adopt any code we wish.

Weaving the Fabric of Awareness

The reason the rishis were able to see this so clearly is that their own experience of the world was beyond the binding influence of any single code of perception. They did not select bits and pieces from the field but saw it as a whole. And what did this wholeness look like? When the rishis turned their attention toward the field to see its totality, they found that the field was pure awareness, the same "mind-stuff" that fills our heads.

"Pure" means without form and can be equated with the motionless silence being contacted in meditation. Existing without form in the field, pure awareness starts to vibrate and in so doing turns itself into the visible universe. A thought can be seen as a vibration inside this mind-stuff, and so can an atom, although an atom is outside our heads and has all the marks of matter. These marks are only trick effects, the rishis declared. Atoms, molecules, photons of light, stars, galaxies—all of creation—are fashioned from the same thing, pure awareness.

This, the core insight of ancient India, is too sweeping to take on faith, and it can only be tested in a higher state of consciousness. However, we have a linking concept, the field, which can at least take us to the boundary of the rishis' world.

Over the last fifty years, the concept of the field rose to prominence in physics when it was realized that matter and energy have no fixed, concrete existence. Because you can hold a tennis ball in your hand, common sense tells you that you must be able to hold the smallest part of a tennis ball in your hand, too. But the elementary particles that are the smallest bits of matter are not solid or fixed.

To see a tennis ball accurately, one has to imagine it being like a swarm of bees. Each bee is flying so fast that it forms a streak of light, like a sparkler waved around in the dark on the Fourth of July. Besides leaving a visible trail, each bee also leaves a trail you can feel. Thus, even though the bee moves out of sight as soon as you try to spot it, your eyes and hands still see and feel where it has been.

In crude form, we have uncovered the basic tenet of quantum reality, the famous Uncertainty Principle, which says that elementary particles, although they appear to exist in a definite place in time and space, cannot actually be found there. Every time you try to catch a bee, it disappears, so that all you have is trails. Physicists were not entirely happy with the notion that everything in existence is constantly slipping away, but they learned to live with it, however uneasily. Instead of having a solid particle to hold on to, they were left with a set of possibilities, and if all the possibilities were lumped together, the result was a field.

In essence a field is only a set of variables to be measured. One can probe it for the various sorts of trails that the whizzing particles are leaving in their wake. When that is done, what comes out is a highly precise, scientifically useful set of descriptions. A quark can be described as having this or that property—mass, momentum, symmetry, spin—all of which can be computed with beautiful mathematical accuracy. Strangely, one can know everything about the flying bee without ever stopping it. That is why a tennis ball seems totally secure, solid, and real on one level, where the senses operate, and totally ghostly and unreal at a deeper level, where the senses cannot go.

Like a rishi, a physicist maneuvers between existing things, possible things, and nothing. Lord Krishna can use the word "field" with the same intent as a physicist: both are trying to convey a sense of nature's wholeness. A field is the most complete way to describe anything, from an atom to a star, because *all* possible descriptions are embedded in it. This implies that anything your eye can see could be anything else. In fact, there is no way out of this peculiar conclusion, since at the level of the field, seeing and creating merge. The renowned Princeton physicist John Wheeler writes: "We used to think of the universe as 'out there,' to be observed as it were from behind the screen of a foot-thick slab of glass, safely, without personal involvement. The truth, quantum theory tells us, is quite different. . . . The observer is increasingly promoted to participator. In some strange sense, this is a participatory universe."

Like every great insight, the discovery that the universe has no fixed structure can seem frightening, but the uncertainty principle is just as much a creativity principle. Words like "void," "nothingness," and "interstellar space" do not have to generate fear; they are the creative stuff of everyday life. "I like the story of the three baseball umpires relaxing over beer one afternoon and comparing notes," Wheeler writes. "One umpire says, 'I calls 'em as I sees 'em.' The next umpire says, 'I calls 'em as they really are.' The third umpire says, 'They ain't nothin' until I calls 'em.' "

The rishis promoted the creative act of seeing even higher than did the quantum physicist. First of all, they expanded the influence of the observer beyond the infinitesimal range of the quantum field, which is from 10 million to 100 million times smaller than an atom. The hide-and-seek of a quark became the hide-and-seek of life as a whole—the Vedic seer pulled forth new tomorrows from the field, whole packages of reality that could not exist without him.

Physics has barely entered this enlarged domain. However, controlled studies have shown that ordinary people actually do project their thoughts into nature's workshop. Two researchers from Princeton's engineering department, Robert G. Jahn and Brenda J. Dunne, have shown that volunteers set down in front of a machine can influence its workings with the power of attention. The experiment is recounted in Jahn and Dunne's rigorously documented book, *Margins of Reality*.

Typically the machine being influenced was a random-number generator, a computer that spewed out strings of 0s and 1s in random order. Over the long run, the number of 0s would be the same as the number of 1s (just as tossing a coin eventually produces as many heads as tails).

The volunteers were asked to tilt the machine's output toward either more 1s or more 0s simply by desiring it. They put their minds on what they wanted the machine to produce and succeeded remarkably well. They achieved deviations from randomness on the order of 18 percent, although even the most sophisticated quantum theory cannot explain how they accomplished this.

In related experiments, the Princeton team showed that ordinary people could also broadcast messages to others telepathically, no matter how far away the receiving person was. In some cases, it was observed that the relayed messages were received up to three days *before* they were sent. The startling implication is that the fixed boundaries of space-time are only conveniences of the mind, not absolutes. We could easily be living in a three-dimensional movie projected by our minds, as the age-old Indian scriptures maintained.

In truth we *are* the three-dimensional movie. It is not separate from us but mingled with our mind-stuff, so that the only way to see it without being fooled is to see the seer. Every person can declare, along with Lord Krishna, "Know me as the field and as the knower of the field." The poet Tagore sensed exactly what it was like to accept his own cosmic status:

> The same stream of life that runs through my veins night and day runs through the world and dances in rhythmic measures.
> It is the same life that shoots in joy through the dust of the earth in numberless blades of grass and breaks into tumultuous waves of leaves and flowers.

If the field is all there is, then the inconceivable impulse driving the universe must also be in every speck of matter and every grain of thought. No, it must be in the mere *possibility* that matter and thought could exist. As the rishis conceived of it, the location of all creativity is in pure awareness, but then so are we and so is everything.

"Mistake of the Intellect"

I have dwelt on the parallels between Vedic thought and modern physics because there has been a great deal of past misunderstanding in this area. It became fashionable in the late Seventies to claim that quantum theory was anticipated by the insights of mystics, principally the sages of Buddhism and Taoism. Many people took this to mean that Eastern wisdom could be interpreted in terms of modern physics, and vice versa. Hope arose that a bridge would be built between East and West, and through a mingling of insights, both world views would profit.

Very soon, however, there came a backlash from professional physicists, among others, decrying the whole notion. To them, the quantum field is a hard fact, while a mystic's visions are at the extreme of softness. It was argued that the complex and highly specialized mathematics which predicts the behavior of such things as quarks and leptons has little or nothing to do with human behavior. To suggest that the mind has a quantum basis was fantasy, since thoughts and subatomic particles exist in totally separate realms. These could not be bridged by physics, nor did most physicists even wish to try. (Although they kept quieter about it, traditional Buddhists were equally dismayed, since they saw their religion as centered on the salvation of souls mired in the cycle of rebirth. They did not see the relevance of quantum theory to this goal, and therefore their desire to build a bridge was minimal as well.)

I hope I will not simply make matters worse by pointing out that to discuss the ancient sages in terms of *either* mysticism or quantum theory deprives them of their true originality and purpose. The Vedic seers, like their later counterparts in Taoism and Buddhism, were not mystics; they were wide-awake observers of the same world we all live in. They did not deal solely in subjective visions and insights; their minds were focused on the junction-point where subjectivity and objectivity meet. This gave them a unique perspective from which to observe their own consciousness as it transformed itself into the rocks, trees, mountains, and stars we all perceive "out there."

I have done my best to provide convincing proof that reality is everyone's personal creation. People will never grasp this solely on an intellectual level—it must be experienced and internalized. The intellect, by raising barriers of doubt, denial, and fear, has reduced direct spiritual experience to an empty mysticism, making it much harder for people to realize how necessary such experience actually is. If I can take the risk of defining it, a spiritual experience is one in which pure awareness reveals itself as the maker of reality. What could be more relevant to our lives? Reality is pouring from us like dreams from a dreamer or light from a bonfire. Once we gain control over this process, we can restore ourselves to a state of freedom and fulfillment; in other words, we can put ourselves back in paradise.

The loss of spiritual experience, in both East and West, has shattered the higher aspirations of human life. "All your suffering is rooted in one superstition," a guru told his disciples. "You believe that you live in the world, when in fact the world lives in you." The ancient rishis went even further and declared that perfection in every area of life was sacrificed because of *Pragya Aparadha*, "the mistake of the intellect."

The intellect's need to explore the world, which began in the remote past and reached its peak in modern times, eventually took us so far into the diversity of creation that the source of creation—our own awareness—was lost sight of. Inner experiences of bliss and infinite expansion, of complete freedom and boundless power, became "mystical." No one has such experiences as a matter of course; indeed, it seems to take years of meditation to get back to the state of awareness where these experiences become remotely possible. By now, the hard reality "out there" has become so compelling that spirit is allowed little if any power at all. Perhaps the existence of spirit was a superstition all along.

As dismal as it may sound, the current state of spiritual atrophy does not have to become permanent; the "mistake of the intellect" can be corrected. In fact, there is cause for tremendous optimism here. To narrow our problems down to a single cause is a breakthrough in and of itself. How then do we correct our mistake? Not by giving up the intellect altogether, which would only result in mindlessness. The intellect must be restored to its proper place in the total balance of awareness. Repeated experience of pure awareness allows this healing to take place.

When all its aspects are in balance, human awareness

finds itself living both halves of life, the absolute state of the Self and the relative state of the self. By remaining in contact with our core of pure awareness, we can fully appreciate the beautiful and diverse world "out there." The mirror of nature will give us back the reflection of our own inner joy. The poet W. B. Yeats wrote, "We are happy when for everything inside us there is a corresponding something outside us." The word "correspondence" means a flow of communication as well as a similarity between two things. When awareness is completely balanced, communicating with the outside world is instantaneous and automatic. It happens with the touch of thought.

The South African writer Laurens Van der Post recalled a day when he went traveling among the natives in the bush country. He came to their camp and found the men sitting around an old tribesman whom Van der Post particularly liked. The old man was sitting still with his eyes closed, deeply absorbed. When Van der Post asked what he was doing, one of the onlookers said, "Ssh, he's doing something important. He's making clouds." The rishis say that you and I were born to be cloud-makers, too. But until we regain control of our inner nature, we will never solve the imbalances that have been inflicted on nature as a whole.

The Circular Trap

I find it significant that so many people are currently involved in the issue of addiction. To me, addictions stand for the deeper conflict between maintaining one's old conditioning and breaking free. The addict's "habit" is but an exaggerated version of all habits, which cling to outworn realities rather than allowing new life to flow in. The root causes of addiction are hotly debated, but one aspect of the syndrome is that it brings pleasure to people who cannot find it any other way. As Alice Miller observes, "People who as children successfully repressed their intense feelings often try to regain— at least for a short time—their lost intensity of experience with the help of drugs and alcohol."

I think it is obvious that many people have anesthetized a huge portion of their feeling self. To show strong emotions is rarely considered an acceptable form of behavior in our society, while paramount importance is placed on self-control. As a result, many of us may reach the point where we panic at the first sign of emotion starting to well up. Repeating the denial of emotion imposed upon us in childhood, we now exert enormous pressure to deny ourselves.

Addiction "solves" this problem by permitting pleasure while at the same time insuring that the pleasure is furtive and guilt ridden. One of my patients, whose facade of correct deportment is impeccable, for many years led a secret life haunting the worst heroin dens in Boston. "I played various characters when I went to the shooting galleries in the ghetto," he said.

"Sometimes I drove my BMW and wore a three-piece suit; other times I had on army fatigues or the rags a street person would wear. I saw people die, begging for heroin to the very end. I was under close surveillance by both the police and the pushers, neither of whom could figure me out. I slept in abandoned houses with other junkies and walked the streets with ten-year-old kids who had orders to shoot on sight anyone who tried to rip off their stash of crack.

"You won't be able to really grasp what it means when I tell you that I had a twenty-bag-a-day heroin habit," he said with an unfathomable look in his eyes. "The common junkie has a two- to five-bag habit, maybe ten. When a person is hooked on that much, his chances of recovery are less than one percent. I shot twenty bags for over a year and survived."

This man is very frank about the enjoyment that his addiction brought him, at least at the outset. From the moment he first injected heroin, long-lost pleasure flooded him. Being able to play various characters as he moved through the junkie's shadow world gave him a secondary source of forbidden pleasure. By having to be real to no one, he could temporarily forget his massive self-doubt, which told him that he might not be real to begin with.

Although lurid on the outside, his addiction was not essentially different from that of the cautious alcoholic who sneaks a shot of whiskey before brushing his teeth in the morning. Both are hooked on the alluring combination of enjoyment and guilt. The essence of any form of compulsive behavior is helpless repetition, which pleasure alone would not be strong enough to incite. Alcoholics and heroin addicts, food bingers and compulsive thieves all return again and again to the very behavior that they would judge shameful in another person.

Often it is pleasure itself that they find shameful; therefore, they have no alternative but to seek pleasures that have built-in dissatisfaction. As one psychotherapist put it, "You can never get enough of what you don't want in the first place." Even the most intense pleasure is not addictive as long as the person indulging in it has a clear idea of what pleasure is. But a certain kind of personality has no choice but to mix feeling bad with feeling good. A guilty pang accompanies the jolt delivered by the drug, and without the guilt, the jolt would lose its allure.

Addicts are pitied and reviled in our culture, and society has not decided whether they are to be considered sick, deviant, or both. There is a deeper ambiguity as well. To contemplate the helpless loss of self-control represented by full-blown addiction is horrible but secretly tempting. Who would not have a flood of pleasure coursing through his body if he did not have to pay too high a price? This is not sheer escapism on our parts. At the heart of addiction, I would propose, lies a deep nostalgia for pleasure that echoes a legitimate need. Despite what our conditioning might tell us, to seek pleasure is not bad. Everyone's life is driven by the spur of desire. But hardly anyone can enjoy deep satisfaction untainted by feelings of guilt, selfishness, or a vague premonition that "this is too good to last."

If addicts are indeed playing out a fantasy we all share, then they may be neither sick nor deviant. I would like to apply the diagnosis provided by the rishis and say that addiction is basically the result of a mistake. The addict is caught in a circular trap of his own devising; he cannot get enough pleasure to finally abolish his guilt; he cannot suffer enough guilt to keep him from the next fix. Rather, the two impulses circle each other in an endless dance.

What we have here is another example of the mistaken

intellect—the circular trap depends upon the addict's belief that his divided awareness cannot heal itself. Yet the rishis maintain that awareness is all-powerful, which means that it should be able to heal anything, including itself. Let us see if a solution to addiction might lie in this direction.

Evelyn Silvers, a Los Angeles therapist who specializes in drug addiction, has learned to create a remarkable phenomenon with her patients that releases them from the bondage of their cravings. Using the simplest sort of suggestion and guided thinking, she induces her patients to manufacture "brain drugs" that appear to act exactly like the heroin, alcohol, cocaine, or tranquilizers that they have been ruining their lives to buy or steal.

Earlier, in 1976, Silvers had focused on a different problem, chronic pain. Widespread excitement had been generated by the recent discovery of the body's internal painkillers, or endorphins, which were analyzed as being many times more powerful than morphine and other opiates. Inspired by this breakthrough, Silvers found that she could get long-term sufferers of migraines, arthritis, and lower-back pain to produce highly effective pain relief on command.

This may seem like a simple application of the body's painkillers, which all of us call upon. But our use is not voluntary, and few if any researchers in the field claim to know how endorphins are actually switched on. They are highly unpredictable chemicals. Under certain circumstances, such as being wounded in battle or being injured in a highway collision, the body may feel no pain for hours, while at other times a minor headache or dental pain may be impossible to suppress.

Faced with this baffling unpredictability, Silvers devised a disarmingly simple approach. She told her patients in an authoritative voice that the brain's inner pharmacy could treat any disorder. She would be giving them a simple technique for tapping "brain drugs" that would successfully deal with the most intractable chronic pain. Next, she told each patient to close his eyes and to imagine that he was creating a supply of endorphins inside his head but without releasing it. The painkilling dose had to be built up to the appropriate level. For the next few minutes she kept her patients in suspense as they felt the dose becoming bigger and bigger, until finally she gave a signal, and each person mentally injected a flood of endorphins into his bloodstream.

At this point, almost everyone felt a surge of pain relief sweep over them, as if morphine were being fed into them through an IV needle. Chronic pain that had resisted all previous treatments improved dramatically or disappeared entirely. When the patients were sent home to use the "brain drug" technique on their own, many were able to wean themselves completely off prescribed painkillers. Remarkably, Silvers made the further observation that if a patient with chronic pain was also a drug addict, using the technique seemed to sweep away all drug cravings along with the pain. This occurred even among patients who had been abusing drugs for twenty years, and there seemed to be no withdrawal symptoms. By 1986 Silvers was confident enough to test her methods on a group of hard-core addicts.

She selected twenty adults who had spent from five to forty years hooked on cocaine, alcohol, Valium, or heroin, either alone or in combination. They were desperate people, almost all of whom had gone far beyond getting any satisfaction from their fixes. They continued on drugs basically to escape their deep feelings of guilt and to alleviate the constant physical pain that their abused bodies were afflicted with. Most had completely ruined their family life and career.

Silvers taught the group her standard technique, but after telling them that the brain produces its own painkillers, she went on to say that it produces the exact equivalent of any drug sold on the street. Besides giving an addict a lifetime supply of pure drugs with no side effects, the brain's pharmacy would make it unnecessary for him to feel guilty. Silvers told the group: "You have been using drugs for a very good reason. The drugs that get abused are precisely those that mimic the natural substances which the brain uses to make people feel normal. When we say that we feel a certain way, our mood is always produced by one brain chemical or other—there is no state of mind without a biochemical foundation.

"In the brains of an addicted person, the internal drugs for feeling normal—happy, calm, balanced, and in control—

are in short supply, either because of a hereditary or spontaneous shortage, or because taking outside drugs lowers the brain's ability to produce its own supply.

"Your addictive cravings have been telling you that your brain was having a problem, and your habit was a way of solving it. Although drug abuse has dangerous consequences, it is nothing to be ashamed of in itself. You were just medicating yourself, like a diabetic taking insulin."

Here Silvers was mixing astute therapy, the power of suggestion, and rather tenuous science. Neuroscientists have not yet proved that the brain produces the equivalent of some addictive drugs (alcohol, nicotine, and cocaine, for example), much less that such substances can be delivered on command. But there is no doubt that our cells are outfitted to latch on to street drugs. That undeniable fact implies that addictive substances must fulfill some purpose that is closely matched by a chemical we make inside ourselves; otherwise, we would have to assume that nature gave us a receptivity for street drugs millions of years before they arrived on the scene, which seems highly improbable.

After Silvers delivered her talk, the members of the group closed their eyes, mentally built up a massive dose of their favored drug, and released it when she gave the signal. What followed was astonishing. The eyes of the subjects glazed over; each person was lost on a different trip, according to the kind of drug he was addicted to. The cocaine addicts felt a rush that left them speechless. They laughed quietly and later said that they had relived childhood memories. The Valium addicts became so tranquilized that they stuttered at the beginning of words. The alcoholics sprawled in dreamy relaxation and lost their inhibitions; they talked calmly about threatening subjects that had aroused massive defensiveness before.

In every instance the drug fix was so strong that Silvers had to wait twenty minutes before the group was coherent enough to describe their experiences. All were elated and convinced by what had happened, although they had approached the session quite skeptically. "For years the drug has been in control of you," Silvers assured them, "now it will be the other way around."

I find this a superb example of how awareness can heal. When Silvers told addicts that their guilt was unfounded, she set the stage for an outlook most of them had not entertained but were eager to accept. Once a plausible tool was offered, the mind allowed itself to break out of an old boundary. My explanation assumes that the brain acted as a neutral agent here; having no will of its own, the brain would have been capable of continuing the addiction or abandoning it. The brain cannot free itself; it needs instructions from the mind.

Silvers follows the current trend to seek explanations within the brain's chemistry, but she admits that the exact brain mechanism she has been tapping is unknown. She places great weight on the notion that feeling like a normal person depends upon a proper balance of many interconnected neurochemicals. This seems undeniable, but it bypasses the mystery of how a single technique could tap into brain chemicals that are not even known to exist. Besides, could an addict's brain, so grossly impaired by outside substances, really cure itself through chemical means? As I see it, the wound of addiction was cured instead by a new ingredient in awareness.

The brilliance of her whole method was that it gave the mind-body connection credit for doing anything it wanted to, even in the face of people's enormous conditioning. As support for the view underlying Silvers' method, consider the power of the placebo effect. If you give a dummy drug to a group of cancer patients, telling them that they are receiving a potent form of chemotherapy, a large percentage will exhibit the typical side effects of chemotherapy. They will feel intensely nauseous after taking the drug; their hair will begin to fall out and sometimes falls out completely.

Clearly we were not born with a fixed brain mechanism for losing our hair at will; nor do chemotherapy drugs mimic natural substances in the brain. In order for the placebo to work, the mind created something new—it was not dependent on the brain's known abilities. Rather, the brain was the mind's infinitely resourceful servant, able to carry out what it was told to do. When Silvers offered these addicts a drugless fix, they discovered on the spot that addiction was not a prison but an illusion. Years of pain, frustration, and demolished self-esteem were suddenly irrelevant. "Curving back upon myself," Lord Krishna expounds to Arjuna, "I create again and again." This is not only a transcendent god speaking, but the creator inside each person.

11

∻∻∻∻∻∻∻∻∻∻∻∻

The Field of Power

In India, if a person appears to be living in a state of grace, people will admiringly say, "Let him walk where he likes, flowers will grow under his feet." I'm sure Sidney has never heard this poetic saying, but it could easily apply to him, now that he has stepped into a wonder world.

"I was the last person who should have started performing miracles," he began, talking in a soft, musing voice. "In my circle, you know, religion means next to nothing. I abhor 'the gradual descent into woolly mysticism,' as Stephen Hawking so aptly put it, and I agree with Freud that people who pray to an all-loving Father in heaven are probably compensating for the father that did not love them enough on earth.

"I was sitting in a café last year telling a student, 'If you are completely honest with yourself, you will never claim to know that you have a soul.' Medieval physicians used to weigh their dying patients to test if the body became lighter as the soul departed. They never found anything, of course. But metaphysics is the hardest superstition to kill. Newton himself believed that the affairs of the universe take place inside God's mind—he never produced evidence for that contention, either.

"Think of all the spiritual titillation we would be forced to abandon if the 'other world' and its 'higher beings' had to prove their existence instead of being taken on faith! By the time I turned twenty-one, I had dropped the whole archaic vocabulary of God, soul, sin, atonement, redemption, and immortality as so much excess baggage."

"But now you do possess a soul?" I asked in puzzlement.

"Believe it or not, I think I do." He laughed and spread his hands in the air to ward off invisible objections. "Let me just tell you what has happened, and you judge."

"All right," I said. I've known Sidney for five years, as a friend and occasional patient. If he had found his soul, it would be worth hearing about. Sidney is forty-seven and looks at the world with the most alert gaze I have ever met. He is a fluent and diverse writer and sometime professor who takes his stance against any kind of orthodox dogma. His words, which pour out like Niagara, are always memorable. Now here we were, seated in another café, taking shelter from the rain one gray Saturday in Cambridge.

"A few months ago," Sidney said, "it became quite clear to me that my normal mind was breaking apart."

"You had a psychotic episode?" I asked, startled.

"Let us say that I brushed up against a state of mind that I would have unhesitatingly labeled as disturbed in someone else," he replied. "But again, I leave the judgments to you. Early last winter I started noticing some strange 'coincidences' in my life. One day it was snowing when I had to walk to the grocery store. As I stepped outside my apartment, a patch of sunlight appeared at my feet, and I couldn't help but notice as I went down the street that it moved with me.

"I took a left turn at the end of the block; so did the patch of sunlight, which measured perhaps ten feet across. I stopped at the traffic light and waited for it to change—and when I crossed the street, so did the light! It accompanied my steps to the very door of the grocery, and if this was not strange enough, when I came out fifteen minutes later, it reappeared and followed me home again. What was I to think?"

Before I could respond, he rushed on. "No, wait. The next day I went downtown to buy a portable typewriter, only to find that the price had gone up by twenty dollars since I had called in the morning. I objected to the clerk and the store manager, but to no avail. Feeling intensely irritated, I bought the typewriter anyway, so as not to waste the trip, and when I stepped outside the door, do you know what was there?"

"A patch of sunlight," I ventured.

"A twenty-dollar bill, right at my feet!" Sidney proclaimed, ignoring me. "Insignificant as these incidents may sound, I began to feel increasingly funny about them."

"Funny?"

"Yes—there was a certain tone to these incidents that I would have to call *playful*, as if I was being shown a particularly amusing trick by a clever child—no, by an intelligence I couldn't see or contact. But let me go on. A week later I was riding alone in the car. It was after dark, and I was in the country, coming back from a house I had never visited before. One winding rural road led to another, and after half an hour I admitted to myself that I was hopelessly lost.

"The few houses I passed were all dark and I began to feel anxious, when all at once my awareness was no longer inside my head—it reached out in front of me, about the length of the car's headlights. Just as I noticed this phenomenon, a further expansion took place, and my awareness now pooled out in all directions. It was a very delicate feeling. How can I possibly describe it? I was simply everywhere, and without thinking about it, I gave up driving my car. I still held the wheel and pushed the pedals, but the feeling of conscious effort was gone. I became this pool of awareness gliding through the night, not caring where I was bound.

"I arrived at crossroads and turned this way or that, apparently at random, yet in ten minutes I came out onto the highway at precisely the turnoff that led back home."

"Would you call that an experience of your soul?" I asked quizzically.

"If the soul is our portion of an invisible world, then perhaps I was projecting myself into the territory of the soul. My invisible extension was alive, and it was undoubtedly me. Everything felt vibrant in its presence—the car, the land, the sky. A scrap of verse comes to mind—where's it from? 'The stars are wide and alive, they seem each like a smile of great sweetness, and they seem very near.'"

"How do you feel now?"

"Not like that anymore. There's been a change, a ripening. I continue to be intensely conscious all the time, and as the days go by, there is a sporadic ecstasy that comes over me. In those moments, the quality of my life becomes sacred. Pardon me for sounding so awkward; I am new at speaking like this."

"I'm happy for you," I said, and added, "You still seem like yourself, if that is a worry. You've always known a lot about yourself, and I'm not surprised that you are getting to know even more."

He gave me a grateful look. "I want to tell you about a very unusual occurrence. Are you bothered by the idea of miracles?"

"I'm not sure. You implied something in that vein already, didn't you?"

"Yes, but you've looked into this area yourself?"

"I don't seek it out, but stories seem to come my way. I've met people who tell me in all confidence that they used to fly as children. They floated down the staircase when no one else was at home and left their dolls on top of tall wardrobes, which mystified their parents. Then one day they told Mommy their secret, only to be assured that flying was impossible. After that, the ability disappeared.

"Of course flying is a very extraordinary claim," I said, "but quite a lot of people seem to flirt with unusual powers. They can visualize lost objects and go right to them if they really need to. They answer other people's thoughts before they are spoken. In a haphazard way, most of us can foretell the future, although our correct predictions remain mixed up with assorted projections from our unconscious minds, wish fulfillments and false premonitions. I wouldn't feel comfortable saying where ordinary life leaves off and miracles begin."

Sidney seemed relieved, but when he started speaking again, it was with marked hesitancy. "My nights have been sleepless recently, not from anxiety but because I seem to be —what shall I say?—filled with light. The pressure of ecstasy makes me get up and walk around restlessly; sometimes I put on my coat and go out into the street. Would you believe it, I dance to the moon! I was in this heightened state one night when I ran across a bedraggled woman lying on the sidewalk near my home. She was asleep, rolled up in a filthy blanket, and I heard her mumbling, 'Mother, Mother, Mother.'

"It was very pitiable, and intuitively I had no doubt that like many homeless people, she was mentally ill. Her voice sounded desperately crazy; it carried such an intensity of suffering that I couldn't bear it, yet at the same time I felt more ecstatic than ever. I leaned down and gently woke her up. She looked at me, frightened, but she didn't pull away. Without knowing why, I told her, 'You don't have to suffer anymore.'

" 'What?' she said, completely bewildered.

" 'I'm here to help you,' I said. 'You're not crazy anymore, are you?' She was taken aback, and yet there was a sane look in her eyes that I am sure was new. She shook her head, as if to make sure of what was inside, and didn't say anything. 'Tell me,' I insisted, 'do you still feel crazy?' In a quiet, normal voice she replied, 'No.'

" 'Look,' I said, 'I don't know why this is happening, but let's just say you are very fortunate. You're going to be all right from now on.' " Sidney stopped.

"This really happened to you?" I said, amazed. He nodded. "But can you really be sure she was cured? It does sound like a manic episode on your part, you must know that."

"Yes," he admitted. "I cannot prove anything, and it wasn't possible at the time for me to analyze what was taking place between the two of us. My heart started pounding, and I felt an overpowering urge to run away. I heard the woman call after me, 'What kind of person are you?' But by that time I was halfway down the block; five minutes later I was back in bed, shivering. I've never seen her again."

Invisible Powers

I have no proof that Sidney's experiences are true, or even sane. He still seems balanced to me: his personality has not been thrown into shock or disarray by his "miracles." As he talks he does not float in the clouds of grandiosity, nor has he suffered from the backlash of depression and disillusionment that typically follows an episode of mania. The fact that he is trying to integrate these remarkable happenings into a new view of himself reassures me, because that means they have been nourishing rather than destructive.

However, the backlash may be just around the corner. It is dangerous to rush into a wonder world. At best, people like Sidney are jewels without a setting, as Maharishi once called them. That is to say, they lack a context that will make sense of the transformation they have gone through. I can understand why Sidney calls his strange episodes "miracles," but he has lapsed into a conventional religious vocabulary for want of a clearer and more precise one. He needs new words, and with them, he needs explanations that apply directly to his situation.

In this light, it is not all that important to decide whether I "believe" in Sidney's story or not. Other people's revelations are unshareable to begin with. If I stood beside Sidney while he was simply gazing at a daffodil, his perception would be just as ephemeral, unreachable, and private as anything he told me about. The critical thing for each of us is to understand our own revelations.

The first step, I think, is to dispel the aura of wonder-working that surrounds the unfoldment of higher states of consciousness. A disciple once complained to his guru, "If you are enlightened, why don't you perform miracles to prove it?" The guru answered, "Because there are no miracles, unless you consider all of life a miracle. I am beyond miracles. I am normal."

Isn't that the wisest perspective? Human awareness has never lost its capacity to open up into the invisible world, and we can be certain that a farmer in the time of Zoroaster looked up at the stars, suddenly near and alive and smiling, with the same awe as Sidney. When you point out to someone that he is not the first person to enter a state of grace, the news comes as a great disappointment at first—in our heart of hearts, we all hunger for the uniqueness of sainthood. But on sober reflection, people who experience wonders are very relieved to know that they are not alone. Indeed, to find that there is a magnificent, broad, endless river of spirit running through the tumult of human existence brings tremendous joy.

"Should I try to encourage these experiences?" Sidney asked at one point, "or should I turn my back on them? They are incredibly seductive, and yet, I can see that they might be too alluring. I could plunge into complete fantasy. Who knows, I may already be there."

"No, you're not lost in fantasy," I said. "You are walking a fine line that your past experience has not prepared you for at all." I urged him to stop hanging out in mental space by himself; he needed a safety net. The entire range of spiritual experiences has been catalogued and analyzed in the ancient traditions of wisdom. The Vedic rishis stand as the most authoritative commentators, being the most ancient, but any continuous, living spiritual tradition has one great advantage —it provides a map of the journey and identifies the destination.

The reason this is so important is that an experience of healing or communion or expansion is usually part of a larger journey as well, pointing the person toward an unseen goal. The ecstasy of one miracle is nothing compared to the ecstasy of complete spiritual transformation. This perspective makes all the difference between growth and chaos. Instead of drifting from one experience to another, one sights a purpose—a higher state of consciousness—and aims for it. The Vedic seers were unwavering in their belief that fulfillment is the natural tendency of life. Growth, evolution, the bewildering activity of the mind are not chaotic. They are trying to break out of the finite and into the infinite.

Without applying any kind of esoteric terminology, we can say that for Sidney, reality is widening, breaking out of the usual patterns that bolster our sense of what is acceptable and tolerable. Even to bend these boundaries can create a feeling of vertigo, as if the ground itself and not just our assumptions was being cut out from under us.

One time a young patient entered my office with the startling words *"Namaste kya hal hai, Doctor sahib?"* It would not be at all startling for an Indian to say, "Greetings, doctor, how are you?" but this man had blue eyes and curly blond hair.

"Where did you learn to speak Hindi so well?" I asked curiously. "You hardly have any accent at all."

"I picked it up in New Delhi," he replied. "I was at Hindu

College for a while, and I was born and raised in Kashmir." I accepted this explanation, and we went into his medical complaint, which was minor. After writing out a prescription, I was about to close his file when I noticed that it read, "Place of birth: Santa Barbara, Calif."

"Wait a minute," I said. "Didn't you say you were born in Kashmir?"

"That's right."

"But your chart says you were born in Santa Barbara."

"I should have explained," he murmured without missing a beat, "I was born in Kashmir last time."

"Oh. Is that also when you learned Hindi?"

"Right." His tone of voice remained blandly matter-of-fact. My first instinct was to keep asking him questions to see if he would give me a few overt signs of mental disturbance.

"I notice that you work as a bartender at a hotel downtown," I said. "That's not a very pure place, I mean for someone who is sensitive enough to remember his past lives."

"I know," he sighed, "but I stay there out of nostalgia. It reminds me of the officer's mess at Mhow." Mhow was one of the most famous military outposts established by the British in central India. It is still so large that most Indian army officers can count on being stationed there at least once in their careers.

"You remember Mhow, too?" I asked.

"Sure," he said cheerfully, "that's where I was killed." We continued to chat amiably in this vein, as if nothing unusual was going on, and after a few minutes I reluctantly let him go. At the time, I felt guilty that I hadn't injected him with 100 milligrams of Thorazine to calm his hallucinations before committing him to a psychiatric ward. Now I find it difficult to separate his strangeness from my own discomfort, which was making him seem strange. It is a mark of our times that all manner of "impossible" things are surfacing before our very eyes, like ancient sea creatures that were given up as extinct but were only sleeping in the depths.

What we can hope to do is to clarify where these reemerging experiences actually originate. There is an age-old tendency for humans to look outside themselves whenever the everyday logic of the world crumbles. One day there is ecstasy where none existed before. Who could cause such a drastic transformation but a divine agent located in the realm of heaven? Heaven and earth come closer together, however, through the physicist's concept of the quantum field. There is no such thing as being outside the field looking in, whether it be God looking down on man or man up to God. We are all part of the field; the field is existence itself, flowing in, around, and through everything. It is the arena where all possibilities unfold.

The field is omnipresent and omnipotent. It invisibly unites two quarks that are light-years apart; it blends individual and cosmic existence, the natural and the supernatural. When their awareness was fully expanded, the ancient rishis were able to declare, echoing Lord Krishna, "I am the field." They saw that their own individual consciousness was identical to the consciousness that upholds the universe. They were conferring the quality of omniscience upon the field—and that gives pause. In the West, to be all-knowing is an attribute exclusive to God, unless you accept that the field is a proper home for the divine. But why shouldn't it be?

The idea that the sacred is outside us makes no sense in quantum terms, because it takes our participation to construct all experience, from the sacred to the profane. When my father was stationed at the big army cantonment at Jabalpur in central India, Prime Minister Nehru came for a one-day visit. It was the early Fifties, and Nehru was considered the savior of India by us and everyone we knew. The whole town poured out to greet him. People milled as thick as ants as far as you could see. Men climbed trees to catch a glimpse of Nehru's open jeep trundling through the street, and agile little boys filled the top branches.

I was just seven and had no clear idea why my father and mother were standing there, mute members of a silence so loud that it was nearly deafening. But I am quite clear that the crowd was silent, and as Nehru approached, standing up on the back seat of the jeep with a rose in his hand, a wave of reverential awe swelled before him. My mother began crying, and as fate would have it, Nehru threw his rose almost at her feet. No one ran forward. The silence endured, and my mother slowly walked over and bent to gather her flower. The

next day people came to our house to see the rose in its silver
vase, and without fail they could not speak when they laid
eyes on it.

What I know now is that their exalted feelings came from
an inner source, not solely from Nehru, perhaps not at all
from him. The crowd participated in a collective reality; they
felt an emotion and let it sprout into independent existence,
until it resided even in a casually tossed flower. This does not
make their sacred feeling unreal, far from it. Whenever a flow
of consciousness moves up from the depths of the human
spirit, great transformations can occur with dramatic speed.
Tearing down the Berlin wall signaled a new rise of freedom
that was taking place among nations. But what is a nation
except a collection of individuals? Politics is what happens
"out there" in response to shifting mental events "in here."
The Berlin wall first had to come down inside people's awareness before it could come down physically.

We do not think of political change in this way mainly
because people are not generally united in their inner perspective. Sometimes, however, a surge of consciousness carries everyone along. Gandhi inspired millions of Indians to
gather silently as a means of protesting British rule; they did
not do anything other than stand or sit together for a time, yet
that in itself created a sort of witness very like the silent witness I tell my patients about. Just to look at your enemy in
peace creates a huge moral effect, because he sees himself in
your eyes. The silent witness reflects the truth that he must
come to terms with in the end.

I do not want to equate collective consciousness only with
emotions or morality; rather, it is the mind we all share beneath the superficial layer of our individual minds. This
shared mind creates our shared world. Therefore, the world is
a map of all that people agree to be real, with the exclusion of
all that they agree to be unreal. The reason that seemingly
impossible things are surfacing again in our culture after
their long sleep is that our collective consciousness has agreed
to let them in. A deep censoring mechanism is losing its
power over us. When the censor is abolished altogether, there
will be no limit to what can be allowed in, for at the level of
the field, all possibilities exist in unmanifest form.

"You are the sole cause of everything in creation," a guru assured his disciples. "All is because you are." The statement reeks of the worst arrogance if we claim that the Big Bang needed our blessing before it could happen. I don't think that is what the guru was saying. He meant that human consciousness and cosmic consciousness are one. The field dances and waits for us to join it. It constantly folds and refolds itself, like an infinite wool blanket tumbling in a dryer at infinite speed. Under these conditions, every point in the universe is everywhere at once, sharing in the omnipotence, omnipresence, and omniscience of the whole field. Everyone has a right, then, to consider himself the center of the cosmos, holding untold powers in his hands.

What the Twins Could Do

Any ability to command nature is called a *siddhi* in Sanskrit. The word means "power," and it refers to powers that have been perfected in consciousness. Healing the sick is a siddhi, and like the supernatural feats that yogis are supposed to be able to perform—flying through the air, turning invisible, reading the past and future—the key to mastery is a shift in awareness. A person suddenly knows how to do something impossible, as simply and easily as I know how to lift my arm. A shift in awareness does not require force. A person who has achieved the level of consciousness where siddhis are natural can breathe change into things as softly as you or I wish and dream, using no more energy than it takes to stir a thought. The basic principle here is that reality is different in different states of consciousness. If I see a tree in my dreams, I can jump over it or make it turn blue or fly over it into the sky. What gives me such powers is the dream state. If I had no other state of awareness to compare it to, the dream state would constitute the only reality I know and accept as valid.

On waking up, I find that I cannot jump over a tree anymore, but why not? According to the rishis, what holds me back is not the tree but the arrival of waking-state consciousness. It has propelled me into a world that obeys different laws of nature. "You think that a dream tree is inside your head," a rishi might argue, "while a real tree is outside you. But this notion can only occur to you *after* you wake up. As long as you are in your dream, the tree seems to be outside you, just as it is in a waking state. In truth, what you take to be the only 'real' tree should be called a waking-state tree. If you cannot jump over it, perhaps you need to wake up from waking. Then you would discover that this tree, too, was in your head."

A siddhi seems particularly amazing when it crops up among people whose minds lack ordinary abilities, much less extraordinary ones. In his much-praised essay "The Twins," Oliver Sacks describes two brothers, identical twins, who were able to perform prodigious feats of mental calculation, despite the fact that they repeatedly tested with IQs no higher than sixty. When Sacks first met them in 1966, the twins were in their mid-twenties and already mildly famous. In appearance they resembled a grotesque Tweedledum and Tweedledee—equally rotund, with thick glasses, bobbing heads, rolling eyes, and various uncontrollable tics and twitches.

Although the twins lived in a private mental world closed to outsiders, Sacks found them pathetically eager to launch into one of their "routines":

> The twins say, "Give us a date—any time in the last or next forty thousand years." You give them a date, and, almost instantly, they tell you what day of the week it would be. "Another date!" they cry, and the performance is repeated. They will also tell you the date of Easter during the same period of 80,000 years. . . . Their memory for digits is remarkable—and possibly unlimited. They will repeat a number of three digits, of thirty digits, of three hundred digits, with equal ease.

The literature on idiot savants is vast; the twins' astonishing talents do not make them unique. Instead, they fall into the well-studied class of "mental calculators," which includes people, both retarded and normal, who can recite from memory the number π to 3,000 decimal places, or tell you how many cubic inches there are in a solid measuring 7,345,278 yards on one side and 5,478,234 yards on the other. (One eight-year-old savant was posed such a problem and instantly replied, "Do you want the answer backwards or forwards?")

But, to my knowledge, Sacks is the first observer who had the insight that the twins were not calculating at all—they were *seeing* numbers. Their minds rummaged in the land of numerals the same way we rummage for old faces in our memories, but with amazing precision, clarity, and speed. The argument Sacks makes is simple. On their own, the twins could not perform basic arithmetic. Adding four plus four baffled them, and it was only after years of training that they could reliably make change in order to ride the bus. The standard explanation for "calendar idiots" is that they have memorized a shortcut, a special mathematical formula or algorithm, that is programmed to give dates without the calculator having to run through the calendar year by year. This is how one would program a computer to name the date of Easter over a period of 80,000 years.

But is it really possible, Sacks wonders, for the twins to calculate at all, even using a shortcut, when they cannot add simple numbers? On the other hand, their ability to visualize had been proven over and over. If you named any day in their lives after the age of four, they could tell you the weather, the incidents occurring around them, and the important political events on that day. Sacks also took careful clinical note of the look on their faces when they were coming up with their extraordinary answers: "Their eyes fix and move in a peculiar way as they do this, as if they were unrolling, or scrutinizing, an inner landscape."

This look of "seeing," complete with eyes rolled upward and a flat, monotonous delivery of the answer, as if reciting from a printout, may seem similar to the look of someone who is mentally calculating, but how could one account for two other facts? First, the twins could "see" prime numbers that were ten and even twenty digits long. Thirty years ago, extracting very long prime numbers was a laborious feat even for the largest mainframe computers, and there was no known shortcut. Yet here were the twins, giggling in their corner, extracting such long primes that Sacks could not check them in a standard mathematical reference book.

Even more mysteriously, it was observed that only one of the twins had been fascinated by numbers at first, early in childhood, and later had somehow passed on his prodigious talents, with no loss of accuracy, to his brother. Duplicate masters in every way, the twins sat for hours in a corner by themselves, murmuring long strings of numerals and gurgling with shared delight over some arcane find that no one else could comprehend.

It is hard to escape the conclusion that the twins in fact possessed a siddhi, one well known in ancient India, called *Jyotish Mati Pragya*—the ability to see into the light. At a subtle level, the rishis say, everything is made of light; light is the finest level of appearance before creation dissolves into pure consciousness. By some means or other, the twins attuned their minds to this level of awareness. And they appeared to know that this was what they were doing. Sacks writes, "If you ask them how they can hold so much in their minds—a three-hundred-figure digit, or the trillion events of four decades—they say very simply, 'We see it.'"

The twins' methods give us a model for how siddhis work in general. A siddhi is a mental ability, no different from ordinary thinking except that it runs deeper. One has to go right to the edge where pure consciousness is about to emerge into its created forms. To put it in the language of physics, a local intention begins to have nonlocal results. Instead of being confined inside my skull, my desire to see a twenty-digit prime number radiates into the field, and the field brings back the answer.

It is not "me," in the most local sense, who has worked out the solution. The field is acting upon itself, folding question and answer together until they meet in time and space. My role is simply to issue the orders, leaving the field to compute, instantly and automatically, whatever result I want. The secret to any siddhi is that you tap into the cosmic computer using the brain as your keyboard.

Siddhis can come spontaneously, as happened to the twins, but more often they have to be cultivated. (The third part of rishi Patanjali's definitive treatise on Yoga, the *Yoga*

Sutras, contains the classic teaching on how to attain siddhis. In modern times, Maharishi has revived the same techniques in an advanced program taught as a follow-up to TM.) The first stage is meditation, which brings the mind into the transcendent; the second stage is to hold onto the transcendent while thinking a specific thought. This sounds like a complete contradiction, and it is. The transcendent by definition is silent and void of thoughts. But the rishis discovered centuries ago that a person can entertain two states of awareness at the same time.

A siddhi throws together everyday awareness with transcendent awareness, and when the two are completely blended, nature begins to respond to one's most casual desires as commands. In itself, this is a wondrous development, but it serves a higher end, which is to rob ordinary reality of its power to keep people ensnared. This is always the aim of Yoga in all its phases. "Once you realize that the world is your own projection, you will be free of it," a guru told his followers. "Everything existing around you is painted on the screen of your consciousness. The picture you see may be ugly or beautiful, but in either case you are not bound by it. Rest assured, there is no one who has forced it on you. You are trapped only because of your habit of mistaking the imaginary for the real."

This is how reality appears from a higher state of consciousness. The siddhis are an essential part of reaching such a state, a stepping-stone. They allow us to experiment with the world illusion. A friend recently told me this story: "Several years ago I took my car on a camping trip through the Far West. One morning in Montana I woke up thinking how splendid it would be to see a rainbow. Not that I had much hope for one—the day was dark and overcast. We started climbing a high mountain pass near Glacier Park that was shrouded in mists. Suddenly, the mists parted, moved aside by invisible stagehands, and a glorious rainbow connected two peaks directly in front of me, as if the gods had fashioned a sparkling bridge of light.

"It was a dazzling sight and an interesting coincidence. We moved down the Rockies to Wyoming, and the next day I saw an impressive rainbow in the Tetons, leaping down into the waters of Jackson Lake. Another rainbow appeared the following day in the Green Mountains, another near Aspen the day after that. This went on for six days. On the seventh I found myself deep in a desert canyon in Utah. There had been no rain for weeks; the July sky was broiling hot and completely free of clouds. Around noon I looked up and saw an impossible vision, a small but vivid rainbow arching over the narrow white sandstone arroyo we had camped in. What could have caused it?

"I am not the kind of person who jumps to miraculous conclusions, and a few days later a park ranger told me about an interesting phenomenon: If the sun is hot enough, its heat can cause a temperature inversion over the desert. Humidity rising up from the canyons remains trapped by the cooler air above, and at times there are enough water droplets in a thin layer over the canyon rim to create a rainbow. So in the end, there was a natural explanation for everything I had seen. Nature herself had the means to make rainbows. Yet I am left believing that she also has the means to make them when and where I want."

The Mind of the Fire

The rishis felt completely comfortable with a quantum fact, that our solid world is basically built up from vibrations in empty space. However, we are not yet comfortable with a Vedic fact, that this space that permeates everything is intelligent. It is *Chit Akasha,* or "mind space." Mind space is inside our heads and gives rise to thought "in here," but it exists outside our heads as well. Nietzsche offered a remark that challenges Western logic to the core when he said, "All philosophy is based upon the premise that we think, but it is equally possible that we are being thought."

Because our conventional system of logic holds that thinking is always internal, we do not see the natural processes taking place all around us as a kind of thinking, but that is just a cultural bias. We could see Chit Akasha everywhere, and if we did, we would realize that everything in nature is a transformation of mind space from one guise to another. The rocks, mountains, oceans, and galaxies are constantly being thought, just as much as we.

To give a concrete example, there is the phenomenon of firewalking, which caught the popular imagination as a fad several years ago, but which has persisted in various traditional cultures as a mainstay of spiritual experience for centuries. Anthropologist Loring Danforth's *Firewalking and Religious Healing* is a fascinating account of one of these firewalking cults, the Anastenaria in northern Greece.

No one knows how the cult began. One legend holds that a raging fire broke out in the village church at Kosti in eastern Thrace untold centuries ago. Bystanders heard loud cries coming from inside the empty building. Amazed, they realized that it was the painted icons of Saint Constantine and his mother, Saint Helen, who were calling to be rescued. A few courageous villagers recklessly rushed into the fire, and when they emerged with the icons in their arms, neither they nor the saints had been harmed.

In memory of this miracle, the devotees of Saint Constantine celebrate his name day, May 21, by walking into a pit of burning coals, and not just walking: they perform a stomping dance on the red-hot cinders, holding aloft icons of the two saints. Perhaps a hundred devout firewalkers, called Anastenarides, are scattered throughout a few villages in northern Greece; almost all of them trace their roots back to Kosti.

To show their unshakable faith and their contempt for the fire, the Anastenaria dancers pick up glowing embers, smashing them into a shower of sparks with their bare hands. One devotee named Stephanos spent five months mesmerized before his home fire, putting out the live coals with his hands hour after hour until his mother begged him to stop, for fear that she would not have any fire left for baking her family's bread.

Without their religious faith, the Greek firewalkers are certain that they would be burned. They each "belong to the saints," having surrendered themselves to divine authority in exchange for their extraordinary powers. Walking into the fire sets a person aside from normal society for the rest of his life;

he is said to have an open road, which means that the saints can guide him anywhere they choose.

One of the firewalkers is a peasant farmer named Mihalis. He recounted how he feels during his fiery dance: "If you have an open road, then you don't feel the fire as if it were your enemy. You feel as if it were your husband or your wife. You feel love for the fire; you have courage. What you see isn't a mountain; it's nothing. That way you go in freely. But if you go in of your own will, then you have fear and doubt. It seems like an enemy, like a mountain. If your courage is from the Saint, then you really want to go into the fire. The power comes from outside. You're a different person."

At the outset of this book I mentioned that some paranoiacs can no longer draw the line between their own mind and God's. In their madness, these people take personal responsibility for averting wars and natural disasters. Mihalis and his cohorts are caught in a similar confusion, but from the opposite pole. They cannot accept that their power to walk on fire is personal, or even specifically human. They insist that it must come from God, through the saints' intercession. It would be inexplicable to them if someone walked on the coals without being devout.

In fact such a person appeared in their midst. In 1985 a tall, smiling, handsome American arrived on Saint Constantine's feast day in the village of Langadas, where the Anastenaria rite is performed. At a restaurant he showed around a photograph of himself firewalking in Oregon, and he was immediately permitted to join the local ceremony. The year before, an Italian spectator had attempted to enter the fire and had been severely burned. The Greek firewalkers took this as confirmation that one cannot defy the fire without the saints.

But this year's visitor was something no one had ever seen, a firewalk instructor. Outside the confined world of the Anastenaria cult, firewalking had become a star turn in the human potential movement, with firewalk "seminars" being held every weekend throughout the West Coast. In its New Age guise, walking into the fire was a form of psychotherapy. It was considered a liberating experience, perhaps endowed with spiritual overtones but not narrowly religious. Therefore, when the visitor, named Ken Cadigan, entered the Anastenaria fire, two worlds collided.

At first there was no open conflict. "Ken managed to make his way through the crowd to the site of the firewalk together with the Anastenarides," Danforth writes. "He danced around the fire with them for a few minutes. Then, after [their leader] Stamatis crossed the fire, Ken went across too. He was dressed in white and held his hands high over his head. 'I didn't have the dance down right,' he said. 'I just went boogying across.'"

We do not know what went through the minds of the Greek firewalkers, but a sinister gesture ensued. "After Ken crossed the fire two or three times," Danforth writes, "he saw Stamatis motion to another Anastenaris to take Ken through the fire with him. The Anastenaris grabbed him by the arm, but Ken broke free. He went back into the fire again, and this time he stayed in for a long time; he really *danced* in the coals. Just then the Anastenaris grabbed his arm a second time, held him in the fire, and stepped on his foot. . . . Ken broke free again and left the fire."

The local crowd had been cheering for the tall stranger, and several reporters now besieged him with questions. How did he walk on fire without being a devotee? Had he been burned at the end? Cadigan joked about the incident and refused to attribute any malice to the man who had accosted him. Privately, however, he was sure that the Anastenaris had pushed him into the coals hoping he would be burned. In fact, he had been.

One of the peculiarities of firewalking is that belief plays such a critical part in it. A skeptic can enter the fire one step behind a believer, and only the skeptic will be burned. An experienced firewalker can be distracted by someone shouting at him from the sidelines and suddenly get burned also. Since the fire is the same temperature for all (hot enough to sear flesh in a matter of seconds), one is convinced that awareness must be playing a crucial role.

There are reports of people who have been severely burned when they rashly stepped onto the coals despite an inner voice that tried to halt them with a sharp warning of "Don't do this!" At the same sessions, others have walked in without harm. There is no scientific explanation for what causes these variances, or for that matter, for how the feat of firewalking is accomplished. In this instance, when Cadigan was drawn into the ugly mood of his assailant, he lost his power to remain unharmed. Danforth notes that even though Cadigan's burns went deep enough to expose the nerves in his foot, he felt no pain either on the fire or afterward.

As he gathered his data, Danforth moved among the Anastenarides, who buzzed with talk after the American left. Quickly and reflexively the Greek firewalkers retreated into rationalization: they claimed that their visitor had walked too quickly across the coals, that he had not really danced, that he had left the ceremony early because he had been burned. In this way the cultists retained their ties to the saints and their exclusive right to an open road.

Yet the main theme of their spiritual life—acquiring power and freedom in the fire—is the same espoused by New Age practitioners. "You are burned by fear, not by fire" is a popular sentiment among American firewalkers. In both camps the fire is a symbol for inner barriers that one must break through in order to prove that reality is more than the senses perceive. But we have to probe deeper and ask, "What is the link between the subjective world of the firewalker and the burning coals?"

The firewalker *thinks* he can enter the fire safely, and therefore he can. His thought causes the fire to become harmless, which implies that the fire *understands* him. The Greek firewalkers accept this assumption: they frequently say that the fire beckons them. They know to walk onto the coals only after the fire says "yes." It is difficult to avoid the conclusion that the fire is in fact intelligent.

If the idea of intelligent fire is too shocking, we could say that one continuous field of mind-stuff links the firewalker and the fire. When a person thinks, that is one vibration in the field; when the fire cools down, that is another. So it is all field speaking to field, without any mystery to it. Mihalis does not really walk into the fire; he walks into the outskirts of his own mind.

Two Fullnesses

It is hard to deny that our reality remains stubbornly intact because our logic is stubbornly rational, geared solely to the events of the waking state. A dreamer can fly because defying gravity in a dream is just a matter of altering one's brain wave patterns: everything that occurs in a dream, no matter how bizarre, is clearly self-generated. Yet the same holds true in waking state, with a difference. Sitting in my chair this minute, I might think, "I want to fly," and nothing will happen. I lack the power of a dreamer, or so it seems, and the reason, I tell myself, is that certain laws of nature have been set aside out of my control, gravity being a prominent example.

However, the rishis would argue that this setting aside is itself a human act. What holds me down to earth is not the fact that gravity is a law of nature. It is the *choice* of laws that happen to be in effect. When a person has reached a higher state of consciousness, he realizes that such choices are always being made and can also be unmade. For every natural law that holds me down in my chair, another, still asleep in the field, would allow me to fly.

Gaining the siddhis means gaining freedom of choice. The rishis say, *"Purnam adah, purnam idam,"* which means, "This is full, that is full." The word *this* signifies the manifest reality I see all around me; the word *that* signifies the unseen world of the transcendent, the world of Being, the field. Both worlds are full—i.e., infinite—and if I do not like the natural laws that trap me here, I can find alternatives inside the field. I don't have to defy the current set of laws, but only wake up a new one. This is how fire can be convincingly hot at one time and cold the next.

The doctrine of "This is full, that is full" causes the yogi to declare that nature is perfect. He is not referring to the picture that reality presents today, nor is he glossing over the gross imperfections that create suffering. The cruelty and violence we see in our world cannot be called perfect by any means. But another kind of world is also available, at the touch of Being, and that fact overrides the evil we are witness to in daily life. Nature is perfect because it contains all possibilities.

The point was made thirty years ago in a fascinating exchange between Maharishi and a skeptical questioner who stood up in a London lecture audience:

> Q: I do not accept that the workings of nature's intelligence are already perfect. I could make the universe along more humane lines, with less suffering, less pain.
>
> Maharishi: Then there would not be any consistency in your universe.
>
> Q: We do not need consistency.
>
> Maharishi: Oh! Then you cannot run anything whatsoever in a systematic way—it will only be chaos. For example, in your universe, you would touch fire and the fire would not burn you. Likewise, you would put rice on the fire to cook, and the fire will not cook it!
>
> Q: But there are those who walk on fire and the fire does not burn them.
>
> Maharishi: That is also the work of almighty nature: that which is hot under certain circumstances is also cool under other circumstances. So if you were going to create the same situation in your universe, you now find that it is already here! A small mind will only create half a world. Unable to see the whole, it only sees parts of the whole.

We are just beginning to abandon the parts to accept a vision of the whole. Seventy years ago the great quantum physicists of Einstein's generation postulated that "local reality" was a dubious proposition. "Local reality" is a term that describes separate events leading independent lives in time and space. An atom of oxygen on Mars is local because it has nothing to do with an atom of oxygen on Venus, just as a suffering man in China has nothing to do with me. On the human level, this arrangement has never seemed satisfactory, because in sympathy I do suffer with the man in China.

Before the advent of quantum theory, the same could not

be said of two atoms. In order for them to be in sympathy, one would have to negate the millions of miles of void that separate them. Common sense says that emptiness is empty; by definition it cannot have anything in it. Today, however, it is known from radio telescope observation that the universe has organized itself along orderly lines across vast distances. Stars at one end of the cosmos obey the same structural laws and pass through the same life stages as those at the other end. It can also be proved in the laboratory that certain elementary particles are paired like twins (according to a principle called "spin type"), and a change of spin in one is instantly matched by an equal but opposite change in its mate, whatever the distance between them. They are connected by a telephone wire that happens to be made of nothing.

Such strange behavior defies ordinary logic. It has led physicists to say that the quantum realm is not only stranger than we think but stranger than we *can* think. The rishi disagrees. To him, a quantum and a thought are remarkably alike. The fleeting, invisible impulses of the mind can turn into concrete, locatable neurotransmitter molecules like dopamine and serotonin. Where can you stand to watch an emotion turn into a molecule? Nowhere—you cannot see or touch an emotion; you can barely pin it down in time, and it has no home in space whatever. Molecules can be objectively seen, stored, and manipulated. They are easier to deal with than emotions, and therefore scientists always assume that the reality of molecules should be the benchmark, while the reality of emotions is somehow inferior.

In the quantum world this situation changes. A quantum event is also invisible, fleeting, and unpredictable, just like our thoughts. Before the sun throws out light, where is the light? Photons come out of nowhere; they cannot be stored. They can barely be pinned down in time and have no home in space whatever (that is, light occupies no volume and has no mass). The similarity between a thought and a photon is very deep.

Thinking is a quantum activity, which is why it permits us to control the laws of nature. Because he is enlightened, a rishi does this far better than I do, but I am not without talent. Consider the calcium that builds a femur, clavicle, or any other bone. The calcium in my body is not fixed in place but constantly flowing. It moves from bone to bone as need dictates (when you wear a new pair of shoes long enough, for example, your leg bones change their inner structure to adjust to your new gait). Calcium also moves out of our bones into the blood, and my skin and urine are sloughing calcium into the world while I take in new quantities through food. I control this constant flow with great precision, even though I am unaware of how I do that.

The white cliffs of Dover, which are made of calcium carbonate, could be entering my bones today, via the sheep that graze on their slopes and then go to market. At every step of the way, from cliff to grass to sheep to lamb roast to blood and finally to bone, the calcium atoms remain unchanged. I don't resemble a cliff or a sheep, however, because once the calcium enters me, it must be transformed. It suffers a sea change into me, a complex structure of intelligence. This change occurs at the quantum level, where everything in creation is given its identity. Even as the calcium flies in and out, circulating in me like leaves in the wind, I remain myself, solidly structured in my quantum mechanical body.

I have read that with every breath one breathes, one takes in several million atoms breathed out by Christ, Buddha, Confucius, and every other luminary who ever lived (there is plenty of room for this, since we breathe in 10^{22} oxygen atoms at a time, or 10 followed by 21 zeros). Also, a few millionths of every breath I inhale today left the lungs of a peasant in China yesterday; his exhalation takes barely twenty-four hours to travel halfway around the globe and mix into my local atmosphere.

This is a marvelous fact, but more marvelous is that I do not turn into Christ, Buddha, or a Chinese peasant. My identity is grounded in the field, and when raw matter enters me, I stamp it with my influence. If I turn afraid, so does my calcium; when I die, I release my calcium to freedom before another mind captures it again. In this way, local mind and universal mind are constantly cooperating.

What the rishis saw so clearly was that the quantum field is a creative source for each person to play in, like a mud bank waiting for a child to make mud pies, mud dolls, or mud houses. You cannot see any objects in the featureless mud, and yet in a sense all objects have the potential to be in it. The most famous sentence in the Upanishads declares, "I am That, thou art That, and all this is That." A quantum physicist could not quibble with these assertions, once he translated the word "That" as "the field."

Despite the infinite power and vastness of the field, it doesn't take a great leap to command it—we do that every time we have a thought. But to gain real mastery, to make our deepest desires come true, we must commit ourselves to reach a higher state of consciousness. Like any force in nature, the force of awareness can be weak or strong. It is strongest in people whose minds are identified with the field, weakest in those whose minds are stranded on the surface of life. To identify fully with the field, then, is a practical definition of what it means to be enlightened. Only then do the hindrances of local reality disappear. One is free at last to join the creative play of the universe.

When people find that their desires are beginning to come true, in defiance of how reality is supposed to behave, the sudden influx of power brings with it vaulting emotions—people feel jubilant and triumphant; they feel fused with the very heart of nature ("I was like an orphan who found the way home," one woman remembers). Fear becomes meaningless, replaced with immense relief at the true simplicity of life.

Simplicity is the key. The rishis lived by a code that depends upon magic rather than struggle. Maharishi expresses this code beautifully:

Keep your desire turning back within and be patient. Allow the fulfillment to come to you, gently resisting the temptation to chase your dreams into the world. Pursue them in your heart until they disappear into the self, and leave them there.

It may take a little self-discipline, but be simple, be kind. Attend to your inner health and happiness. Happiness radiates like the fragrance from a flower and draws all good things toward you.

Allow your love to nourish yourself as well as others. Do not strain after the needs of life—it is sufficient to be quietly alert and aware of them. In this way life proceeds more naturally and effortlessly. Life is here to enjoy.

Just by being ourselves, we are borne toward a destiny far beyond anything we could imagine. It is enough to know that the being I nourish inside me is the same as the Being that suffuses every atom of the cosmos. When the two see each other as equals, they will be equal, because then the same force that controls the galaxies will be upholding my individual existence. If a man claims to be enlightened, I only need to ask, "Do your desires effortlessly come true?" If he says yes, I can accept that his thinking has turned magical.

But I would also ask a second question, "On what scale do you have your desires?" If he says his desires are for himself, I will know that he has not broken free of local reality. On the other hand, if he says that his desires are for the world, I will know that the entire universe works on his behalf. He has mastered nonlocal reality—he is a citizen of the field.

12

~~~~~~~~~~~~~~~~

What It Means to Be Whole

$\mathbf{T}$o give them the benefit of the doubt, Nick's parents did not deliberately set out to destroy him. Quite the reverse: from the time Nick was born they treated him like a little god. All the toys a rich family could provide were laid at his feet, and the slightest wish was instantly granted. His infant goos and gurgles delighted his mother so much that she could not bear to let him out of her sight. If she was forced to tear herself away for even half an hour, Nick's grandparents stepped in to take her place, and they, too, loved him so much that they never let him out of their sight, either.

For three years Nick accepted as normal the constant gaze of adult eyes. He was much too little to suspect that he might be under guard. Then one day his mother took him aside and tried to make him understand something important. Thirty-five years later, he still remembers the intense emotion in her voice.

"You came out of me, and you are a part of me. That will always be true," she said. "But your father and I want you to know something. You didn't come the way other babies did. You were adopted." Nick smiled, delighted by this new word. He was not old enough to wonder how he could have come out of his mother and been adopted at the same time. He only knew that he was even more special than before. "I'm adopted! I'm adopted!" he kept repeating, and he immediately rushed off to tell his best friend the good news. It took two years before he fully grasped what being adopted meant.

"My parents have always held on to me very tightly," he told me, "and little by little I became aware that their love was colored by a great deal of desperation. They were obsessed with me. The reason I was constantly watched was that they had this morbid fear that I would be kidnapped by my real mother, like a fairy-tale prince stolen in the night by gypsies."

Keeping Nick under constant watch was the only way his parents had of handling their fear of losing him. In itself, this anxious, doting attention might not have been too destructive. But, as soon became apparent, there was much more involved.

"There's something wrong with my father," Nick said. "I guess you could call him a misogynist, a woman-hater. He would be shocked to hear that, because he is very affectionate towards my mother, and he makes a great show of acting extremely romantic around her, particularly in public. But in subtle ways he constantly degrades and belittles her. I have never seen him strike her, but it became clear to me as a young child that she lives in fear of him and is helpless to do anything about it."

The same fear crept into Nick's own life as he passed the toddler stage. He discovered that his loving father, who hugged him so tight and showered him with gifts, could fly into a blind rage without warning. At the most unexpected moments he would lash out, and the inhibitions that kept him from physically hurting his wife did not apply to his little boy.

"My father hit me a lot, for reasons that I could not figure out. I never really did anything that bad. My mother and I bent over backwards to placate my father, to always stay on his good side, but if I said something in a tone of voice he didn't like, or if I hesitated to obey one of his orders, he would slap my face or spank me hard, very hard."

Nick has guilty memories of hiding the bruises that his father inflicted with his hard spankings, of feeling like an innocent victim and yet at the same time being inexplicably ashamed whenever he was punished. "I want to be fair to my father," he carefully explained. "He didn't push the violence to extremes. I wasn't battered. What hurt so much was not how hard he hit but where the punishment was coming from. What had I ever done to him to deserve his contempt?"

The fact that he was beaten for the most trivial infractions—not picking up his socks, leaving his room untidy—made it impossible for Nick to sort out why he was being punished. Whatever the emotions were that drove his father, they were too alien for a small child to comprehend, and much too powerful to defend himself against. Although Nick's mother feebly tried to intervene, his father's rage ruled the house basically without opposition.

Unable to fight back physically, Nick took his cues from his mother and turned his energies to keeping the peace. Without protest he was drawn into a conspiracy of silence, preserving the facade of being a perfect child nestled in a perfect family. "When I grew up, I found out that we were living out a pattern of denial that is very common in families like ours. But at the time, I had nothing to compare my situation to. My mother knew what was going on, but she turned her back, and soon I had to accept the bitter fact that she would not try to protect me, no matter how bad things got."

Throwing himself into the role of model child, Nick became the kind of offspring parents dream of having. He was an intelligent, sensitive boy, well behaved and diligent in his schoolwork. He grew up to be magnetically good-looking, and other boys looked up to him as a natural athlete and a born leader. Success followed success, and yet festering underneath it all, like rotten wood covered with gold leaf, was a feeling of dread that never left him.

"I learned to keep our secret at any price, particularly from my grandparents—they were Greek immigrants who looked on me as the bright, blond hope. Everyone expected the world of me, and I wanted above all to oblige. At five years old I felt like a little adult. I understood adult feelings and adult ambitions, and the adult need to guard yourself from exposure. The strain inside me was enormous, because everyone in my family was basically living through me."

The deeper Nick's parents buried their own severe emotional problems, the more necessary they found it to manipulate him. His psyche became the stage for playing out their hidden frustrations. "I accepted that I was the sacrificial lamb. What Mommy and Daddy felt, I felt, too. That was my job, to be a buffer between them. I knew it was unfair. I wasn't being allowed any feelings of my own, the child's feelings that my friends had. I was never simply happy or simply sad. My emotions were complicated, because they were grown-up emotions shifted from my parents onto me."

No child is prepared for such pressures, and Nick soon became profoundly confused about the most basic issues of feeling and identity. "I remember calling out in anguish when I was six, asking God why I was being tormented in this way. But what could I do? My mother said I came out of her, and yet she said I was adopted. My father claimed that he loved me, and yet he beat me for no reason. And their whole motive, so they said, was that they wanted me to be a real son to them.

"In some strange way, it all came down to my being adopted. Whenever he hit me, my father seemed to be saying, 'Damn it, you may not be my son, but if I wallop you hard enough, I'll make you mine.' "

Above the Play of Opposites

So far, I am telling Nick's story as he told it to me, from the viewpoint of a thirty-eight-year-old man who vividly remembers the pain of his childhood but who has worked it through. Nick came to me during the last phase of treatment for a serious addiction, at a time when he was beginning to meditate—this has become the anchor for his healed sense of self. Our talks turned on inner issues; the strictly medical problems of being an addict are over with. Forthcoming as Nick is today, the terror of his world as a child can only be guessed at by an outsider. Its real texture and feelings are not apparent in the man I see before me.

The adult Nick is a very understanding person. He has read the books on dysfunctional families and been through the groups. Today he can talk sympathetically about his aged father, the same man who emerges as a monster in his tale.

"My father is seventy now, but he is still emotionally brittle. It's hard to bring up those years without upsetting him," Nick said. "In order to love my parents as they are today, I have accepted responsibility for my past, all of it. I want to get on with my future."

Nick spoke these conciliatory words near the end of our long first interview. The whole time he had been talking, his voice had remained perfectly, almost uncannily calm. But just hearing about his father's aggression had set my own heart pounding. I suddenly realized that I felt more outraged by Nick's story than he seemed to be—and that gave me pause. When an adult is entrusted with a guilty or shameful secret, it may cause extreme psychological distress, but at least he has a formed personality to absorb it. Nick has never been a person separate from his secrets. They were molded into his psyche from his earliest years. I couldn't help but wonder how much of himself Nick had to smother in order to become so accepting.

This was not a subject I intended to probe. After years of painful effort, Nick has made himself into something admirable—he is a good man, sane, kind, and tolerant. But being good is not the same as being whole. The two can be exact opposites, in fact, if goodness is the outcome of a war in which one part of the self must defeat another. Whatever wholeness is, it is not a war. It is a state of mind above conflict, not touched by evil, immune to fear. This degree of psychological freedom may seem unreachable, but the very concept of wholeness means not split into parts, even the basic dualities of good and bad, love and hate, black and white.

Since reality can be divided endlessly, how can wholeness possibly exist, and if it does, how can it be integrated with the fragmented world? The ancient rishis set out to answer these questions, and what they found was this: the human mind can be either silent or active. In that regard, duality is unavoidable. "The play of opposites," as the Upanishads calls it, cannot be abolished. But opposites can coexist without challenging each other—and that is the secret. For wholeness to be a living reality, one must learn how to expand beyond the field of duality, encompassing the most diametrically opposed qualities of life: good and evil, joy and suffering, love and hate.

Thinking about Nick, I realized that his upbringing had fostered a "solution" that many other people have adopted, putting all their energy into making life perfect on the outside while shoving all their fear, anger, and guilt out of sight. In any case, it is not the repression of pain that worries me, for psychiatry has explored that mechanism extensively. But what about the other pole? By pretending that everything was perfect, Nick developed a profound disillusion that anything could *really* be perfect. He equates perfection with deception. Sadly, so do most people.

One of the greatest shocks I had as a young doctor came when I saw how divided most of my patients were. They preserved a public facade up to the very moment I ushered them in from the waiting room. The instant I closed the door, however, the public self crumbled. An overwhelming flood of pain came my way, far more pain than their disease could have caused. A lifetime of pent-up rage, self-doubt, grief, guilt, and remorse poured uncontrollably from these people. I would do what I could, and after half an hour, they just as quickly recomposed themselves, and the public person once again marched out into the waiting room, bidding me good-bye with a cheerfulness that was chilling.

This is exactly what it means to be fragmented, to live under the sway of opposites. It is a condition so far removed from healing that perfection—which could be seen as simply the natural state of life—looms as an enemy. Many neurotic patients go into therapy wanting to be "cured." But the last thing they want is to cry their hearts out or show vulnerability or grieve over lost love or whoop with joy. Yet that is what normal people do if they are in touch with themselves. The deep problem facing not only Nick but everyone is how to break free of boundaries when being a prisoner is the only comfortable way we know how to live.

First of all, one has to be honest enough to admit that life is not perfect already. Although this may sound like the easiest step, it is often the hardest, because it has to be accomplished on the feeling level. Looking around and saying calmly, "Yes, we could do with some improvements here," has nothing to do with buried emotions, feeling trapped, angry, disappointed, humiliated, and in pain. Deny it as they will, everyone has such feelings. The reason I can risk this blanket generalization is that I see no one living a perfect life, and since perfection is both natural and possible, something must be denying it and holding it back.

Once a skeptical disciple was visiting his guru. Modern gurus do not all live in caves, and this one happened to inhabit a tiny apartment in Bombay.

"Is there really any difference between you and me?" the disciple demanded. "I look at us, and I just see two old men sitting in a room waiting for their lunch." The guru replied, "Your level of awareness forces you to see yourself as an old man sitting in a room. But to me, this room and everything in it occupy the smallest speck on the horizon of my awareness."

"Even if you have adopted that perspective, we still live in the same world," the disciple argued.

"No, your world is personal, private, and unshareable. No one else can enter it, because no one can hear or see things exactly as you do; no one else can have your memories, thoughts, and desires. And they are all you have. My world is consciousness itself, open to all, shared by all. In it there is community, insight, love. The individual contains the totality, which makes him real. You are unreal. This private reality you accept without question, bounded by these four walls, by your isolated body and your conditioned mind, is imaginary. It is nothing but a dream."

"Then why do you bother to be here?" the disciple grumbled.

"I don't have to be in your dream," the guru replied, "since I know the truth: I am infinite. But it gives me pleasure to visit your dream, because I may coax you to wake up."

A Speck of Consciousness

For thousands of years, the metaphor of waking up has been applied to describe what it means to move from a state of ignorance to a state of enlightenment. When a person wakes up, he opens his eyes and sees, which he couldn't do while asleep; he moves from a completely inert state of consciousness to one that is alert and responsive; he regains the sense of identity that was lost in sleep. The contrast delivered when a person becomes enlightened is said to be just as stark. But there is a subtle point to grasp: waking up also implies a natural process that does not have to be forced. You do not choose to wake up in the morning—it dawns on you—and despite the sleepy resistance you may put up, eventually you are awake. The rishis believed that spiritual awakening was just as natural and inevitable.

The enlightenment that dawned upon the ancient sages was different from yours or mine only because it came earlier. If only we knew it, we are already moving out of deep sleep. The process is happening at its own pace, often with little, if any, outward sign. Here I think of Nick again. When he was seventeen, he took stock of himself in a poem that shows a keen understanding of the knots that tied up his personality. He also foretold much of his tempestuous future. The poem's hero is a tormented sailor about to journey toward unknown shores:

> *Days and nights of peace*
> *Have turned into success and frustration.*
> *Oh, demonish powers have betrayed my wits,*
> *I am haunted by nothingness.*
> *Away! Away!*
> *I must leave to destroy this self-destruction*
> *Within my aching soul.*

The words are feverish but true: given his chaotic childhood, the young Nick had nothing solid to stand on but his lonely ship—his self—and his great enemy was the threat of self-destruction that recurred throughout his young adulthood. Within a few years he found that the fantasy of escape, which might be viable in a romantic poem, did not work in real life.

Very early on he learned that he would have to struggle just to survive. Constant struggle—against his family, against drug addiction, against his inner demons—has remained the main theme of his existence. Therefore, more than anyone else I know, I would like Nick to see a way out that is beyond struggle. To find that way out, we have to focus on those rare islands of calm when he did not experience struggle. These were the portents of wholeness that his psyche was trying to gain.

If wholeness can be recognized by how it feels, the appropriate feeling is fulfillment. Anything that is deeply fulfilling gives a person the sense of his own completeness. If only for a moment, one reaches a state where "I am" is enough, without cares, without the craving for anything more. One is content to live on life itself, just the air, sunlight, trees, and sky. One lacks for nothing. Being here is the highest reward.

When I was seven I had an experience of this kind that has served as a talisman ever since. Every day I shared a small family ritual with my mother and younger brother Sanjiv, who was four. My mother would draw us close to her while she read verses from the Ramayana, the epic tale of Lord Rama. There is no exact equivalent of this work in the West. It contains the battles and adventures required of an epic, but the Ramayana is also scripture. Rama is both an exiled prince and an incarnation of God. It is impossible to separate his humanity from his divinity, and while Sanjiv and I were captivated by Rama's exploits in battle, the same verses would raise my mother to a pitch of devotional exaltation.

Nor were we just reader and listeners. The Ramayana is recited to music, and my mother would sit at a small harmonium picking out the tunes for each verse. Sanjiv and I sang along, and wherever the music went, so did our emotions. Rama's saga moves from the wildest ecstasy to the depths of despair, touching every emotion in between. When my father walked in the door after work, dressed in his starched army uniform, he never knew whether his wife and children would have tears rolling down their cheeks or be shrieking with delight.

Being a canny storyteller, my mother ended each day's recitation at a suspenseful point in the tale. One day she stopped after the demon Ravana, the arch villain of the saga, shoots Rama's brother Lakshman on the battlefield. Lakshman lies near death, and the only remedy for his poisoned wound is an herb that grows on the mountainsides of the Himalayas. Unfortunately, the battle is taking place in Sri Lanka, hundreds of miles south. Rama's greatest ally is the monkey king Hanuman, who by incredible good fortune can, as he now reveals, fly. He instantly volunteers to bring back the herb that will save Lakshman's life. Hanuman flies to the Himalayas, but when he arrives he cannot find the plant he needs. He searches high and low, knowing that every second is precious. Still the herb is nowhere to be found. Hanuman is beside himself with frustration.

This is where my mother closed the book, leaving us to go to bed that night tingling with dread and anticipation. I had begun to identify myself and Sanjiv with Rama and his younger brother and so felt particularly anxious for Sanjiv. The next day my mother sang to us of how the clever monkey king solved his dilemma. He ripped the mountain up by its roots, bore it through the air to Sri Lanka, and laid it at Rama's feet. The herb was found, and to our joy, Lakshman's life was saved in the nick of time.

Unable to contain our feelings, my mother, brother, and I rushed out into the courtyard. Still singing, we joined hands and began to dance in a ring, faster and faster. I got dizzy and sat down in the dust, laughing. When my head quit swimming, I looked up. Everything I saw had taken on a feeling of utter rightness. I was in the middle of a perfect world, sparkling with clarity and joy. The sky, the sunlight glancing off the trees, the nearby sounds of Delhi traffic, and my smiling mother bending over me fused into an image of complete fulfillment.

Many times since then I have referred back to that momentary feeling, which never fails to remind me of its truth, as enduring in my mind as Rama himself. But what sets this experience apart from the other joys I have felt is that Ravana the demon was included in it. I loved him for shooting Lakshman! His evil enabled good to triumph; it made Rama's whole adventure possible. This was the closest I came, before I knew of spirituality, to grasping the sage's serenity at the rightness of life as a whole. I experienced that the beauty of the totality far exceeds the beauty or ugliness of any single part.

Few people have carried fulfillment far enough to be able to say whether complete, lasting satisfaction is built into human nature, although that is exactly what is claimed in higher states of consciousness. Nick experienced a glimpse of fulfillment for the first time when he was sent to an experimental high school in Vermont. As part of their curriculum, the students spent weeks hiking and mountaineering; they learned self-reliance by camping alone in the woods.

"I would be left on my own for days at a time, and it gave me a sense of self that I had never had," Nick recalled. "There were hours when I was very quiet inside. I felt protected, and remaining at peace with myself seemed like a real possibility." This interlude spent communing with nature made a lasting impression on him, but returning home exposed him once more to the emotional turbulence of his family. His sense of self became tenuous again, glimpsed only in fleeting moments.

A few years later, Nick's father pressured him to drop out of college and take over one of the construction firms that he owned. Nick proved extremely successful at this, but before long he faced his first emotional crisis as an adult. For years, whenever he dared to open his heart to someone else, Nick instantly felt strong pangs of distrust. This was predictable, given that the models of love he learned from as a child, his father and mother, were also powerful models of betrayal. The fused emotions of love and distrust were imprinted on his psyche, and he found it nearly impossible to separate them.

At first this imprint remained at the unconscious level, while Nick went through the normal adolescent rites of dating and casual intimacy. Disaster struck when he turned twenty-five and plunged into a sudden marriage with a woman named Clare. I have almost no sense of what she was like, since Nick says little about her now, except that he divorced her after two stormy years together.

Apparently their period of compatibility lasted little longer than the honeymoon. Nick quickly discovered, to his horror, that he was preprogrammed to treat his wife the way his father treated his mother. "I was under tremendous pressure at work, having discovered too late what a huge mistake I made by going into business for my father. He was a worse tyrant than ever, and when I came home in the evening, I found myself taking my revenge on Clare. I would snap at her and start arguments over nothing.

"Beneath this irrational behavior, which upset me terribly, I wanted to do exactly the opposite, to open up and treat her as a confidante. But there was always a great resistance inside me, like a rock in the middle of my chest."

This is the tragedy of a fragmented self. Certain feelings become impermissible, because the past has made them too threatening to incorporate into oneself. The rock in the middle of Nick's chest was part of him, but it had split off so completely that it felt like a thing, a piece of nonself that could not be moved. "Every time I tried to share a feeling with Clare, I had a dreadful premonition that she would betray me. The two impulses locked together, and I really believe that the most extreme torture could not have forced me to tell her what I was feeling. Like an oyster, I would die if my shell was pried open. Frustrated by what she perceived as my rejection, Clare became estranged, and soon we drifted apart completely."

Nick's marriage ended in failure, but at least he could sense that the war inside himself was not total. A speck of consciousness hovered above the fray. One knows this because Nick saw himself creating the conflict that trapped him, even though he lacked enough awareness to free himself. It would be years before this speck of consciousness became more powerful. For the moment, it only intensified his suffering, because he could see all too clearly how he was victimizing Clare.

Life in Unity

To grow from a speck of consciousness to complete self-awareness is a natural process, although few people get to the end of it. If you close your eyes and sit quietly, you will experience the same feeling of "I am" that a yogi has, but this fundamental sense of self can be very limited or very large. It can be so fragile that a crisis will easily shatter it, or it can be so firm that you could build the world on it.

The fragmented self pretends to be firm and solid, but the rock inside is made of pain, denied emotions, and guilt. This repressed pain eventually makes itself known, either by causing suffering or by bringing up a mirror image (in this case, Nick's wife) which reveals the presence of pain even if the feeling itself cannot be faced. But denial is incredibly powerful. Any reality, however punitive, can be seen as acceptable, even ideal. I was very moved when I read a sentence from one of the Christian church fathers: "God has placed souls in Hell, but in His mercy He allows them to believe that they are actually living in Paradise." This would not be merciful if there was no escape from hellish situations. But if one believes that every person is working his way through the process of awakening, then nothing could be more merciful than letting everyone think that his stage of growth is the best.

All this is to preface the notion of "false unity." There is a huge difference between different states of consciousness, but each one tends to feel as if one has found unity. "Unity" means a sense of being in touch with reality, of seeing things as they are. The most deluded paranoiac, who believes that Martians are going to invade tomorrow, pities the rest of us who cannot share his grasp of reality. Likewise, the saint who sees God in a fallen sparrow has no choice but to accept that his awareness is not shared by everyone, either.

Because we all harbor the secret belief that our level of awareness must be the right one, it seems all but impossible to credit that there is, in fact, a state of *true* unity. The rishis called it *Brahmi Chetna*, "unity consciousness," and declared that it was the goal toward which all other states of consciousness are evolving. Anyone who has a speck of self-awareness is heading, however haltingly, toward it. The difference between me, a man who lives in ordinary waking consciousness, and a man in unity is that I see the world dominated by differences: billions of separate fragments cluster together to form my reality. A man in unity sees these fragments, too, but underneath them he perceives wholeness. To him, the world with all its diversity is just one thing.

A world made of only one thing sounds strange, but the

rishis found it glorious, because what they beheld in all directions was their own awareness. Creation became a mirror showing them themselves. The objects seen by the eye were no longer made of inert matter. They breathed with life; their being flowed seamlessly into the rishi's own. Although usually invisible, this living consciousness could shine forth at times, making a table or tree seem to glow from within or filling the air with a shower of golden sparkles.

Visible or invisible, a world suffused with awareness becomes indescribably intimate to a person in unity. There are no separations anymore. Without stretching out a hand, one can feel the texture of a distant wall. The heave of the earth as it turns on its axis can be felt under one's feet. Even touching a star becomes a direct experience. "Since everything is made of consciousness alone," the Upanishads jubilantly declare, "there is nothing in creation that is not myself."

The mind's shift into unity is as radical as the change from waking to sleeping, or sleeping to dreaming. A book can barely suggest what happens, but imagine a British explorer brewing a cup of tea in the Arctic. One thing, the molecule H_2O, surrounds him on all sides, in the form of his ice floe, the snow covering it, the Arctic Ocean over the horizon, the clouds above, the boiling water in his kettle and the steam rising from it; even the explorer's body is two-thirds water. The eye alone could not reveal this unity. It takes a specific state of awareness, one that has been educated in the basic principles of physics, to experience so many different things, by turns hard, soft, cold, hot, white, blue, invisible, visible, moving, and still, as transformations of one fundamental substance.

Because of what he knows, the explorer can manipulate part of reality. He can make ice into water, or water into steam, and so on. The state of unity goes one better: any aspect of reality can be changed, not by manipulating molecules or atoms, but by manipulating the fundamental layer of awareness that ties all of nature together. By a simple but breathtaking stroke, if I can change my mind, and if the world is made of the same stuff as my mind, then I can change the world.

We are speaking of a natural unfoldment of the mind's

deeper layers. The rishis claim that wrapped up inside us is the capacity to command every force of nature, to influence every atom in the universe. Is all this really believable? Our present state of awareness keeps us convinced that we are small and helpless. One person is insignificant compared to the might of natural forces. An all-powerful and merciless environment does not care for his fate. Terrible things happen at random to people who do not seem to deserve them, and everyone feels swept along by circumstances beyond his control.

To accept such a reality is the most crippling kind of ignorance, according to the rishis, because it fulfills its own prophecies. If you are unaware of Einstein's general theory of relativity, your ignorance will not change relativity one jot, but if you are ignorant about your own self, your self will shrink to fit your conception. For any person engaged in strong denials of pain and anger, the picture of reality presented to him will be twice as deluding, because whenever he makes a move to release his pain, it will hurt, and escaping hurt is his whole reason for denying in the first place. Ignorance is the most circular of circular traps.

Fortunately, awareness is not only self-healing, if given the chance, but a certain part is already healed. This part is the sense of Being, of "I am," which no one can ever sacrifice or destroy. Only a person in unity sees Being in all directions, but we each have a seed of Being inside, the starting point of our evolution.

Brain scientists have stumbled across this aspect of awareness in their exploration of the brain and wondered what they were confronting. Beginning in the 1930s, the renowned Canadian brain surgeon Wilder Penfield spent several decades probing the brains of epileptic patients with an electric needle.

This procedure (which was entirely painless) enabled Penfield to talk with his patients while their cerebral cortex was being stimulated. When the needle touched various parts of the cortex, which controls the higher functions of thought, all kinds of experiences were evoked. Any moment from the past might return, not with the vagueness of a memory, but replayed exactly as if it were happening again.

Penfield recounts the experience of a young South African who burst out in astonishment because he perceived himself far away, laughing with his cousin on a farm back home, while at the same time being fully conscious that he was lying on an operating table in Montreal. It was very exciting for Penfield to discover that completely formed, totally convincing reality could be evoked from the brain. The farm, the sun, and the patient's cousin were as real as life. But what intrigued Penfield far more was the fact that this man did not believe he *was* in South Africa. His consciousness maintained two tracks at once, and he was quite clear that only one was true. In other words, he could tell that a brain picture was not convincing enough to constitute reality. Something stood aside and judged the picture without becoming wrapped up in it.

Similarly, Penfield could touch a specific spot on the cortex that caused the operating room to change visually, to become suddenly much larger or much smaller, but the patient knew that this was an optical illusion, even though it was the only thing he could see. He didn't say, "The room is getting bigger," but "I am seeing the room appear to get bigger." This may sound like a fine distinction; however, to Penfield it proved something immensely important, that awareness can be studied apart from the thoughts and images that usually fill it.

In other words, some aspect of the mind is not imprisoned in the world of duality. It maintains a steady state of conscious intelligence; it just is. This core of undisturbed clarity is awareness itself, in its purest, simplest form. Whether he realizes it or not, every person's mind is anchored in clarity. Pure awareness remains unaffected even in the midst of life's most wrenching events (brain surgery being one of the most wrenching, by any measure). Although we cannot alter our core of pure awareness, lose it or destroy it, we can forget it. As part of being free creatures, each of us has the choice whether to put his attention on the changing part of the mind or on the unchanging part.

What the rishis discovered is that a whole mind, one that has risen to a higher state of consciousness, fuses these two different modes of attention. One mode follows the activity of the world; the other remains motionless within its own nature. A person is beyond all suffering when he can think and act without disturbing the silent clarity of his mind. As the rishis put it, the full moon's reflection breaks apart on a windy lake, but that does not break up the moon itself. In one poetic image, they captured exactly what Penfield discovered with his probes.

Like any other wound, hurt awareness has to heal of its own accord. This means that for many people, the initial stages of evolution will remind them of pain, anger, and guilt they would rather forget. But awareness is like an army that advances together, leaving no stragglers; all the old pain must be confronted. As Maharishi points out, "enlightenment" means that every part of the mind receives light; there are no dark corners, and nothing remains that is frightening to look at. Meditation does not confront us with our old hurts head on, however. Each hurt has left its mark in the nervous system, and it is these physiological scars that get released.

In this way, the growth to enlightenment proceeds without wrenches. There is no pressure to grow at a certain speed. Franz Kafka, whose literary reputation centers on his portrayal of acute suffering, once wrote a brilliant affirmation of the path to enlightenment: "You do not need to leave your room. Remain sitting at your table and listen. Do not even listen, simply wait. Do not even wait, be quite still and solitary. The world will freely offer itself to you to be unmasked; it has no choice, it will roll in ecstasy at your feet." Reading this passage, I feel the breath of reality. It beckons without disturbing its own stillness, and to know what it whispers, I must become just as still myself.

Struggle and Expansion

Nick's next phase, occupying his late twenties and early thirties, was to wrestle with the speck of consciousness that had revealed itself off and on since his childhood. Outwardly, this was the most chaotic time of his life, in which his urge to be free of his demons expressed itself in twisted ways, often as

self-destructive behavior. At some deep level, however, wholeness was mysteriously growing.

The divorce from Clare was not a friendly one, and it was
soon followed by an acrimonious legal dispute with Nick's
parents, who claimed title to his house and bank account.
These had been transferred to them as a legal ploy during the
divorce proceedings, but after Clare departed with a modest
settlement, Nick's parents flatly refused to return his property. His father coolly challenged him to file a lawsuit, claiming that he could tie Nick up in the courts for years.

In a fury, Nick walked out of the family business. Having
managed to gain money from a trust fund, he fled to Italy,
where he spent a kind of fantasy year learning to race cars on
the grand prix circuit. He drove recklessly, pushing the sport's
dangers to the limit, but his self-destructive streak was just
beginning to emerge. Soon he came back to Boston and raised
the ante on his life by turning to cocaine. The same mixture of
danger, thrills, and rage that he had felt driving a race car
now became much sharper edged.

The compulsion to stay on cocaine was immense. Nick
had reached the point where keeping up the facade of normal-
ity, which he had been so good at when he was five, became
nearly impossible now that he was thirty-five. Despite his intense efforts to channel his energies into productive outlets—
he ran five miles a day, swam two more miles in the pool,
worked out at the gym, and kept up a large circle of sympathetic friends—he found that despair and rage inexorably
crept into his mind, tingeing every other impulse. His buried
secrets were claiming their revenge.

Nick broke out of his addiction by slow stages, but at each
stage the common theme was his expansion of awareness.
What gives any form of mental torment its sinister power is
that people have a mistaken notion about themselves. We
think that we are being tortured by grief, depression, fear, and
despair *as if* some foreign enemy were attacking from within.
Yet there are no enemies within. There is only mind-stuff. Like
a kind of universal modeling clay, this invisible substance
molds itself into all our thoughts, feelings, and desires.

The problem is that mind-stuff can enact dramas in which
it plays opposite roles. It can play victim and torturer at the

same time. Nick told me that he was staying in a Jamaican hotel a few years ago, spending a week scuba diving. He was temporarily off all drugs and had never been in better shape physically. As he stepped into the shower one morning, he suddenly found himself dropping to his knees, crying, totally beside himself. A wave of despair welled up from some dark recess. "God," he cried out loud, "why is this happening to me? Should I kill myself? Do you exist? Please, please, if you are God, take my torment away!"

He related this terrifying moment, as ever, in a controlled, pleasant voice, but I was brushed by the emptiness he had felt. "Do you think God heard you?" I asked after a moment.

"I don't know," he said. "I can't say that God is real to me. I could have been crying out to fate or to the void."

"So as far as you're concerned, your voice didn't reach anyone?" I asked.

"I don't know," he repeated.

"But at least we know someone who heard it," I said.

"We do?"

"You were heard by you," I said. "Why not begin there? Instead of wondering if there is some almighty agency who can save you from suffering, at least we can begin with your need to understand yourself, to truly listen and know who you are.

"Whenever we cry out, our voices reach ourselves. When we are afraid, it is ourselves making us afraid; if we start to tear apart inside, the same mind is doing the tearing and being torn. Experiencing just one side leads to suffering, no matter whether you identify with the actor or the one being acted upon. In reality, there is no actor separate from the acted upon. It is all just you."

Thinking about the pointless suffering that ensues, I saw a sad, bemused look on Nick's face, too. But we weren't meeting to discuss sorrow. The latest phase of Nick's life has been the happiest, because he has realized that he can find a way out of the cruel self-splitting that shaped him in childhood. He realized that if he was ever going to live at peace with himself, he had to dismantle the haunting threats from his past. He was fortunate to find a sympathetic, experienced therapist whom he began to see several times a week. At first Nick's anger toward his father was too violent to deal with. "When I uncorked my revenge fantasies and started talking about killing my father, I sounded so convincing that my therapist said he would have to call my parents to warn them that they were in danger. It took that strong a threat to curb me." It was also necessary to check Nick into drug detox centers off and on; he went through various rehabilitation programs a total of nine times.

Eventually, the turbulence of his inner world began to subside. He no longer feared the sudden eruption of his black rage; he did not wake up at midnight, as he had ever since adolescence, sweating in the grip of a panic attack. The surface Nick—the good little boy who wanted to please—began to realize that the other Nick, seemingly so wild and self-destructive, was in fact a sobbing child whose emotions of grief and terror were legitimate. They did not deserve to be condemned or feared. They deserved to be healed.

A year ago, as he was terminating his therapy, Nick began to meditate. It came as a revelatory experience, because all at once he recovered the clarity that had been lost twenty years earlier, the last time he was by himself in the Vermont woods. Even though his experiences of inner silence were brief, when he came out he felt as if he had contacted a source of deep fulfillment. It was his first experience of a whole self in many years, and also the first satisfaction that rendered his shame, guilt, and self-loathing totally irrelevant.

"I have had a recurring image of myself as a swimmer caught out alone in the middle of the ocean," Nick said. "I am thrashing around, while shadowy monsters are rising up toward me from below. But the first time I meditated, this sinister image changed. It dawned upon me that I was the swimmer but also the sea, and the monsters were nothing but me, too."

After a long pause, he unexpectedly began to tell me a story: "I had been searching for my real mother for thirteen years. It became extremely important for me to find her. I thought that maybe my addiction was related to my bloodline; I also just wanted to look into a face that might be like mine. All kinds of reasons motivated me. But nothing happened.

Years went by; I spent a fortune on investigators, some of whom were outright charlatans.

"Soon after I began to meditate, I turned on the radio and heard a woman saying that she could track down the parents of adopted children in six weeks. She would not disclose her methods, but I immediately sent her my name. Just as she promised, six weeks later I received the name of my real mother in the mail."

It sounded like a story some writer had carefully contrived: Nick's biological mother actually turned out to be a gypsy, just as he had imagined in the fairy tale he told himself as a child. She had threatened to steal him back when he was first adopted. She continued to hound Nick's parents for several years, attempting to squeeze more money from them (they have not revealed how successful she was).

"All at once, my whole life began to hang together. The impersonal, random world disappeared, and I waked into a world that had meaning. I can't really tell you exactly when this new sense of meaningfulness dawned on me, but once it did, I felt incredibly free. All I wanted to do was to contact my real mother and tell her that everything was all right. No matter what she had done, I forgave her and my adopted parents, everybody."

"But this woman sold you and then tried to practice extortion," I pointed out.

"I was so thrilled to find her," he said, "how could I not forgive her? When I first called up, I was extremely nervous. The woman who had tracked my mother down said to write a letter first, but I had to telephone her. Her name is Eva Z——, and I pretended to be a distant relation. After a while she became suspicious and asked me how I knew so much about the Z——family without ever showing up at their gatherings.

"I came right out and asked her, 'Did you ever have a son?' Without hesitation she said no. We fenced around a bit, and then I pushed her harder. 'Did you give birth to a baby boy on August 5, 1953, and give him up for adoption to a wealthy couple in Glen Rock, New Jersey?' Sounding twice as suspicious now, Eva again demanded to know who I was. 'I'm your son,' I blurted out.

"She didn't even pause. 'You may never believe this,' she

said, 'but I love you.' All at once my heart melted. We both broke down crying. She wanted to see me immediately but I stalled. I needed time to soak in the fact that I had really found her after thirteen years of searching.

"Two weeks later we met, and it was wonderful. Eva looks like me; her two daughters look like me. She has a beautiful laugh. Once, she couldn't stop laughing for ten minutes, and I anxiously tried to calm her down. She brushed me away, saying, 'Leave me alone, I just want to laugh.' We went dancing, and I held her in my arms. She would smile and look up at me, and I thought, 'She's my mother, right here in my arms. I am holding her and touching her.' How could I not forgive her?"

Nick paused to collect himself. He had found out the secret of his birth, which opened a deep well of emotions inside him, but there was more to it. He was caught up by the wonder of a heart that is just beginning to know itself, which is a second birth. I thought about how much I have changed, too. My hard belief that life is merciless, like a mill wheel impartially grinding out birth and death, is gone. To see things that way is to accept the appearance and miss the essence. Come closer, and the world looks much more like a wish, a great desire coming true all around us, with our own wishes and desires woven into it.

In this human life we cannot stop the wheel from grinding, but at some other level we have all the power. We are nature's privileged children. Once we fix upon our deepest desires, they must come true. That is why the great wish of the world is unfolding in the first place.

Nick and I sat silently, sharing a conception of life so delicate and so thrilling. He had nothing more to say, but I could still hear what I had missed before and never wanted to forget. For the first time, sheer joy had been rising in his voice.

Recommended Reading

I have limited the following list to books that are both informative and enjoyable. Most of the titles were mentioned in the text of this book. All have helped me to bring together in my own mind the scattered fields of medicine, psychotherapy, quantum physics, and consciousness.

Crichton, Michael. *Travels*. New York: Knopf, 1988.

Hawking, Stephen M. *A Brief History of Time*. New York: Bantam, 1988.

Laing, R. D. *Wisdom, Madness, and Folly*. New York: McGraw-Hill, 1985.

Langer, Ellen J. *Mindfulness*. New York: Addison-Wesley, 1989.

Locke, Stephen, and Douglas Colligan. *The Healer Within*. New York: E. P. Dutton, 1986.

Maharishi Mahesh Yogi. *On the Bhagavad-Gita*. New York: Penguin, 1969.

———. *Science of Being and Art of Living*. New York: Signet, 1968.

Miller, Alice. *The Drama of the Gifted Child*. New York: Basic Books, 1981.

Noonan, David. *Neuro: Life on the Front Lines of Brain Surgery and Neurological Medicine.* New York: Simon and Schuster, 1989.

Penfield, Wilder, et al. *The Mystery of the Mind.* Princeton: Princeton University Press, 1975.

Sacks, Oliver. *The Man Who Mistook His Wife for a Hat.* New York: Simon and Schuster, 1985.

————. *Seeing Voices.* Berkeley: University of California Press, 1989.

Selzer, Richard. *Mortal Lessons.* New York: Simon and Schuster, 1987.

Yalom, Irvin D. *Love's Executioner.* New York: Basic Books, 1989.

Index

About the Author

Trained in India and the United States, DEEPAK CHOPRA, M.D., has practiced endocrinology since 1971 and is a Fellow of the American College of Physicians. He is President of the American Association for Ayurvedic Medicine and Director of the Maharishi Ayurveda Health Center in Lancaster, Massachusetts. His previous books are *Creating Health* (a selection of the Prevention Book Club), *Return of the Rishi* (a selection of the Literary Guild), *Quantum Healing*, and *Perfect Health*. His writing has been published in twenty-two languages and he lectures widely in the United States, Europe, the Soviet Union, Japan, and India.

Requests for information on workshops and seminars by Dr. Chopra or any personal correspondence can be addressed to:

QUANTUM HEALING PROGRAMS
P.O. Box 598
S. Lancaster, MA 01561
(800) 858–1808